Social Security Law in the United Kingdom

Social Security Law in the United Kingdom

Third Edition

Stephen Hardy

This book was originally published as a monograph in the International Encyclopaedia of Laws/Social Security Law.

Founding Editor: Roger Blanpain
General Editor: Frank Hendrickx
Volume Editor: Willy van Eeckhoutte

Wolters Kluwer

Published by:
Kluwer Law International B.V.
PO Box 316
2400 AH Alphen aan den Rijn
The Netherlands
E-mail: international-sales@wolterskluwer.com
Website: lrus.wolterskluwer.com

Sold and distributed in North, Central and South America by:
Wolters Kluwer Legal & Regulatory U.S.
7201 McKinney Circle
Frederick, MD 21704
United States of America
Email: customer.service@wolterskluwer.com

Sold and distributed in all other countries by:
Air Business Subscriptions
Rockwood House
Haywards Heath
West Sussex
RH16 3DH
United Kingdom
Email: international-customerservice@wolterskluwer.com

ISBN 978-94-035-1163-4

e-Book: ISBN 978-94-035-1222-8
web-PDF: ISBN 978-94-035-1223-5

The Author

Professor Stephen Hardy, LLB, PhD, SFHEA, FRSA, MCIArb, Barrister, has been a legal academic for over twenty years, specializing in European Union (EU), employment, commercial and social welfare law. As a practitioner, he has acted in some landmark employment and public law cases, as Counsel for the United Kingdom (UK) Government and for many UK trades unions. Above all, as a scholar, he has written over 300 refereed articles and 25 books in the field of EU social policy and social-economic rights, as well as having been General Editor of Sweet & Maxwell's Encyclopaedia on Employment Law for over a decade. Since 2011, he has been a judge of the First-Tier Tribunal (Social Entitlement Chamber), as well as being a judicial mentor. He is also an academic member of the UK's Administrative Justice Council.

The Author

Table of Contents

List of Abbreviations

AA (65+)	Attendance Allowance for the over 65s
AC	Appeal Cases
All E R	All England Law Reports
BA	Benefits Agency
C	circa (about)
C, Cd, Cmd, Cmnd	Command Paper (Official Government Document)
C.A.	Court of Appeal
CA	Carer's Allowance
Ch	Chapter
CMEC	Child Maintenance Enforcement Commission
CPAG	Child Poverty Action Group
CSA	Child Support Agency
CTB	Council Tax Benefit
CTC	Child Tax Credit
DLA	Disability Living Allowance
DSS	Department of Social Security
DWP	Department for Work and Pensions
ECJ	European Court of Justice
Ed.	Edition
EEA	European Economic Area
ESA	Employment and Support Allowance
EO	Employment Officer
EU	European Union
FC	Family Credit
FES	Family Expenditure Survey
GA	Guardian's Allowance
GB	Great Britain
GBP	Pound Sterling (£)

List of Abbreviations

HASSASSA	Health and Social Services and Social Security Adjudication Act 1983 HB Housing Benefit
HC Paper	House of Commons Paper
HL	House of Lords
HCP	Health care Practitioner
HMRC	Her Majesty's Revenue and Customs
HMSO	Her Majesty's Stationary Office
IB	Incapacity Benefit
IS	Income Support
JSA	Job Seeker's Allowance
MOD	Ministry of Defence
NHS	National Health Service
NI	National Insurance
No	Number
P	Probate Reports
PT	Primary Threshold
PAYE	Pay-as-You-Earn
PIP	Personal Independence Payment
s.	Section(s)
SAP	Statutory Adoption Pay
Sch	Schedule
SDA	Severe Disablement Allowance
SERPS	State Earnings-Related Pension Scheme (now called Additional State Pension)
SMA	State Maternity Allowance
SMP	Statutory Maternity Pay
SPP	Statutory Paternity Pay
SPVA	Service Personnel and Veterans Agency
SSA	Social Security Act
SSAA	Social Security Administration Act 1992
SSCBA	Social Security Contributions and Benefits Act 1992
SSP	Statutory Sick Pay
ST	Secondary Threshold
TSO	The Stationery Office
UC	Universal Credit
UEL	Upper Earnings Limit
UK	United Kingdom
Ufi	University for Industry
WFTC	Working Families Tax Credit

WRA	Welfare Reform Act (2007, 2012, 2016)
WRPA	Welfare Reform and Pensions Act 1999
WTC	Working Tax Credit

List of Abbreviations

Preface to the Sixth Edition

It has been two years since the last edition of this volume of the *Encyclopaedia* was revised. During that period, significant changes have been made to the UK's Social Security system. Most notably, the full implementation of Universal Credit (UC) across the UK. Further, the impact of the benefit cap has emerged. Also, the case law developments in Housing Benefit (HB) and family policy (namely child tax credits (CTCs)) have been momentous in challenging Government thinking as well as causing a remodelling of those laws.'

Therefore, key reforms updated in this edition are:

- UC full-service implementation and challenges to the UK's UC 'flagship' new benefit.
- the impact of the benefit cap;
- tax creditl appeals; and
- EU migrants' benefits after BREXIT.

More significantly, as we approach the BREXIT deadline, the impending implications of the UK without an EU, in terms of social security co-ordination and exportability is looming with much uncertainty.

Lastly, as ever I am indebted to my family for their support; constructive editorial advice from my Editors and Publisher; and wise counsel given by my academic and my judicial colleagues.

Any errors remain mine and the usual disclaimers apply.

Stephen Hardy
June 2018

General Introduction

§1. General Background

1. In common with the other volumes in the *Encyclopaedia*, the purpose of this volume is to provide the reader with an account of the law of social security, in this case as it relates to the United Kingdom (UK). The function of this General Introduction is to provide a brief analysis of the context within which the British (i.e., England, Wales, Scotland & Northern Ireland) social security system is currently found. As is the case in other countries, in particular those with well-developed (and therefore very costly) social security systems, there is considerable debate in the UK about how the social security system should develop. In particular, much consideration is being given to the extent to which the individual should look to the State to provide social security benefits and the extent to which the individual should be encouraged/forced to provide such benefits for himself/herself.

2. Before further progress can be made, however, it is necessary to consider what is meant by the concept of 'social security' in the British context.

I. Definition of Social Security

3. The concept of 'social security' is defined somewhat differently in Britain from the way it is defined in many other countries, in particular the countries of Western Europe. In the UK, 'social security' covers the provision of a range of benefits, usually payable in the form of cash, which are paid to individual claimants who qualify for the receipt of such benefits under rules prescribed by the British Government, made under the authority of Acts of Parliament. According to Beveridge, the acknowledged founder of the UK system of social security: 'Social security must be achieved by co-operation between the State and the individual. The State in organizing security should not stifle incentive, opportunity, responsibility by each individual to provide more than the minimum for himself and his family.'[1]

4. Health care, which in many other countries is regarded as falling within the scope of the social security system, is *not* included in the conceptual framework of the British social security system (although of course health care, provided through the National Health Service (NHS), *is* a central feature of the British Welfare State).

1. 'Beveridge Report', Cmd 6406, 1942, para. P.

In addition, a number of other services provided by the State might be regarded as forming part of the social security system in some countries but in Britain are regarded as related to but conceptually distinct from the social security system. These include, for example, services provided in relation to employment and training, or in relation to health and safety at work.

5. Over the last decade, there has been a profound shift in how the relationship between tax and social security is perceived. The central role that tax credits now play in the social security system illustrates the point most forcibly. This text focuses principally on 'social security' as it has been traditionally understood in the UK, as now developed by this association with the tax system. The primary focus is still on cash benefits. Accordingly, UK social security law regulates the delivery of benefits, either in cash (e.g., Job Seeker's Allowance (JSA), IS, Employment and Support Allowance (ESA), Personal Independence Payment (PIP)) or in kind, that is, by the provision of free or reduced-cost goods or services (e.g., free dental care or milk/eye care tokens). Such benefits are payable as a form of occupational or social welfare. In the twenty-first century, the development of social security law has been dominated by three themes: the rise of social insurance during the twentieth century since the National Insurance Act 1911; debate over welfare reform, the form of benefit regulation has always been controversial since the Social Security Act (SSA) 1980. Such a debate has been exacerbated by the Welfare Reform Acts (WRAs); and, the need to simplify what has become a very complex and formal benefits appeal process and legal system. To that end, the 1998 SSA commenced the tide of change towards developing a new decision-making and determinations, introducing the concept of 'stakeholder welfare'.[2]

II. The Purposes of Social Security

6. The social significance of the social security system of any country can only be understood by a consideration of the varied purposes of that system. It should not be assumed that all countries view the purposes of social security in the same way; different countries may have different understandings of the social, economic and other purposes of the social security system, depending, for example, on the historical and political juncture at which the social security system was developed.

7. In the British context, a number of purposes for the social security system may be identified:

- *the prevention of destitution* – for example, by the provision of means-tested benefits creating a financial 'floor of entitlement' or 'poverty line' below which those living in Britain should not be allowed to fall;
- *the provision of additional resources to meet defined expenses* – for example, the payment of benefits to the disabled to help meet the additional cost of providing care facilities or enhancing the quality of their lives;

2. *See* JSSL, [1997] Vol 4, Issue 2, pp. 47–48 & [1998] Vol 5, Issue 3, pp. 104–117.

- *the provision of substitute income* – for example, the provision of short-term benefits to replace earnings from work to cover periods of sickness or in the longer term to cover retirement from employment;
- *the exercise of industrial discipline* – for example, through the withholding of unemployment benefits where persons have left employment without just cause, or refuse to take alternative employment, or through the withholding of benefits to the young who refuse to undertake additional training after leaving school;
- *the application of other forms of social coercion* – for example, linking entitlement to social security benefits to requirements to receive job training or to apply for employment;
- *the encouragement of social responsibility* – recent Governments have given increasing emphasis to the importance of individual social responsibility as a precondition to support from the Welfare State;
- *the encouragement of labour mobility* – successive UK Government has promoted the mobility of workers to 'go where the jobs are', alongside the European Union (EU) advancing the free movement of workers across the European Economic Area (EEA);
- *the achievement of broader social objectives* – such as the redistribution of income from richer to poorer or the enhancement of social solidarity or assisting the process of economic reconstruction; and
- *responding to the social consequences of an economic system* based on the principles of the 'free market'.

8. What is important to appreciate is that not only is there a *range* of objectives but also they are by no means necessarily consistent, the one with the other. The complexities and potential inconsistencies of such purposes must be recognized if any sophisticated understanding of the social importance of the social security system of countries in general, and Britain in particular, is to be achieved.

§2. Historical Background

I. Social and Economic Background

9. The poor may always have been with us, but the same cannot be said of laws seeking to regulate or alleviate poverty. The current UK system of social security law is often presented as a development of the post-war political consensus that saw the advent of the Welfare State. However, the roots of this system run deep and can be traced back to the English poor laws, enacted during the reign of Henry VIII. Latterly, the Poor Law Amendment Act 1844 provided the first framework for adjudication, fraud prevention and entitlement. As with many other advanced capitalist countries, the UK has, over the last sixty years, undergone profound social and economic change. The heavy manufacturing industries that were so significant in generating the wealth of the nation in the last years of the nineteenth century and the first half of the twentieth century have been replaced by more service- and information-based industries. Within the UK, many formerly State-run enterprises have been privatized. There has been increasing political emphasis on the importance of 'the market' as the conceptual basis for economic policy.

10. One consequence of these structural changes has been that levels of unemployment have tended to run at rather higher levels, compared with those experienced in the years immediately following the end of the Second World War.

11. There have also been major changes to the composition of the workforce. In particular, the participation of women in the workforce is far greater than it was in the immediate post-war years. The nature of employment has also changed, with many more jobs now being held on a part-time basis.

12. Furthermore, many full-time jobs are currently offered on a limited term basis only. Increasingly, workers cannot anticipate a single career with one company for the bulk of his/her working life. The labour market is much more flexible than it was fifty years ago. This is not without social consequences. There are indications that this has led to much higher levels of stress, not only among the unemployed but also for those in employment.

13. In addition, there have been other very important demographic and social changes. Average life expectancy has continued to increase; at the same time, the overall birth rate has been falling, though this trend has recently been reversed. These developments have major social and political implications, in particular for pensions' policy (and also for the costs of running the NHS).

14. Since the end of Second World War, there has been a marked increase in levels of divorce, resulting in family networks of much greater complexity and also significantly increased numbers of lone-parent (usually women) families.

15. All these factors – changes in the labour market, demographic change, social change – have had major impacts on the social security system, and in particular on levels of demand for social security benefits and thus on social security expenditure.

16. The very existence of a mature system of social security, especially support for unemployment, has, of course, been one of the factors which have enabled successive British Governments to adopt policies which have led to these structural changes – for example, reductions in subsidies to declining industries and the programme of privatization of nationalized industries.

17. At the same time, these social and economic factors have themselves helped to shape current debates about the future development of the social security system in the UK. In particular, there is now a sharp debate about the extent to which policies developed for the circumstances of the immediate post-Second World War period (and themselves based on the legacy of the 1930s depression) remain appropriate in an era of significantly increased economic prosperity.

II. Historical Background

18. There is substantial literature on the history of social security in the UK (*see* below *Select Bibliography*). This section of the general introduction highlights a limited number of points only.

19. Five hundred years ago, the widespread assumption was that poverty was the result of individual human weakness – in particular a refusal to work, or sickness or disability – rather than caused by structural weaknesses in social or economic organization. Limited assistance was given to the poor by organs of the State, in particular by the local parish, under the provisions of the old Poor Law, dating back to a Statute of 1601. There were crude attempts to subsidize the wages of the agricultural poor, known as the 'Speenhamland system'.[3] The main institutional providers of assistance, however, were charitable institutions who did provide some help, often coupled with the imposition of strict moral conditions.

20. In 1834, the Poor Law was remodelled and made more punitive in nature through the introduction of the notorious principle of 'less eligibility'. Assistance would be offered, usually through the workhouse, but only to a level at which the recipient of assistance was in a less favourable (or 'less eligible') position than that of 'the independent labourer of the lowest class'. This very restrictive provision could be alleviated for the 'deserving poor', such as the sick, disabled and elderly, who were perceived as being more obviously the victims of their personal situation rather than affected by their own moral delinquency.

21. During the latter part of the nineteenth century, as the adverse social and public health effects of industrialization became more apparent in the slums of Britain's major cities, a number of studies of the poor were published which rejected the view that people were poor simply because of their own moral failings; in particular, it came to be understood that unemployment, and thus poverty, was as much the result of macroeconomic factors as of individual weakness.

22. At the same time, interest began to be shown in Bismarck's experiments in 1890 with social insurance in Germany. In 1905, Lloyd George, the then British Prime Minister, became convinced, after a visit to Germany, that social insurance offered the best way to bring protection against undeserved poverty. It mirrored the familiar concept of private insurance but ensured that all citizens fell within the scope of the scheme.

23. The first National Insurance Act, introducing what now seem to be very limited schemes of unemployment insurance as well as a rudimentary system of National Health Insurance, was enacted in 1911.

3. For a detailed history, *see* M. Neuman, *The Speenhamland County: Poverty and the Poor Laws in Berkshire* 1782–1834 (New York: Garland, 1982).

24. Between the two World Wars, there was a limited expansion of social insurance to the elderly and sick, as well as some expansion of the scope of unemployment insurance. Most notable, however, was the failure – during the severe economic depression of the late 1920s and early 1930s – of the scheme of social insurance to operate, as initially intended, on truly actuarial principles. People were unemployed for far longer than the social insurance scheme contemplated; thus, the scheme could not afford to meet the full demands made upon it. In 1934, a means-tested scheme of Unemployment Assistance was introduced for the benefit of those who had exhausted their entitlement to Unemployment Benefit or who had not come within the scope of the scheme at all.

25. This structure, of social insurance benefits combined with a 'safety-net' of means-tested provision, formed the basis for the famous Beveridge Report,[4] which called for the slaying of five 'giants' on the road to post-Second World War reconstruction, namely, want, disease, ignorance, squalor and idleness. This of course implied that the policies of the Welfare State should encompass a much broader range of issues than simply social security: proper health services, education services, public health services and a lively economy with full employment were all part of his vision. The bulk of his report however considered the social insurance scheme.

26. Such was the political and popular support for the scheme that it led to the enactment of the main post-Second World War statutory framework of the National Insurance Act 1946, the National Insurance (Industrial Injuries) Act 1946 and the National Assistance Act 1948. These Acts created the structure for a comprehensive scheme of contributory benefits 'from the cradle to the grave', together with the means-tested National Assistance – replacing Unemployment Assistance. In addition, administrative fragmentation was ended; for the first time, National Insurance (NI) was to be administered by a single Department of State – the then Ministry of National Insurance – rather than the variety of Departments hitherto involved.

27. Unlike other European models of social security, Beveridge had argued, and the post-Second World War Labour Government had enacted, that social insurance should provide 'flat-rate' – rather than earnings-related – benefits in return for the payment of 'flat-rate' contributions. Beveridge's view was that this was the best way of ensuring that the State provided a *basic minimum* while providing encouragement to citizens to make additional provision for themselves through the medium of savings or private insurance.

28. There was, however, one important respect in which the Beveridge 'blueprint' was not adopted by the then Government. He had argued that the level of benefit should be set at an officially determined 'poverty line' – based on a calculation of the amount of cash needed weekly to purchase a basket of essential goods. On this view, means-tested subsistence benefits would have played only a residual role

4. 'Social Insurance and Allied Services', Cmd 6404 (London: HMSO, 1942).

to cover those who for one reason or another fell outside the contributory framework. The 1945 Labour Government rejected this proposal, primarily on the ground of cost. The officially defined 'poverty line' was set at a higher level than that for Unemployment Benefit. Thus, the possibility of means-tested National Assistance being simply a residual 'safety-net' was never a practical option.

29. It was recognized however that, whatever its limitations, the scheme would be expensive. Beveridge's view was that the cost could be met by economic growth based on a policy of full employment.[5]

30. In the early years after 1945,[6] the political rhetoric that poverty would be eradicated under the new social security system was widely believed. But increasingly, evidence was presented indicating that, far from the social security system eliminating poverty, there was still a substantial section of the population which was living at or below the officially defined poverty line. The impact of this on the children of those families was particularly noted.[7]

31. At the same time, it became apparent that a number of groups were not effectively covered by the scheme; in particular, the disabled who were never able to get into employment and thus never able to build up a contribution record; and lone parents who, with the increasing incidence of divorce and relationship breakdown, were having to rely on means-tested benefits to enable them to acquire a basic level of subsistence income.

32. The political rhetoric of the 1960s was rather different. There was increasing criticism of the concept of means-testing, implying a need for State officials to pry into individuals' financial circumstances. This was said to stigmatize recipients of means-tested benefits, as well as deter many who should have received those benefits from claiming them.[8] There was also criticism of the role of 'discretion' in social security provision, particularly in the context of the means-tested National Assistance scheme. Adopting concepts developed in the United States,[9] there were calls for the elimination of discretion – said to give officials too much power to determine the nature of individual lifestyles – and the adoption of a 'right' to social security.

33. Key UK social reformers also campaigned for the reinstatement of the Beveridge principle that contributory benefits should be set at the poverty line level, thus eliminating the need for means-tested benefits. But the cost of this was still judged by politicians to be far too high. Instead, in 1966 the National Assistance scheme was abolished, replaced by a new Supplementary Benefits Scheme. Section

5. Set out in the White Paper, 'Employment Policy', Cmd 6527 (London: HMSO,1944).
6. *See* R. Lowe, *The Welfare State in Britain since 1945* (London: Macmillan, 1993).
7. *See* B. Abel-Smith & P. Townsend, *The Poor and the Poorest* (London: Bell, 1965).
8. A. Deacon & J. Bradshaw, *Reserved for the Poor: The Means-Test in British Social Policy* (Oxford: Blackwell, 1983).
9. *See*, for example, the very influential article by C.A. Reich, 'The New Property', *Yale Law Journal* 73 (1964): 733.

1 of the Supplementary Benefits Act provided that everyone over the age of 16 should have a 'right' to Supplementary Benefit. However, the new statutory language was largely cosmetic. The reality was that little had changed: the benefit was still means-tested, and officials still had considerable discretionary powers which were associated with the scheme.

34. During the 1960s, there were also the first moves away from the Beveridge principle of flat-rate contributions in return for flat-rate benefits. In order to raise more revenue for the scheme, earnings-related contributions began to be introduced though with only a very modest benefit enhancement.

35. In the early 1970s, a number of these issues were addressed more directly by the Government. First, the dependence of the elderly on means-tested benefits to bring them up to the State poverty line (as a result of the low level of the retirement pension) led to a number of attempts to introduce a new State-run scheme for retirement pensions. After abortive attempts at enacting new legislation in 1969 and 1973, the SSA 1975 was finally passed which introduced new measures whereby all those in employment, who were themselves not already members of an occupational pension scheme that provided benefits at least as good as the State scheme, were required to join a State Earnings-Related Pension Scheme (SERPS). The scheme was not to come fully into force until 1998, while participants built up a sufficient contribution record.[10] This was not, however, the last word. The challenge of providing a level of retirement pension which the State could afford has not gone away.

36. Second, the same Act of 1975 abandoned any idea of returning to the Beveridge idea of flat-rate contributions; instead, the Act enshrined the principle of earnings-related contributions which is still in force today.[11] In many cases, these contributions lead only to entitlement to flat-rate benefits. (Indeed, as will be seen in Part II, some contributions now lead to the creation of no entitlement to social security benefit at all; they are taxation in all but name.)

37. Third, for the first time a new social security benefit – Family Income Supplement – was introduced (in 1970) to subsidize the low wages of families in work. This was the forerunner of the tax credits that are now a central feature of the British social security system.

38. Fourth, there was a major enquiry into one-parent families – who emerged as one of the groups not adequately catered for in the Beveridge scheme – which recommended the introduction of a new social security benefit, the Guaranteed Maintenance Allowance,[12] though this proposal was not taken forward.[13]

---

10. For changes to the SERPS scheme, *see* below Part VIII.
11. For further detail, *see* below Part II.
12. 'Report of the Committee on One-Parent Families', Chairman: The Hon Mr. Justice Finer, Cmnd 5629 (London: HMSO, 1974).
13. *See* below Part IV Family Allowances: Child Benefit and Child Support.

39. Fifth, and perhaps the most significant change to the social security system which took place in the 1970s, was the introduction of a new system of Child Benefit, replacing the former very inadequate system of Family Allowances.[14]

40. Towards the end of the 1970s, attention began to focus on the costs of the discretionary additions being paid to recipients of Supplementary Benefit. A review by officials in the Department of Health and Social Security (as the Ministry of National Insurance had by then become) concluded that there should be a move from a discretion-based scheme to a rule-based model. This was implemented by the incoming (Thatcher) Conservative Government in 1980.

41. Particular critical attention was also given to the genesis of aspects of the adjudicatory structure for the UK social security scheme, in particular the poor quality of many appeal tribunals handling appeals relating to Supplementary Benefit (*see* further Part XI).

42. In the 1980s, the then Thatcher Government in the UK introduced a new rhetoric into public debate about the Welfare State. She expressed a desire to reduce levels of individual dependence on the State, to increase incentives to get people back to work, to 'target' benefits to those who needed them most and to encourage the individual provision of welfare. Instead of the Beveridge model of universal benefits, Conservative Government rhetoric suggested a more limited role for the Welfare State, and within that, social security provision.

43. One early manifestation of the determination to change the approach to funding occurred in the housing field, where general subsidies for the cost of building public sector housing were reduced, to be replaced by a new HB, targeted by means-testing those – both those out of work and those in low-paid employment – who rented accommodation, either from public sector (local authority or housing association) landlords or private sector landlords.

44. In the mid-1980s, UK social security policy was subjected to a more comprehensive and wide-ranging review under the then responsible Minister, Norman Fowler.[15] The Green Paper (Consultation Document) that was the outcome of the review reflected much of the ideology of the 'new right' and argued for a more focused social security system, with more targeted benefits. There was also increased emphasis on trying to create a social security system which 'the country could afford'. In particular, the demographic trends of an ageing population with lower numbers of working age led the Government to conclude that there had to be a new approach to the State Earnings-Related Retirement Pension Scheme.

---

14. *See* further below Part IV.
15. *See* the Green Paper 'Reform of Social Security', vols. 1 and 2, Cmnd 9517 and 9518 (London: HMSO, 1985).

45. The review led to the passing of the SSA 1986, which provided encouragement to individuals who were in SERPS to opt out of it and instead to buy their own private pensions.[16]

46. In addition, major changes were made to the means-tested 'safety-net'. Supplementary Benefit was abolished and replaced by Income Support (IS). While there were enhancements to benefits for claimants with children and for the disabled, there was also a draconian curtailment of benefit entitlements for the 16- to 17- year-old school-leaver group who – broadly – were denied benefit unless they undertook vocational training. Family Income Supplement was also abolished and replaced by Family Credit (FC).

47. As a separate exercise, in the early 1990s, there was a rationalization – and in many respects an improvement – in the range of benefits available to the disabled, a group rather ignored in the Beveridge plan, but whose claims for improved provision had been increasingly heard during the 1970s and 1980s.

48. An attempt to reduce the dependence of lone parents (typically mothers) on social security payments and to increase the level of support for children from the absent parent (usually fathers) was made with the introduction of the extremely controversial scheme of Child Support, operative from 1993.

49. In the same year, an official report[17] was published on the costs of social security in the UK, which showed not only how expenditure on social security had increased during the past fifteen years but more significantly projected rates of growth into the future. This led the Government to consider yet more ways of trying to bring social security costs under control.

50. Thus, a new regime for the sick was introduced in April 1995, with the introduction of Incapacity Benefit (IB) to replace sickness benefit and invalidity benefit. In the Autumn of 1995, significant changes to the extent to which social security payments could meet the housing costs of the poor were introduced. In 1996, JSA replaced Unemployment Benefit and IS for the unemployed. Further changes were also introduced in relation to provision for pensions in old age, further encouraging individuals to make private provision for themselves, and not simply relying upon the State to provide. More attention was paid to getting the unemployed back to work.

51. In 1997, the New Labour Administration launched their own review of social security. In the resulting Green Paper,[18] they drew a picture of a system in crisis: it was said to foster high levels of inequality and social exclusion, despite operating at a very high cost. Moreover, it constructed barriers to work and was open to

16. This is discussed further below in Part VIII.
17. *The Growth of Social Security* (London: HMSO, 1993).
18. 'New Ambitions for Our Country: A New Contract for Welfare', Cmd 3805 (London: TSO, 1998).

fraudulent abuse. There was substantial overlap with the diagnosis of the (Conservative) Fowler review of the 1980s, clearly indicating that the former Conservative Government was far less able to tackle what it saw as the problems with the social security system than its political rhetoric had suggested.

52. Over the last two decades, there has been a string of new Government reports and legislative initiatives that have changed much of the detail of the British social security system. Under the former Labour Governments of Tony Blair and Gordon Brown, the most important developments were: first, strengthening links between entitlement of the unemployed to social security and taking steps to ensure that those out of work receive help to get into the labour market; second, making substantial effort to reduce levels of poverty through widespread use of tax credits; third, trying to achieve a more sustainable structure of the benefits available to retirement pensioners – these included (in 2002) replacing SERPS with Additional State Pension, a scheme designed to improve retirement pensions for those in lower paid employments and some, such as carers, who were not in the regular workforce; fourth, major change in the benefits payable to the long-term sick and disabled; and fifth, significant change to HB.

53. Under the Coalition Government, 2010–2015, led by David Cameron, yet further major reform has been announced, including a complete restructuring of the tax credit system, reform of HB and major changes to the reform of the law on pensions, including in particular making the age at which men and women become entitled to State Pensions the same, increasing the age at which entitlement to State retirement pension arises, and making workplace pensions compulsory. Underpinning all these measures are the constant – if conflicting – challenges of providing for an increasingly ageing population, encouraging those who can work to do so, and keeping the costs of the system under control.

54. The most significant of these developments are considered further in the context of specific benefits below. Here, they are set out in outline so that the reader who is unfamiliar with the British social security system get an idea of present issues and future challenges facing the British system. One may also consider the extent to which problems faced in the UK are reflected in their own country.

55. More recently, the majority Conservative UK Government, since 2015, has sought to widen its existing welfare reform programme, culminating in the 2016 Welfare Reform and Work Act which makes provision for reports on progress towards full employment and the apprenticeships target, as well as to enact a newly revised benefit cap and change social security and tax credits. This grand scale reform seeks to further the Government's intentions to make sure claimants are better off in work than on benefits and create a simpler, fairer benefits system. Through its flagship policy of Universal Credit (UC), the Government has replaced six main benefits fully since January 2018 with a single monthly payment for people in work or out of work, enabling the transition from welfare to work. These reforms aim to make the financial benefits of work clearer to claimants while reducing the risks of taking up a job. The recently instituted benefits caps also seeks to promote and incentivize work rather than welfare. Also, with BREXIT, culminating in the UK's withdrawal from the EU under Article 50 of the TFEU, post-BREXIT, the social security rights of EU twenty-seven migrants to the UK will continue to be determined by their residential status in the UK, and it is this status which will no longer be decided by EU law.

§3. Sources of Social Security Law

56. Although the policy underlying the British social security system is the result of political debate, the legitimation of that system and the authority to put it into effect derives, as is the case with most other social policies, from detailed statutory provisions. A note about these sources of law is set out below.

I. The Legal Systems of the United Kingdom

57. Although relatively small in geographical terms, the UK is a densely populated country made up of distinct national entities: England, Wales, Scotland and Northern Ireland. Within the UK, there are three separate systems of law in operation: (i) in Scotland, the legal system is based on Civil (Roman) law, in the European tradition, rather than the common law of England and Wales; (ii) in Northern Ireland, there is essentially a common law system, but with important differences from the laws of England and Wales and where Statute law has individual characteristics reflecting the fact that Northern Ireland has its own legislature (the Northern Ireland Assembly); and (iii) in England and Wales, there is also a common law system, supplemented by a vast body of complex and detailed statutory provisions.[19] The constitutional position has been complicated by devolution under the Scotland Act 1998, the Wales Act 1998 and the Government of Wales Act 2006. In relation to both Scotland and Wales, certain legislative powers have been devolved to, respectively, the Scottish Parliament and (to a lesser extent) the Welsh Assembly Government. All jurisdictions are in addition subject to the law emanating from the European Community. Although these distinctions are important in some areas of the law, for the purposes of this work the distinctions are not a matter of particular significance. Broadly, the same (statutory) rules of social security law apply throughout the UK. Those interested in the detail will find that there is a separate body of statutory provision relating to Northern Ireland; in addition, many of the main statutory rules analysed in the following chapters make special provision for Scotland and the particular social and legal circumstances found there. However, for the purpose of this work, designed to provide an introduction to the British system for those not familiar with that system, the law is in essence the same. Therefore, at the risk of offending readers in Northern Ireland and Scotland, the discussion in this entry in the *Encyclopaedia* is in terms of the law applicable in England and Wales alone.

19. More detail can be found in M. Partington, *Introduction to the English Legal System,* 6th edn (Oxford: Oxford University Press, 2011).

II. Sources of Social Security Law

58. British social security law is to be found in the following principal sources of law:

- *primary legislation* – Acts of Parliament;
- *secondary legislation* – Regulations and Orders in Council;
- *case law* – decisions of the courts and the Upper Tribunal (Administrative Appeals); and
- *European law.*

59. Primary Legislation: Under the (unwritten) British constitutional system, all acts of officials have to be legitimated by the authority of Acts of Parliament, which have been the subject of debate and voting through both Houses of the British Parliament – the House of Commons (HC) and the House of Lords (HL). Modern practice – given the time needed for bills to pass through Parliament and become Acts of Parliament – is for Acts of Parliament to provide a framework of legislative authority, which gives Ministers – in the case of social security, the Secretary of State for Work and Pensions – power to make further, secondary legislation (*see* paragraph 61).

60. In 1992, there was a major consolidation of this primary legislation into the Social Security Contributions and Benefits Act 1992 (SSCBA) and the Social Security Administration Act 1992 (SSAA). These have been further amended by recent WRAs. However, the rapid development of policy, noted above, has led to many more Acts being passed through the Parliament. In this text, any law referred to as an 'Act' is one of these examples of primary legislation.

61. Secondary legislation: In addition to Acts of Parliament, which set out the legal framework, the British legislative tradition is that the detail of rules of entitlement to benefits, rules relating to contributions and rules relating to the administration of the system are contained in secondary legislation, made under the authority of the Acts of Parliament, but which – in the main – have not themselves been the subject to detailed debate and voting in the Parliament.[20]

62. There are two principal types of secondary legislation: *regulations* and *orders*. The technical difference between the two is of no relevance to this work.

---

20. Most regulations are laid before the Parliament and made subject to what is known as the 'negative resolution' procedure, that is to say they come into effect on a date set out in the regulation, unless a resolution is passed in Parliament which prevents this from taking place; given the fact that the Government has a majority in the Parliament, it will be realized that this hardly ever takes place. A small number of regulations are made the subject of a 'positive resolution' procedure, whereby the regulation is laid before Parliament but only comes into effect if Parliament approves it after a debate and a vote. In practice, such debates do not focus on the detail of the proposed regulations, but provide Members of Parliament, particularly in the opposition parties with an opportunity to criticize Government policy on social security. Again, given the Government's majority in Parliament, such regulations are invariably approved and thus come into force.

What is important is that readers understand that reference to either in the text is reference to secondary legislation, made by Ministers acting under the authority of the primary Act of Parliament.

63. An important distinction between Acts on the one hand and Orders and Regulations on the other is that, under the British Constitution, legal challenges to the validity of Acts of Parliament (Statutes) are not countenanced by the courts, save in the rare instance where an Act is found to be in conflict with a rule of European law, but Orders and Regulations may be subject to challenge in the courts, and on occasion are so challenged, on the ground that there was no statutory authority for a particular provision in an Order or Regulation and therefore should be declared invalid on the ground that it is ultra vires the terms of the Act of Parliament. More significantly in the field of social security law in the UK – a raft of Regulations exist. Similarly, a raft of EU regulations pervades this important area of EU social policy.

64. *Case law*: Despite the amount and detail of the statutory provision associated with the British social security system, there can always be found rules which are unclear or which do not deal precisely with specific factual situations. Thus, procedures exist for decisions to be appealed. Although most cases are appealed on the basis of the facts of the case, a minority do involve issues arising from the correct interpretation of the law to the particular case. In this context, questions of law may be determined not only at first instance by officials but also on appeal by specialist tribunals, the Upper Tribunal (formerly the Social Security Commissioners) and, in rare instances, the ordinary UK Courts. If a case reaches either of these last two levels, there is always the possibility that the decision will be reported. Such reported decisions, offering authoritative interpretations of the law, are part of the law of social security to be taken into account by those whose task is to apply the law.

65. *European law*: Although European law is not directly relevant to social security law, there have nonetheless been certain important respects in which European law, in particular the foundational rules relating to equal treatment, and rules relating to the position of migrants, have had a significant impact on the development of British social security law.[21] From 2020, post-BREXIT, social security rights will no longer be decided by EU law. National sovereignty over the substance of social security provisions will thus remain intact

21. T.K. Hervey, *European Social Law and Policy* (London: Longman, 1998); T.K. Hervey, 'Social Security: The European Union Dimension', in *Social Security Law in Context*, ed. N. Harris (Oxford: Oxford University Press, 2000); and, C. Barnard & S. Peers, *European Employment Law* (European Union Law: Oxford University Press, August 2017).

Part I. The Institutions

In the context of this entry in the *Encyclopaedia*, discussion of the institutions relevant to the administration of British social security law is to be found below, in Part XI, Chapter 2.

Part II. Contributions and Financing

Introduction

66. Since a primary objective of the social security system is to make payments, by way of the social security scheme, cash benefits to those citizens of the UK/EEA who find themselves entitled to those benefits in a variety of statutorily defined circumstances, it is obviously essential that – insofar as benefits are paid for directly by the State – the State is able to raise the finance necessary to enable such benefits to be paid. This chapter considers the sources of that finance.

67. In the UK, there are two primary sources of public finance for the social security system which are considered here: first, contributions and second, general taxation. A third source of funding is private funding. This has played a very important role particularly in the context of providing financial protection for people in old age – pensions. The use of private finance in other areas, for example to offer financial protection against industrial injury, sickness or unemployment, has been more controversial, but, given the changing shape of British social security policy also requires brief consideration here.

Chapter 1. Contributions and Credits

68. As noted in the General Introduction, the Beveridge 'vision' for social security in Britain was that it should be based on the concept of 'social insurance'. Drawing an analogy from the premiums paid into private insurance schemes, the primary source of funding in the Beveridge scheme of social security benefits was to be the 'NI contribution' paid weekly by both employers and employees into the NI Fund.

69. Once these contributions were paid into the NI Fund, the fund in turn would be used to finance the payment of those benefits to which entitlement had been established by an appropriate contribution record. Under the Beveridge plan, contributions were to be 'flat-rate' and would be used to fund the payment of 'flat-rate' benefits.

70. As also noted in the General Introduction, the commitment to flat-rate contributions could not be sustained. They simply did not raise sufficient revenue to meet the demands placed upon the NI Fund. There was also the realization that the economic effect of flat-rate contributions was that the burden of them fell more heavily on poorer-paid workers than on the better-paid; in economic terms, it was a 'regressive' form of taxation. Thus, during the 1960s and 1970s, it came to be accepted that contributions should be paid on an 'earnings-related' basis. While certain contributions do, remain payable on a flat-rate basis, the bulk of social security contributions are now earnings-related, varying with the earnings of the contributor.

71. The basis of the present contribution system was established by the SSA passed by Parliament in 1975. It is now consolidated into the Social Security (Contributions and Benefits) Act 1992, Part 1. The current situation is that there are *six* separate classes of contribution payable by contributors, the precise class or classes depending on the employment category into which the individual contributor falls.

72. The contribution classes are:

- Class 1 contributions, paid by both employed earners (the 'primary' contributors) and their employers (the 'secondary' contributors);
- Class 1A contributions, paid by employers only;
- Class 1B contributions, also paid by employers only;
- Class 2 contributions, payable by the self-employed;
- Class 3 voluntary contributions, paid by those who seek to make up a contribution record; and
- Class 4 contributions, paid by the self-employed.

NI Classes

The class you pay depends on your employment status and how much you earn, and whether you have any gaps in your NI record.

National Insurance class	*Who Pays*
Class 1	Employees earning more than GBP 162 a week and under State Pension age – they are automatically deducted by your employer
Class 1A or 1B	Employers pay these directly on their employee's expenses or benefits
Class 2	Self-employed people – you do not have to pay if you earn less than GBP 6,205 a year (but you can choose to pay voluntary contributions)
Class 3	Voluntary contributions – you can pay them to fill or avoid gaps in your NI record
Class 4	Self-employed people earning profits over GBP 8,424 a year

The Weekly Rates in the UK Are:

England & Wales/NI

PAYE (Pay-as-You-Earn) Tax Rates and Thresholds	*2018 to 2019*
Employee personal allowance	GBP 228 per week GBP 988 per month GBP 11,850 per year
UK basic tax rate	20% on annual earnings above the PAYE tax threshold and up to GBP 34,500
UK higher tax rate	40% on annual earnings from GBP 34,501 to GBP 150,000
UK additional tax rate	45% on annual earnings above GBP 150,000

Scotland

PAYE Tax Rates and Thresholds	*2018 to 2019*
Employee personal allowance	GBP 228 per week GBP 988 per month GBP 11,850 per year
Scottish starter tax rate	19% on annual earnings above the PAYE tax threshold and up to GBP 2,000
Scottish basic tax rate	20% on annual earnings from GBP 2,001 to GBP 12,150
Scottish intermediate tax rate	21% on annual earnings from GBP 12,151 to GBP 31,580

PAYE Tax Rates and Thresholds	*2018 to 2019*
Scottish higher tax rate	41% on annual earnings from GBP 31,581 to GBP 150,000
Scottish top tax rate	46% on annual earnings above GBP 150,000

Class 1 NI Thresholds

Class 1 NI Thresholds	*2018 to 2019*
Lower Earnings Level (LEL)	GBP 116 per week GBP 503 per month GBP 6,032 per year
Primary Threshold (PT)	GBP 162 per week GBP 702 per month GBP 8,424 per year
Secondary Threshold (ST)	GBP 162 per week GBP 702 per month GBP 8,424 per year
Upper Secondary Threshold (under 21) (UST)	GBP 892 per week GBP 3,863 per month GBP 46,350 per year
Apprentice Upper Secondary Threshold (apprentice under 25) (AUST)	GBP 892 per week GBP 3,863 per month GBP 46,350 per year
Upper Earnings Limit (UEL)	GBP 892 per week GBP 3,863 per month GBP 46,350 per year

Class 1 NI Rates

Employee (Primary) Contribution Rates

NI Category Letter	*Earnings at or above LEL up to and Including PT*	*Earnings above the PT up to and Including UEL*	*Balance of Earnings above UEL*
A	0%	12%	2%
B	0%	5.85%	2%
C	Nil	Nil	Nil
H (apprentice under 25)	0%	12%	2%
J	0%	2%	2%
M (under 21)	0%	12%	2%

NI Category Letter	*Earnings at or above LEL up to and Including PT*	*Earnings above the PT up to and Including UEL*	*Balance of Earnings above UEL*
Z (under 21 – deferment)	0%	2%	2%

Employer (Secondary) Contribution Rates

NI Category Letter	*Earnings at or above LEL up to and Including ST*	*Earnings above ST up to and Including UEL/UST/AUST*	*Balance of Earnings above UEL/UST/AUST*
A	0%	13.80%	13.80%
B	0%	13.80%	13.80%
C	0%	13.80%	13.80%
H (apprentice under 25)	0%	0%	13.80%
J	0%	13.80%	13.80%
M (under 21)	0%	0%	13.80%
Z (under 21 – deferment)	0%	0%	13.80%

Class 1A NI: Expenses and Benefits

NI Class	*2018 to 2019 Rate*
Class 1A	13.8%

Class 1B NI: PAYE Settlement Agreements

NI Class	*2018 to 2019 Rate*
Class 1B	13.8%

Class 2 NI: PAYE Settlement Agreements

The 2015 Summer Budget confirmed the Government's intention to abolish Class 2 National Insurance contributions (NICs). This means that since 2016, instead of paying two classes of NICs (Class 2 and Class 4), the self-employed will pay just one (Class 4) in the future. This follows the recommendations of the Office of Tax Simplification and will simplify the NICs system for millions of people.

Class 2 NICs provided the self-employed with access to a range of state benefits: the Basic State Pension, Bereavement Benefits, Maternity Allowance and contributory ESA. To ensure that the self-employed can continue to access these benefits through the NICs system, alternative options were enacted in order to maintain benefit entitlement under a Class 4 NICs entitlement test.

Class 4 NI

Self-employed NI Rates
Two types of NI if you are self-employed:

- Class 2 if your profits are GBP 6,205 or more a year
- Class 4 if your profits are GBP 8,424 or more a year

How Much You Pay

Class	*Rate for Tax Year 2018 to 2019*
Class 2	GBP 2.95 a week
Class 4	9% on profits between GBP 8,424 and GBP 46,350 2% on profits over GBP 46,350

73. Assuming that all the contribution conditions are satisfied, that is to say that sufficient contributions have been paid or credited in relation to the benefit in question,[22] Class 1 contributions establish entitlement to all contributory benefits. Classes 2 and 3 establish entitlement to a more limited range of contributory benefits. Contribution classes 1A, 1B and 4 establish no entitlement to benefit at all; they are simply a means to raise additional revenue for social security purposes.

§1. Class 1 Contributions

74. The shift from the original 'flat-rate' principle to the 'earnings-related' principle is most noticeable in the case of Class 1 contributions. The old rules provided that employees who earned less than a 'lower earnings limit' did not pay contributions. However, this limit was below the point at which such employees began to pay income tax. There is still a lower earnings limit – currently GBP 116 a week, but in order to prevent non-taxpayers paying Class 1 contributions,[23] those who earn below what is called the 'PT' (currently GBP 162 per week)[24] pay no contributions at all, but are treated as though they have paid them. Employees whose earnings are

22. For further details, *see* the discussion of the specific contributory benefits: for example, JSA, Sickness Benefit, Retirement Benefit, Widows' Benefits, discussed in the relevant chapters below.
23. The changes were introduced by the Welfare Reform and Pensions Act 1999 (WRPA) Sch. 9, para. 3.
24. These sums are adjusted annually.

above the threshold find that their contributions increase as their level of income increases until they reach an 'UEL' (currently – 2018 to 2019 – GBP 892 a week).[25]

75. Those whose earnings are above the PT limit and who are not contracted out of the Additional State Pension (formerly called SERPS)[26] pay 12% on the amount of earnings which fall between the PT limit and their actual weekly earnings or the UEL, whichever is the smaller. Thereafter, employees pay 2% of their earnings over the UEL.

76. The employers' contribution is also assessed on a sliding scale. No contributions at all are payable by employers on employees' earnings falling below the statutorily defined 'ST', currently GBP 162 a week. Above that level, the employers' contribution is 13.8% on all such earnings.[27]

77. The effect of these rules on the individual employee is that, assuming that their earnings are above the PT, they are required to pay, on top of any income tax, another defined percentage of their earnings up to the UEL. Over that limit, the percentage falls.

§2. Class 2 and Class 4 Contributions

78. Class 2 contributions are paid by the self-employed (unless their incomes are very low – below GBP 6,205 in the tax year April 2018 to April 2019). These contributions are still flat rate, currently GBP 2.95 a week. However, the self-employed are also liable to pay what are in effect earnings-related Class 4 contributions. These are levied at the rate of 9% on the profits of the self-employed person, which fall between defined lower and upper profit limits (GBP 8,424 and GBP 46,350, respectively in 2018/2019). They pay 2% on profits above the upper profit limit. As with the upper and lower earnings limits, these limits for Class 2 and Class 4 contributions are also revised by the Government each year.

§3. Class 1A and Class 1B Contributions

79. Class 1A contributions were first introduced in 1991.[28] Originally, they were payable by employers in cases where their employees had the use of a company car not only for company business but also for private purposes. This was introduced to

25. Cf. https://www.gov.uk/government/publications/rates-and-allowances-national-insurance-contributions/rates-and-allowances-national-insurance-contributions#class-1-national-insurance-rates.
26. *See* below Part VIII.
27. This again reflects a change from the system which existed prior to the SSA1998. Previously, there were a number of thresholds at which the rate of contribution payable was increased. But this was felt to present a sequence of barriers to increasing workers' earnings.
28. By the Social Security (Contributions) Act 1991; now Social Security Contributions and Benefits Act 1992 s. 1(2)(b) and s. 10.

close a loophole in tax law whereby employers, who were permitting widespread use of company cars and providing subsidized petrol to employees, were regarded as making a form of payment in kind to their employees which was not hitherto regarded as part of the wages on which social security contributions (and indeed tax liability) were based. Since April 2000, Class 1A contributions have been levied on other benefits in kind which are subject to income tax – for example, payments of medical expenses insurance. This class of contributions is now charged at 13.8% of the 'cash equivalent' of the benefit to the employee, which is calculated in broadly the same way as for income tax purposes.[29] The net has since been widened further. The principal objective is clear; anything that counts as income for income tax purposes should also count as earnings for NI contributions purposes. However, the outcome is a network of detailed regulations of considerable complexity.

80. Class 1B contributions were introduced to provide a mechanism to facilitate payment of standard employers' contributions on small non-cash payments made to employees which are dealt with under a PAYE settlement arrangement made with the Inland Revenue.[30] They are now paid at 13.8%, the same rate as other employers' contributions.[31]

§4. Class 3 Contributions

81. Class 3 contributions are still flat rate. These are payable voluntarily by those who need to make up their contribution records – for example because they do not have an adequate work record – for entitlement to widows' benefits or retirement pensions.

New Income Tax Allowances and NI Rates

Income Tax Allowances

	2017–2018	*2018–2019*
	GBP	GBP
Personal allowance	11,500	11,850
Income limit	100,000	100,000
Married couple's allowance (dob before 6.4.1935)	8,455	8,695
Married couple's allowance (minimum amount) (dob before 6.4.1935)	3,260	3,360
Marriage allowance	1,150	1,185

29. Income and Corporation Taxes Act 1978 s. 158 and Sch. 6.
30. SSCBA 1992, s. 10A inserted by SSA1998, s. 53.
31. WRPA 1999, s. 77.

	2017–2018	*2018–2019*
	GBP	GBP
Blind person's allowance	2,320	2,390
Dividend allowance	5,000	2,000
Personal savings allowance (basic rate taxpayers)	1,000	1,000
Personal savings allowance (higher rate taxpayers)	500	500
Annual Individual Savings Account (ISA) subscription limit		
Overall limit	20,000	20,000
Junior ISA	4,128	4,260
Child trust fund	4,128	4,260

NIC Rates 2018–2019

Lower earnings limit, primary class 1	GBP 116/week
UEL, primary class 1	GBP 892/week
PT	GBP 162/week
ST	GBP 162/week
Employees' primary class 1 rate between PT and UEL	12%
Employees' primary class 1 rate above UEL	2%
Class 1A rate on employer-provided benefits	13.80%
Employers' secondary class 1 rate above ST	13.80%
Married women's reduced rate between PT and UEL	5.85%
Married women's reduced rate above UEL	2%
Apprentice upper ST for under 25s	GBP 892/week
Class 2 rate	GBP 2.95/week
Class 2 small profits threshold	GBP 6,205/year
Special class 2 rate for share fishermen	GBP 3.60/week
Special class 2 rate for volunteer development workers	GBP 5.80/week
Class 3 rate	GBP 14.65/week
Class 4 lower profits limit	GBP 8,424/year
Class 4 upper profits limit	GBP 46,350/year

Class 4 rate between lower profits limit and upper profits limit	9%
Class 4 rate above upper profits limit	2%

§5. Credits

82. In situations where a person is not liable to make a contribution, a gap in that person's contribution record arises. In many situations, the gap is filled, at least in part, by a credited contribution or 'credit'.[32] Credits do not perform all the functions of full contributions, but they can assist in many commonly found situations where it would be harsh to penalize a person for an inadequate contribution record.

83. Credits are attributed to an insured person's contribution record in the following circumstances:

- during weeks of unemployment or incapacity for work;
- during periods while the contributor is caring for an invalid;
- during periods a person has been wrongly detained in prison, where his original conviction has been quashed;
- during periods of full-time education or vocational training;
- during periods while in receipt of Statutory Sick Pay (SSP), Statutory Maternity Pay (SMP) or Statutory Adoption Pay (SAP);
- periods while on jury service;
- in certain cases following bereavement;
- men aged 60 or over (who have taken early retirement) (this is being phased out as the pension age for women is increased to align them with the men's pension age);
- years during which a person is entitled to 'home responsibilities protection', for example, because they were looking after a child or a person who is disabled.

§6. The Relationship Between Contributions and Benefits

84. The precise relationship between the contributory principle and those benefits which are contributory in nature is extremely complex. Put simply, the conditions are more demanding for long-term benefits, such as retirement pensions, than they are for short-term benefits, such as the short-term component of IB (in those cases not covered by statutory sickness pay).

85. There are usually two essential conditions. The first demands that actual or deemed contributions should have been paid into the NI Fund (i.e., credits do not suffice); this is to meet the foundational Beveridge principle that there should be a

32. *See* generally, The Social Security (Credits) Regulations, 1975, SI 1975 No. 556 (as amended).

link between building up entitlement during periods in work and the benefits which are payable when a person is, for whatever reason, not able to work.

86. The second condition relates to the value of the contributions which have been paid (or the credits which have been credited). In general, the longer term the benefit lasts, the greater must be the sums that the insured person has paid into the scheme, before there can be a full entitlement to benefit. By contrast, short-term benefits require lesser sums to be paid into the fund.

87. It is not the case, however, that contributions build up on an actuarial basis as would be the case with private insurance schemes. The money paid in by today's social security contributors is used to pay today's social security beneficiaries. This is a frequent source of misunderstanding by members of the public, and an issue which politicians find hard to explain convincingly to the public.

Chapter 2. General Taxation

§1. Direct Provision

88. Part of the income of the NI Fund has always come, not from the contributions just discussed but from a grant paid by the National Exchequer out of general taxation.[33] Thus even in its pure Beveridgean form, the social insurance scheme benefited from some income derived from general taxation as well as the resources available from contributions. Nonetheless, in the seventy years since Beveridge's concept of NI was developed and brought into operation, general taxation has become a much more important source for the funding of social security benefits.

89. There are a number of reasons for this, many of which have been hinted at in the course of the discussion in the General Introduction.

90. First, the financial levels at which (contributory) social insurance benefits have been set have usually been lower than those at which officially defined poverty levels have been set. Thus, in order to bring the available financial resources of the poorest members of the community up to those officially defined poverty levels, there has always been a need to supplement social insurance benefits with non-contributory means-tested benefits for those individuals and families who have no or very few additional monetary resources.[34]

91. Second, this trend has been exacerbated in recent years with the increasing commitment on the part of the Government to 'targeting' social benefits on the neediest, which has resulted in yet further increased use of means-tested benefits, funded out of general taxation.

92. Third, there have emerged new areas of social need which Beveridge did not adequately take into account. In particular, there have in recent years been created a number of non-contributory benefits for the disabled who, by reason of their disabilities, could never get into the workforce and thus could not begin to make the contributions that would be necessary for them to satisfy the contribution conditions which were sketched out above.

93. Fourth, the introduction of Child Benefit in 1975, which is a very substantial benefit in overall public expenditure terms, was in its creation so linked with the abolition of the married man's tax allowance that it became politically essential that this too should be funded out of general taxation and not made a contributory benefit.

---

33. The Exchequer contribution to the Social Insurance Fund was abolished in 1989 (SSA1989 s. 3) but reinstated again in 1993 (SSA1993). Under the present rules, this contribution is determined according to the National Insurance Fund's balance in any particular tax year; under the earlier rules, the contribution was fixed at a defined percentage of revenue from contributions devoted to the payment of contributory benefits.

34. *See* further, Part XI.

§2. Indirect Provision

94. Apart from direct contributions to the payment of social security benefits from tax revenue, the tax system also provides certain important indirect contributions to the overall system of social security provision, in particular through the tax advantages that attach to many occupational and personal pension schemes. The details of these tax rules are complex and beyond the scope of this work. The nature of private occupational pension schemes is considered in a little more detail in the next chapter and below in Part VIII. Suffice it to say here that the effect of such tax reliefs is to add significantly to the total sums available for pension provision; in this sense, therefore, the tax system makes an additional and important further contribution to overall social security provision.

95. The importance of recognizing this source of funding has a wider significance. A number of proposals are being developed within the British political context suggesting, in effect, that individuals should be encouraged to make even more private provision for the circumstances currently covered by the social security system. Insurance cover for unemployment and sickness, as well as further insurance for old age, is among the ideas that are being considered in different parts of the political spectrum. It is, therefore, very likely that one of the developments that will occur within the British social security system in the coming years will be increased incentives to provide personal social security through different insurance schemes.

§3. Retention of the Contributory Principle?

96. There has been some debate in Britain about the value of retaining the contributory principle, given the increasing importance of benefits funded out of general taxation. After all, the fiscal effect is the same; money is taken from individual pockets to fund State expenditure.

97. The response from the Government, however, has been not to alter the basic structure of contributions and taxation. Part of the argument is that citizens are familiar with the contributory principle and would not wish to see it removed. They may even feel that, as with private insurance schemes, the money paid into the NI Fund is actually directly related to the benefits that they ultimately receive from it.

Chapter 3. Pension Provision and the Role of Private Finance

98. Discussions of social security systems have, until recently, largely focused on the provision of benefits provided by the State. Increasing financial pressures have, however, caused successive Governments to consider questions such as how far social security pension provision should be regarded as the exclusive responsibility of the State and how far private provision should be embraced within the framework of social security.

99. This is conceptually controversial, but the relationship between public and private provision must be considered in any modern discussion of the social security system in Britain. While private provision may in the past have been regarded as a matter of individual choice and lacking that element of State regulation thought to be an essential aspect of the definition of social security, this has become increasingly untrue.

100. The issue may perhaps be illustrated best in the context of *occupational pensions*. As noted in the General Introduction, one of the great debates in British social security policy in the 1960s and early 1970s addressed the question of how the elderly could be lifted out of poverty. They were in receipt of the State retirement pension, but this was set at a level which in very many cases was below the official poverty line. Thus large numbers of pensioners had to supplement their State Pension by claiming an additional means-tested benefit – then called Supplementary Benefit.

101. There was evidence[35] that many elderly people would in fact prefer to live below the poverty line rather than claim a means-tested benefit; others were simply ignorant of their entitlements. There was a more political/moral argument as well – that after a lifetime of work it was not right that the elderly should end their days with resources at or below the poverty line. The policy debate, therefore, focused on how a mechanism could be devised for ensuring that those who retired would receive not only the flat-rate retirement pension but also an earnings-related occupational pension.

102. Occupational pensions had long been available to better-off workers in 'white-collar' employment; they were much less available to manual 'blue-collar' workers.

103. After considerable debate, the SSA 1975 introduced the SERPS which would apply compulsorily to all workers who were not already in an occupational

35. *See*, for example, R.E. Lister, *Take up of Means-Tested Benefits (Poverty Pamphlet, 18)* (London: CPAG, 1974); J. Millar, *Take Up of Means-Tested Benefits* (London: DHSS, 1982); A.B. Atkinson, *Take-Up of Social Security Benefits* (London: ESRC, 1984); J.-Y. Duclos, *The Take-Up of State Benefits: An Application to Supplementary Benefits in Britain Using the FES* (London: LSE, Welfare State Programme, 1992); V.C. Fry & G. Stark, *The Take-Up of Means-Tested Benefits 1984–1990* (London: Institute for Fiscal Studies, 1993).

pension scheme. Contracting out of SERPS into a private scheme would be permitted, but only so long as the benefits under the private occupational pension scheme were at least as good as those provided under the SERPS.[36]

104. The effect of 'contracting out' is that the level of payment by both employers and employees under Class 1 was reduced. But, of course, such employers and in most cases employees[37] were making contributions into the private occupational pension scheme. It is because these private arrangements are now regulated by the State, at least in terms of setting the basic levels of contributions and benefits, that occupational pension schemes must now be regarded as part of the social security system.

105. Despite the fact that SERPS was introduced by legislation passed in 1975 (which in turn did not take effect until 1978), it was never designed to become fully operational until 1998, since it would take twenty years for benefits to build up under the scheme. During the 1980s, however, actuarial calculations were undertaken taking into account likely demographic trends into the early years of the twenty-first century. These suggested that with increasing longevity of pensioners combined with diminishing numbers of people of working age, the financial burden on those in employment to fund the pensions for those who had retired would become intolerable.

106. In 1986, the Government introduced new incentives both to encourage the establishment of occupational pensions schemes in employment sectors where before there had been none[38] and also to create the ability of people to join their own approved private pension schemes developed as alternative to the SERPS. In recent years, there has been a major crisis in the pensions industry arising from the mis-selling of private pension schemes.

107. The response of the Blair Labour administration 1997–2007 was not to pour further State resource into SERPS, but rather to provide a new framework for pension provision for those on low and middle incomes in partnership with the private pensions industry.[39] Two particular initiatives were taken. First, the concept of the 'stakeholder pension' was introduced in the WRPA 1999, designed to provide a more secure and regulated form of private pension than formerly existed. Second, a new 'State Second Pension' or Additional State Pension replaced SERPS in 2002

---

36. The Secretary of State for Social Security and the Occupational Pensions Regulatory Authority – replacing the former Occupational Pensions Board – certify whether private schemes do or do not satisfy this test: *see* Pension Schemes Act 1993, as amended by the Pensions Act 1995.
37. Certain categories of employees receive 'non-contributory' occupational pensions. Civil servants are the largest group of workers in Britain in this fortunate position. The pensions of workers in these groups are wholly funded by their employers, in the case of civil servants out of Government resources, that is, by the taxpayer.
38. *See* SSA 1986, and now the Pension Schemes Act 1993.
39. *See* the Green Paper, 'A New Contract for Welfare: Partnership in Pensions', Cmd 4179 (London: TSO, 1998).

by boosting the additional (second-tier) pension of low earners and providing additional pension for the first time for carers and some long-term disabled people with broken work records.

108. Notwithstanding these developments, there remained significant doubts among politicians and policymakers about the capacity of private pension schemes to meet the retirement needs of the least well off, not least because of the difficulty they face in making sufficient contributions into a pension scheme during their working lifetime. One of the responses to this has been that the principle has now been accepted that employees should automatically be enrolled in a workplace pension scheme; provision for the introduction of this is contained in the Pensions Act 2014.

109. Another indication of the importance of looking at private sources of finance in the context of social security can be seen in the fact that since 1991, part of the expense of *SSP* has had to be met directly by the employer. Until that date, SSP had been funded 100% by the State with the employers in effect merely taking over the role of the Department of Social Security (DSS) in administering short-term Sickness Benefit. This trend was (at least from the Government's point of view) taken to its logical conclusion in 1994, from which time employers, in general, have had to bear the total cost of SSP. The present position is considered further below, Part V.

110. In 1997, the same trend was evidenced in changes made to the arrangements under which the State seeks to recover any money paid out in social security benefits to an individual as a result of any accident, injury or disease. Where a third party accepts liability or is found liable to pay common law damages to that individual because of being held to be legally responsible for the accident, injury or disease, that third party (and his/her insurer) becomes liable to reimburse the State for such social security benefits as have been paid to that individual for a period of up to five years, or until the date on which the compensation is paid.[40]

111. The Blair Government believed, and the former Coalition Government from 2010 to 2015 believed, that one of the principles that should guide social security reform is the need to secure a closer partnership between the public and private sectors in the provision of social security. For example, the Blair Government looked to an increasing role for private insurance in pension provision and funding for *long-term care.*[41] The Coalition Government established an independent Commission – the Dilnot Commission – to review policy in this area; its report was published in June 2011.[42] Successive Governments have also sought to encourage more

40. Social Security (Recovery of Benefits) Act 1997.
41. The practical difficulties – both political and economic – in moving in this direction should not be underestimated. For example, the Royal Commission on Long-Term Care reviewed the role of the insurance market in relation to the elderly and concluded that private insurance is not a viable option for funding the cost of personal care for the elderly or the disabled. The Royal Commission called

personal saving, though these efforts have been thwarted by currently very low-interest rates. While the inference to be drawn might be that, increasingly, State provision will concentrate on a residual support, the reality is that the UK is still a long way from reaching that position.

112. In more concrete terms, the previous UK Labour Governments' (1997–2010) desire to shift responsibility for social security from the State to the individual was evidenced in proposals to reduce entitlement to an ongoing social security income for childless widows; to remove most non-contributory, non-means-tested earnings replacement benefits for the disabled (other than those disabled at a young age); to reduce SERPS provision for the better off; and to shift some of the burden of IB to the private sector by providing that income from private insurance schemes will reduce entitlement to that formerly non-means-tested benefit. The present Coalition Government has placed great emphasis on linking personal responsibility to apply for and take employment to the conditions for entitlement to unemployment benefits.

113. Since 2000, one of the main challenges facing Governments throughout the developed world is how to keep levels of public expenditure under control. In the context of social security, this could be achieved simply by abolishing particular social security benefits. However, this is always politically difficult, if not impossible. A politically less damaging option, therefore, may be for Governments to alter the structure of the social security system so as to impose additional funding obligations directly on individuals. It does seem, therefore, that private funding of what we now regard as social security – albeit within a statutory framework imposed by Government – is increasingly likely to occur in the coming years.

---

strongly for personal care to be paid for on a non-means-tested basis out of general taxation. (*See* their report: 'With Respect for Old Age', Cmd 4192 – I (London: TSO, March 1999). This option has been ruled out.

42. *See* www.dilnotcommission.dh.gov.uk/2011/07/04/commission-report/; the Government has not yet decided its response to these proposals.

Part III. Health Care

Introduction

114. It will be recalled from the General Introduction that Beveridge regarded the creation of an NHS as an essential step which needed to coexist with his proposals for a social insurance scheme. Indeed the establishment of the NHS after the end of Second World War has been regarded as one of the most significant developments in the Welfare State in Britain.

115. However, following the Beveridge proposals, the health service has always been regarded in Britain as distinct from rather than a part of the social security system. Unlike many social security systems in Continental Europe and indeed other countries in the world, the provision of health care in Britain does not, for the most part, fall for consideration as a central part of the British social security system. The reason for this is that, in Britain, most health care facilities are provided and paid for within the separate legislative and financial framework of the NHS.

116. The entitlement of individuals to health services derives principally from tests of residence and presence in the country,[43] rather than entitlement based specifically on the payment of statutory (or private) insurance contributions or premiums. Health care is, thus, in principle free to those entitled to it, and the cost of the service is funded out of general taxation, though there is also a contribution made from the NI Fund. It follows that analysis of the British social security system does not involve a detailed understanding of the complex rules relating to health insurance which have to be considered in the overall scheme of social security in other countries of the world.

117. There are, however, obvious links between health service policy and social security policy which may be noted here.

118. First, charges for certain categories of health care are in fact now levied, despite the basic policy of free provision. Noteworthy examples are charges for dental care, for optical care and for the dispensing of prescriptions. This is a trend that seems likely to continue (though since devolution, free prescriptions have been

43. Those coming from overseas who do not satisfy the residence and presence tests are required to pay for treatment.

introduced in Wales, Scotland and Northern Ireland). There are cash benefits available to subsidize the payment of those charges for the poor which should properly be regarded as a part of social security provision, though it may be noted in passing that they do not attract the attention they deserve among British social security policy analysts, and they do tend to be ignored by British social security scholars. In fact, when looked at as a whole, they now combine to create a not insignificant branch of British social security law.

119. Second, there is an important link between social security policy and health care policy in the functional sense that if health care is effective, particularly to prevent sickness and disease, this should help to limit the numbers of those who are in receipt of the range of sickness benefits[44] that are available in the social security system.

120. Third, and notwithstanding these general comments, it is the case that a minority of British people do belong to private health care insurance schemes. Indeed, there are certain categories of treatment that are only available on a private basis and which fall outside the NHS provision. Participation is, however, entirely voluntary and not part of regulated State provision.

§1. The Scope of This Part

121. This Part comprises three further chapters. The first discusses those benefits, mentioned above, which are designed to provide assistance to the poor with their NHS charges. (This is one area where the rules are different in Scotland and Wales from those in England.) The second considers the general – if rather technical – rules of social security law which affect those who become inpatients in NHS hospitals, which have the effect of reducing entitlement to other social security benefits (on the principle that if the State is looking after a person in hospital or similar institution it should not also provide him/her with the cash that he/she would have needed were that person still to be living independently outside the hospital or other institution). The third, though not perhaps entirely appropriate in this Part, looks at those social security benefits payable in situations where health care has been unable to prevent an individual from dying: social security benefits payable on death. Further information is to be found in the leaflet *HC11: Help with health costs* at http://www.nhs.uk/NHSEngland/Healthcosts/Pages/help-with-health-costs.aspx#.

44. For sickness benefits, *see* Part V; for industrial injuries benefits, *see* Part VI; and for benefits for disabled persons, *see* Part IX.

Chapter 1. Health Service Benefits

122. Various forms of assistance are available to assist with paying for the following matters:

- prescription charges for medication;
- dental treatment and the provision of dentures (false teeth);
- eyesight tests and the provision of glasses;
- provision of wigs and fabric supports;
- assistance with fares to hospital (where a free ambulance service is not provided); and
- free milk and vitamins for children.

123. In some situations, entitlement to social security assistance in this context is linked to receipt of another social security benefit;[45] in other situations, entitlement depends on the actual circumstances of the potential beneficiary; in yet other cases, entitlement depends on the application of an alternative means-test. The following examples will help to clarify these points.

§1. Prescription Charges for Drugs/Medication

124. In an effort to stem rapidly rising costs associated with the provision of drugs by doctors to their patients, the Government pursued two policies. First, it sought to limit the freedom of doctors to prescribe whatever drugs they wished; in particular, where drugs are available both under a cheaper 'generic' name and a more expensive 'brand' name, the freedom to prescribe has been reduced.

125. In addition, and more relevant here, the charges imposed on patients who have been given by their doctor's prescriptions for drugs supplied under the NHS have risen very sharply over the last decade. It is largely for this reason that the significance of the 'health social security system' has increased in importance. A number of means for reducing or lifting the burden of these costs are available. (These do not apply in Wales, Scotland and Northern Ireland where, following devolution, prescriptions are free for all.)

I. Prepayment Certificates

126. Anyone, whatever their financial means, who because of a health condition requires a substantial and regular supply of prescribed drugs and thus needs frequent drug prescriptions can, if not otherwise entitled to them free (as a result of the matters discussed below), apply for a 'prepayment certificate' (or 'season ticket'). By paying a lump sum covering a period of either four months or a year, the holder

45. *See* the discussion of the concept of 'passporting', considered below, Part X.

of the certificate will not have to pay any more for his/her prescriptions during the period covered by the certificate, no matter how many prescriptions are needed. This is of financial advantage to anyone needing more than fourteen prescriptions in any period of twelve months and is, therefore, in practice a subsidy for the cost of the prescriptions.

II. Free Prescriptions

127. In addition, certain categories of person and those suffering from defined categories of disease are entitled to free prescriptions.

128. Taking these two matters in reverse order, free prescriptions are available to those who suffer from a continuing physical disability, which prevents them from leaving the home, except with the help of another person; to those suffering from epilepsy, which requires continuous anti-convulsive therapy; to those with a permanent fistula;[46] to those suffering from diabetes mellitus, or diabetes insipidus (and other forms of hypopituitarism), Addison's disease (and other forms of hypoadrenalism), myasthenia gravis, myxoedema and hypoparathyroidism; (since 2009) to those undergoing treatment for cancer. Free prescriptions are also available for the treatment of a sexually transmissible infection; for patients subject to a community treatment order, in respect of any drug supplied to that patient for the treatment of a mental disorder; and for medication for the treatment of tuberculosis when the medication is supplied at a hospital or clinic.

129. It will be seen that this list is very specific. Many other conditions which in practice require constant medication (e.g., asthma) are not included in this list.

130. In addition to those suffering from specific diseases, there are large groups of persons who are entitled to free prescriptions. These are: all those aged under 16 or over 60; individuals receiving IS, income-based Jobseeker's Allowance, income-related Employment Support Allowance or the guarantee credit of Pension Credit (PC) or individuals who have a family member on these benefits; individuals, or their partners, who receive CTC, working tax credit (WTC), or with or without WTC on its own but with the disability or severe disability element, and whose gross annual income is less than GBP 16,105; permanent residents in nursing or residential care who are not responsible for the full cost of that care; hospital inpatients; asylum seekers receiving support from National Asylum Support Service (NASS) or a local authority; war disablement pensioners who need their prescriptions for their war disability; 16 and 17 year olds who are being maintained by a local authority having left care; prisoners/young offenders; and individuals on 'low income'.[47]

46. This is an ulcer. It may arise in a number of situations, including caecostomy, ileostomy, laryngostomy or colostomy needing continuous surgical dressing or an appliance.
47. *See* Regulations 4–6 National Health Service (Travelling Expenses and Remission of Charges) Regulations 2003 SI 2382.

131. This last category is determined by the application of a means-test that is similar to but not identical with that for IS or the income-related element of JSA or ESA.[48] In particular, more housing costs are included. This has the result that those just over the IS limits become entitled to free prescriptions. Also, the disqualifications for voluntary unemployment and involvement in a trade dispute, which apply to JSA and ESA,[49] do not apply in this context. Unusually, however, there is no appeal[50] to a tribunal against any decision that they may come to. Dissatisfied claimants only have the possibility of writing to the Authority to ask for a review of any decision they may reach.

132. As a result of all these exemptions and special rules, it has been estimated that around 90% of all prescriptions in England are, in practice, free.

§2. Dental Treatment and Dentures

133. All NHS dental treatments, including routine preventive check-ups, attract charges which vary depending on the amount of work that has to be done to the patient (except in Scotland where NHS dental check-ups are free). As with prescription charges, many categories of people are entitled to free NHS dental treatment and dentures. These include those listed in paragraph 138, as well as those under 18 (or under 19 and in full-time education), pregnant and new mothers and members of specific schemes. Free treatment is also given to those attending the NHS Dental Service and the Community Dental Service (principally the disabled). Also, in Wales, there are free check-ups for the under 25s and over 60s.

134. Even if a person's resources are above the means-test limits, there may still be an entitlement to a *reduction* of the charge that would otherwise be paid, where the level of the charge is high and a person's income is still low.

§3. Eyesight Tests and Spectacles

135. While treatment for eye disease is free under the NHS, eyesight tests are not, except in Scotland. Nor are spectacles or contact lenses.

136. *Eyesight tests* are nevertheless provided free[51] to those listed in paragraph 138, as well as those under 16, or under 19 if still in full-time education; to those

48. The National Health Service (Travelling Expenses and Remission of Charges) Regulations 1998 No. 551 and the National Health Service (Travelling Expenses and Remission of Charges) Regulations 2003 No. 2382.
49. *See* below Part X.
50. *See* below Part XI.
51. In addition to statutory entitlement, some opticians do, in fact, provide free eye testing as a commercial 'loss-leader'.

aged over 60; to those registered blind or partially sighted; to patients of the Hospital Eye Service; to those who have been prescribed 'complex lenses'; to those suffering from diabetes or glaucoma or with a predisposition to glaucoma; to those over the age of 40 and who are the parent, brother, sister or child of a person suffering from glaucoma; to war pensioners who require the sight test because of their war disability; and to those on low incomes.

137. In this last category, those whose income is low, but not low enough to qualify for a free test, may nevertheless obtain it at reduced cost if their 'resources' exceed their 'requirements' by only a limited amount, that is, if they are just above the means-test limit for tests to be provided free of charge.

138. Where, as a result of the eyesight test, *spectacles and contact lenses* are prescribed by the optician, they are not actually supplied free, but the claimant will be issued with a voucher of a certain value which may be used towards the cost of purchasing the glasses or contact lenses which have been prescribed. The value of the voucher depends on what has been prescribed. By shopping around, the voucher holder may find an optician able to provide what has been prescribed for the price stated in the voucher, but there is no guarantee of that. These so-called full-value vouchers are issued to those in the exempt groups in paragraph 143–147, to those under 16 or under 19 if in full-time education; to Hospital Eye Service patients who need frequent changes of glasses or contact lenses; to those who have been prescribed complex lenses; and to those on low income. Again, 'reduced-value' vouchers may be issued to persons in this last category, where the 'resources' of the patient are only modestly in excess of the 'requirements'.

§4. Provision of Wigs and Fabric Supports

139. Where wigs or fabric support for the spine are prescribed under the NHS, they are covered by the rules on prescriptions above. They can also be provided free of charge by health authorities, General Practitioners (GPs) or hospitals, or social services departments may provide them, which can be subject to a reasonable charge.

§5. Travel Expenses to Hospital

140. Those attending an NHS hospital or clinic for treatment or a disablement services centre will qualify for help with the cost of getting there if they are in one of the groups listed in paragraph 131 (above), or if they are a patient at a sexually transmitted disease clinic which is situated more than fifteen miles from the patient's home, or if they live in the Scilly Isles or the Scottish Highlands and Islands and have to travel more than a specified distance for their treatment, or they are on 'low income'.

Chapter 2. Impact of Health Treatment on Social Security Benefits

141. Where a social security beneficiary goes into hospital for free treatment under the NHS, entitlement to social security benefit is affected in a variety of ways.[52] The basic policy objective is that as people's long-term needs are reduced if they are being looked after in hospital; therefore, they do not need the cash benefits for normal daily expenses. Though understandable in theory, this assumption is not always justified in practice.[53]

§1. Personal Benefits: General

142. In relation to most benefits, no reduction at all is made for stays in hospital lasting no more than twenty-eight days.[54] After these four weeks, as discussed below, payments of Attendance Allowance and Disability Living Allowance (DLA) or Personal Independent Payment (PIP) cease, and this can have a knock-on effect on other benefits with disability premiums (IS, income-based JSA, income-related Employment Support Allowance, UC, PC, HB and Council Tax Benefit (CTB) – these from 1/2018 are housing costs under UC). However, if the person in hospital is a child, their benefits, including Child Benefit, are only affected after eighty-four days in hospital.

§2. Attendance Allowance for Those over 65

143. Entitlement to Attendance Allowance ceases after four weeks in hospital.[55] This has the knock-on consequence for UC/purposes that a claimant who is in receipt of UC loses entitlement to the severe disability premium. His/her carer, where relevant, then loses entitlement to Care Allowance and also, after a further eight weeks, to any UC carer's premium.[56]

---

52. *See*, generally, Social Security (Hospital In-Patients) Regulations 2005/3360.
53. One particularly harsh consequence of the rules arises where the reduction in the benefit level to which the person is entitled has the effect of taking them off the means-tested IS. When they come out of hospital, they find that they have to make a new claim for IS and thus suffer the statutory reduction in entitlement to the payment of housing costs – as to which *see* Part X – which may add further to their financial burdens.
54. After fifty-two weeks in hospital, some benefits will be reduced, but until then (subject to the above) they will be paid as normal. In essence, IS will be paid at a reduced rate, while Housing and Council Tax Benefit, or help with housing costs as part of another benefit will be no longer be paid out. *See* the Social Security (Hospital In-Patients) Regulations 2005/3360 (as amended).
55. Social Security (Disability Living Allowance) Regulations, 1991, SI 1991 No. 2890, Regulations 8 and 10; in the case of children in hospital, the period is twelve weeks.
56. For details of the relevant rules, *see* Income Support (General) Regulations, 1987 (as amended) Sch. 2 paras 13 and 14ZA.

144. By contrast, entitlement to the mobility component of PIP continues if the claimant had a Motability agreement[57] or they have been a patient since 31 July 1995. Otherwise, entitlement to the mobility component also ends after twenty-eight days.

§3. Industrial Injuries Disablement Benefit

145. This is unaffected by a stay in hospital; nor is Reduced Earnings Allowance, where this is in payment.

§4. Benefits for Children

146. Where a child goes into hospital, Child Benefit and any increments to the 'personal benefits' (as defined in paragraph 162 below) remain in payment for the first twelve weeks. After then, entitlement ceases unless it can be shown that the parent is still regularly incurring expenditure on account of the child. Since this includes the payment of fares to visit the child in hospital, the practical consequence is that in most cases the benefits remain in payment.

147. Where the family is claiming IS or income-based JSA, the personal allowance for a child in hospital is reduced after twelve weeks. Thereafter, it is withdrawn immediately in the unlikely event that the child is no longer in regular contact with the family. Usually, however, the allowance ceases to be payable only when it becomes likely that the child will be away from his/her family for more than fifty-two weeks unless it is unlikely that he/she will be away for much longer than that.[58]

§5. Other Benefits

148. Entitlement to JSA is lost as the claimant is not available for work while in hospital, although those in receipt of the benefit before they go into hospital can be treated as available for work for up to two periods of up to two weeks per year. After six weeks in hospital, a more stringent means-test is applied for HB and CTB, and a single person's entitlement to those benefits ceases completely after fifty-two weeks in hospital. In most other cases, for example, Maternity Allowance, entitlement is not affected.

---

57. *See* Part IX. Motability is a charity supporting individuals on higher rate DLA mobility; it can help them to lease or buy a car.
58. Income Support (General) Regulations Sch. 7 para. 3(b), Regulations 16(2)(b) and 16(5)(b) and Jobseeker's Allowance Regulations Sch. 5 para. 2, Regulations 78(2)(b) and 78(5)(c).

Chapter 3. Benefits Payable in Respect of Death

149. A variety of social security benefits is payable in the event of death.

§1. Funeral Expenses

150. One of the circumstances in which the Social Fund is required[59] to make a payment is in relation to funeral expenses. Entitlement to such a payment is strictly means-tested and arises only in the following circumstances, namely, where:

- a person or a member of that person's family has taken responsibility[60] for the costs of a funeral;
- the funeral takes place in the UK or, in the case of EEA workers and their families only, in the EEA;
- the deceased was ordinarily resident in the UK at the date of death;
- the person taking responsibility is in receipt of UC (previously IS, income-based JSA, income-related ESA), WTC which includes the disability or severe disability element, CTC at a rate which exceeds the family element, PC, HB or CTB/ UC Housing costs; and
- the person who has taken responsibility for the costs is sufficiently close[61] to the deceased person and there is no one else who ought rather to take on the responsibility.[62]

151. The claim must be made within three months of the death of the deceased, which can be extended to twelve months if there was 'good cause' for the failure to claim in time.[63]

---

59. Other mandatory payments are: maternity expenses, *see* Part IV; and Cold Weather Payments, *see* Part X. For discretionary payments from the Social Fund, *see* Part X. For administration and adjudication of Social Fund claims, *see* Part XI.
60. It is not necessary that the person claiming should have been a relative of the deceased or indeed necessarily have arranged the funeral; responsibility will usually be recognized by the BA where the person has obtained an estimate of the cost or a bill for the cost from the funeral director. Nor is it necessary for the person to have dealt directly with the funeral director: an agent can act on his/her behalf. (R (IS) 6/98).
61. Either: (i) the partner of the deceased at the time of death; or (ii) the person with responsibility for a child who has died (and there is no other absent parent who is not claiming means-tested benefits); or (iii) the parent, son or daughter; or (iv) another close relative or close friend of a person who had no partner at the time of death. A person who claims under categories (iii) or (iv) must also show that it was reasonable for him/her to take responsibility for the funeral. It is provided that no payment shall be made to such claimants if there are other immediate family members (i.e., parents, sons or daughters excluding any who are still children) who are not estranged from the deceased and who either are not on qualifying benefit, or have capital in excess of the capital limits for a payment. Further it is deemed not to be reasonable for an individual to take on responsibility for a funeral broadly if there is another individual as close or closer to the deceased who for financial reasons would not be entitled to a full funeral payment.
62. Entitlement to a Social Fund payment is extinguished if another liable relative exists who could pay for the funeral, regardless of whether or not that relative is in fact willing to pay for the funeral.
63. The old law on 'good cause' for late claims is considered in Part XI.

152. The amount of the payment covers broadly: (i) the reasonable costs of either burial or cremation; (ii) certain limited associated fees, for example, for documentation and other necessary services; (iii) specified transport expenses for the body; (iv) limited travel expenses to the funeral; and (v) any other funeral expenses, excluding any expenses incurred as a requirement of the deceased's religion. Certain deductions are to be made from any funeral payment otherwise due, for example any sums readily available without formality from the deceased's estate, any payment from a funeral plan, an insurance policy, occupational pension scheme or similar source and any charitable contribution.[64] The reality is that these payments do not now cover the cost of even a modest funeral; the Government has decided that, since 2012, it has been possible for the very poor to make a claim for additional funeral expenses under the budgeting loans scheme associated with the discretionary Social Fund.[65]

§2. Benefits for Widows and Widowers

153. Until 2000, there were three contributory benefits payable on the death of a spouse: Widow's Payment, Widowed Mother's Allowance and Widow's Pension. They were payable to widows[66] only, on the basis of the deceased husband's contribution record. Entitlement was lost if a widow remarried or cohabited with another man.

154. Under the WRPA 1999, all those receiving the former widows' benefits continue to receive the former benefits, while new claimants receive.

I. Bereavement Payment

155. Following enactment of the WRPA, the former Widow's Payment was doubled from GBP 1,000 to GBP 2,000, and now widows, widowers and surviving civil partners are entitled to claim. It is designed to assist with the initial costs of coming to terms with widow(er)hood.[67] The payment is only made if the relevant contribution conditions are met (or the spouse/civil partner died as a result of an industrial injury or disease), but the payment is not means-tested and is tax-free. This benefit is distinct from the Social Fund payment for funeral expenses, which was discussed above. In appropriate cases, entitlement to both sums is possible.

64. For full details of the rules, *see* Social Fund Maternity and Funeral Expenses (General) Regulations, 2005 No. 3601.
65. *See* below para. 655.
66. To be entitled, the widow must be validly married at the date of her husband's death. Divorced women, by definition, cannot be widows. If a husband has disappeared, it may be possible to obtain a court ruling that he is presumed dead; alternatively, where he has not been seen for many years, and there are indications that he may have died, death may be assumed by the adjudicating authorities: *Chard v. Chard* [1956] P. 259.
67. WRPA 1999, s. 54. It applies to widows/widowers whose spouse died on or after 9 April 2001, and also, from 5 December 2005, surviving civil partners.

II. Widowed Parent's Allowance

156. This is a weekly taxable benefit payable where the widow, widower or surviving civil partner is entitled to Child Benefit in respect of a 'qualifying child', or where a widow is pregnant by her late husband at the time of his death or as the result of fertility treatment undergone while living with her husband (this category also applies to pregnant civil partners).[68] Qualifying children must either be living with the claimant or are being supported by the claimant, and include both the child(ren) of the couple, plus any child in relation to whom the late spouse/partner was entitled to Child Benefit and any child in relation to whom the surviving spouse/partner was entitled to Child Benefit at the time of the death.[69] The current maximum amount payable is GBP 117.10 per week.

157. Entitlement is usually dependent upon the contribution record of the deceased spouse. But entitlement will also arise, irrespective of that contribution record, where the death has occurred as the result of an industrial injury or disease. Remarriage or a new civil partnership will end entitlement to the benefit. Claimants also cannot claim if the death occurs after they have reached pensionable age.

III. Bereavement Allowance

158. This is a weekly benefit payable to a widow, widower or surviving civil partner who is not entitled to the Widowed Parent's Allowance because she/he has no dependent children, is over the age of 45 and under pensionable age at the date of death.[70] As with Widowed Parent's Allowance, entitlement is dependent upon the spouse or civil partner's contribution record or the fact that the death was the result of an industrial accident or disease.

159. The precise amount of benefit that is payable depends upon the age of the widow/widower when first entitled to the benefit. The maximum is payable if he/she is over 55 years of age; otherwise it is reduced by 7% for each year under the age of 55 (but above the minimum age of entitlement of 45). If the contribution record was not complete, the level of payment will be further reduced. Payment lasts for one year only.

IV. Means-Tested Benefits for Widows and Widowers

160. Widows and widowers may be entitled to other means-tested benefits.[71]

68. WRPA 1999, s. 55.
69. SSCBA 1992, s. 37(2).
70. WRPA 1999, s. 56.
71. For further information about income support premia, *see* below Part X, Ch. 1.

Part IV. Family Allowances: Child Benefit and Child Support

Introduction

161. This Part considers the range of mechanisms whereby social security law makes special provision for family responsibilities. By in large the benefits in this section have a common theme: the need to compensate claimants for the additional costs they must bear in respect of parenting. To that extent, we discuss four separate issues, all associated with the provision within the social security system of financial assistance relating to the costs generated by the birth and upbringing of children. They are:

(1) financial support provided within the social security system, associated with the birth of children;
(2) financial support, also provided within the social security system, associated with the costs of bringing up children;
(3) (in outline) measures relating to Child Support, introduced by Government to encourage continuing parental support on the breakdown of marriage, in order to reduce the dependence of lone parents on benefits provided within the State social security system;
(4) establishment (and subsequent abolition) of the Child Trust Fund, a development aimed at encouraging saving and giving children a lump sum to use when they reach adulthood.

162. This Part does not consider the forms of financial assistance that may be given to those who have children who are disabled, nor measures relating to the assistance provided for low-income families with children, and these are dealt with in Part X.

Chapter 1. Financial Provision Associated with the Costs of the Birth of a Child

163. Three separate measures are considered in this chapter:

(1) Statutory Maternity, Paternity and Adoption Pay;
(2) State Maternity Allowance (SMA);
(3) Assistance with maternity expenses.

§1. Statutory Maternity, Paternity and Adoption Pay

164. Ever since the National Insurance Act 1946 came into force, the British social security system has made some provision for maintaining the income of women who were in employment but who needed to leave their employment in order to have their babies. Since that date, the importance of the place of women in the job market has been increasingly recognized. In addition to measures of income maintenance which are to be found within the social security system, women have also been given significant rights under employment protection legislation, which guarantee their right to return to work in defined circumstances, after the birth of their children.[72]

165. As a consequence, the original NI benefit – called 'Maternity Allowance' – became supplemented by contractual entitlements to maternity pay, negotiated by trade unions as part of the collective bargaining process, plus, from 1975 a statutorily based scheme of maternity pay. From April 1987, a fundamental restructuring of these arrangements occurred with the introduction of *SMP*. More recently, the Government has legislated to provide for *SAP* and *Statutory Paternity Pay (SPP).*[73]

166. Under the new system, mothers can claim SMP and fathers can claim SPP. A single adoptive parent can claim SAP. Where there are joint adoptive parents, one can claim adoption pay and the other partner can claim paternity pay. Finally, a partner of a single adoptive parent who is not becoming an adoptive parent himself/herself may also claim SPP. Since 2010, there have been two types of SPP: ordinary and additional.

167. For all of these statutory pay schemes, the individual must have been in continuous employment for a set period, which means that the individual must have

---

72. General discussions on the employment rights of women will be found in standard textbooks on Labour Law. For specialist analysis *see*, for example, A.A. Morris & S.M. Nott, *Working Women and the Law: Equality and Discrimination in Theory and Practice* (London: Routledge, 1991); and S. Fredman, *Women in Labour: Parenting Rights at Work* (London: Institute of Employment Rights, 1995).
73. The relevant provisions are now to be found in SSCBA 1992, Part XII, as significantly amended. Under the Work and Families Act 2006, the periods of SPP were extended; the new rules came into force in 2010 and apply to births after April 2011.

been working for an employer who was liable to make Class 1 contributions in respect of them (although a contributions record is not necessary). They must be earning at least as much as the lower limit for NI contributions, and they must also have ceased to work for that employer or another employer. Finally, the parent must have given the correct notice.

168. To claim maternity pay, mothers must have been in continuous employment for twenty-six weeks prior to the fifteenth week before the expected week of confinement. The mother must give notice to the employer at least twenty-eight days before the day on which she expects payment to start, or if this is not possible, as soon as is reasonably practicable. She must also give evidence of the expected date of birth.

169. The same period of continuous employment applies to SPP for birth of a child, but the claimant must also have been employed right up until the date of the birth. The claimant must give notice to the employer setting out when the SPP will start and whether the claim is for one week or two. This notice must be given at least twenty-eight days before the SPP period is to begin or if this is not possible, as soon as is reasonably practicable. Finally, the claimant must tell the employer the expected week of confinement and give a declaration that they will care for the mother while getting SPP and will have responsibility for the child's upbringing.

170. Where the paternity pay is in respect of an adopted child or the claim is for SAP, the parent must have been continuously employed for a twenty-six-week period ending with the week in which notification of an adoption match is received. Furthermore, where the claim is for paternity pay on adoption, the claimant must have been continuously employed from the date of notification up until the day the child is placed with the family.

171. The notice period for SAP and SPP on adoption is the same as for SPP on birth, but where the claim is for SPP on adoption, the employee must also inform the employer of the date they expect the child to be placed with them, the date on which the adopter was notified that the child had been matched with them and a declaration to the effect that the claimant will have responsibility for the child.

172. The notice for SAP must include details of when the SAP is to start, the date on which the child is to be placed with the claimant, a written declaration that the claimant wishes to receive SAP rather than SPP and supporting documents from the adoption authorities.

173. Statutory maternity, paternity and adoption pay are paid by the employer. Entitlement to maternity and adoption pay lasts for a maximum of twenty-six weeks where the baby was born or placed with the claimant before 1 April 2007. Those with babies born or placed after this date can claim for a maximum of thirty-nine weeks. Paternity pay (now called 'ordinary SPP') runs for a maximum of only two weeks; however, where the mother decides to return to work before the end of the thirty-nine-week period, the father can, from the twentieth week following the birth, claim 'additional SSP' which runs until the end of the thirty-ninth week. In other words, parents now have more flexibility as to who should receive the payments.

174. Payment of SMP can commence from the beginning of the eleventh week before the expected week of confinement. If the woman is in fact confined before that time, her period of entitlement starts in the week immediately following such confinement. SPP is more flexible, and as long as notice has been given to the employer within eight weeks of birth (or eight weeks after the start of the expected week of confinement where the birth is earlier than expected), it can be taken at any time. The earliest SAP can begin is fourteen days before the day on which the claimant expects the child to be placed with them, and the latest day is on the day of placement.

175. Where a claimant is working outside the UK, they may still qualify for statutory maternity, paternity or adoption pay. A claimant must be employed, and this includes where an employer is required to pay secondary Class 1 NI contributions, where the claimant is employed within the EEA (in certain circumstances) or where the claimant is a continental shelf worker or a mariner.[74] Entitlement is lost, however, if the claimant is detained in legal custody (e.g., prison). Special rules on notice periods apply where the parents are adopting a child from abroad.

176. There are two rates of SMP.[75] The higher rate is paid for the first six weeks of entitlement only. This rate is set at 90% of the mother's average weekly earnings for the eight-week period before the last payday before the claimant took maternity leave. It is paid to those who have worked full time (defined as sixteen or more hours per week for at least two years) ending with the qualifying week. It is also paid to those who have worked part-time (more than eight hours but less than sixteen hours per week for at least five years) ending with the qualifying week. After the initial six-week period of entitlement ends, SMP is thereafter payable at the lower rate, which is either the earnings-related rate or a statutorily fixed sum (currently GBP 145.18), whichever is lower.

177. Both SAP and SPP are paid at 90% of the claimant's average weekly earnings over the same eight-week period, or at the statutory standard rate (currently GBP 145.18), whichever is lower.

178. It should be stressed that these forms of statutory pay are the *minimum* required by law; employers are at liberty to pay more and may well have entered into collective agreements to do so.

179. SMP, SAP and SPP are regarded as income. Thus, the beneficiary may be required to pay tax and NI contributions out of their statutory pay. At the lower rate, however, no liability to pay NI contributions can arise. During the period of receipt

74. SSCBA 1992, ss 164 and 171.
75. SSCBA 1992, s. 166.

of the lower rate, the mother is entitled to claim NI *credits* in lieu of contributions.[76] Individuals on low incomes can also claim WTC and, where there is a dependent child, CTCs (*see* Part IV).

§2. State Maternity Allowance

180. For women who are or have been in employment, but who do not fall within the rules which entitle them to SMP, there remains the SMA.[77] There is no contribution requirement for the SMA, but the claimant must satisfy an employment[78] and an earnings condition. In addition, applicant mothers must be within the maternity allowance period and must not be working.

181. To meet the earnings condition an applicant must have been in work, either as an employee or on a self-employed basis, on incomes below the NI threshold but above the 'maternity allowance threshold', currently set at GBP 30 per week. SMA is thus available to a variety of groups of workers who cannot claim SMP including the self-employed and those who have not been in employed earners' employment for long enough to qualify for SMP. Furthermore, the claimant does not have to have worked for the same employer throughout the period for which contributions (or earnings) count.

182. As with SMP, entitlement to SMA where a baby is expected before 1 April 2007 lasts for up to twenty-six weeks running, usually, from eleven weeks before the expected week of confinement. Mothers of babies expected after 1 April 2007 are entitled to SMA for thirty-nine weeks. It is paid directly by the Department for Work and Pensions (DWP).

183. Claims for Maternity Allowance must be made within three months.[79] Claims can be backdated for three months, and there is no need for the claimant to demonstrate why the claim was made then rather than at the time of birth. Claimants are entitled to NI contribution credits for the period in which they claim SMA.

184. SMA is paid at either 90% of the claimant's average weekly earnings or a statutory minimum (currently GBP 139.58) whichever is the lower.

---

76. *See* above Part II.
77. SSCBA 1992, s. 35; *see also* the Social Security (Maternity Allowance) Regulations, 1987, SI 1987 No. 416, as amended.
78. The employment condition is that a woman will be required to have worked for some part of at least twenty-six of the sixty-six weeks that precede the expected week of confinement (SSCBA 1992, s. 35(1)(b) as amended *ibid.*).
79. Social Security (Claims and Payments) Regulations, 1987, regulation 19(2).

§3. MATERNITY EXPENSES: MATERNITY GRANT

185. SMP, SAP and the SMA are all designed primarily as a partial replacement for the woman's earnings while she is away from work to have her baby, rather than specifically to cover the special costs that are associated with the fact of the birth of a child.

186. When the National Insurance Act 1911 was first introduced, mothers were entitled to a lump sum grant which, typically, was used to cover the expenses of confinement in a hospital or nursing home. When the NHS was introduced after the Second World War, these costs were met by the State, unless the mother chose to have her baby in a private hospital or home outside the scope of the NHS.

187. Nevertheless under the National Insurance Act 1946, a State 'maternity grant' was created as a social security benefit, which was a one-off lump sum paid as a contribution towards the costs associated with the birth of a child (e.g., clothes, bedding, prams). The value of this benefit was, however, modest and was frozen at GBP 25 in 1969 with the result that, during a period of rapid inflation, its value declined markedly. By the 1980s, there were increasing calls either to revise the sum upwards or to abolish it. Not surprisingly, the Government chose the latter option.

188. From 1987, more 'targeted' arrangements have been in place. Claimants who are in receipt of either IS or WTC (which includes the disability or severe disability element),[80] income-based JSA,[81] CTC[82] or PC[83] are entitled to claim 'maternity expenses' from the Social Fund.[84] The payment had been renamed the *Sure Start Maternity Grant* from 2011. The maximum amount payable is currently GBP 500 (https://www.gov.uk/sure-start-maternity-grant/overview) and is unaffected by any capital the parents may have. A claim must be made within strict time limits: at the earliest eleven weeks before the expected week of confinement, or three months after birth or adoption at the latest. In order to establish entitlement to the Sure Start Maternity Grant, the claimant must also demonstrate that she is in contact with an established health care professional.

80. *See* below Part X.
81. *See* below Part VII.
82. *See* below Part IV.
83. *See* below Part VIII.
84. For full details, *see* Social Fund Maternity and Funeral Expenses (General) Regulations, 1987, regulation 5 (as amended). There is an entitlement to this benefit if the qualifying conditions are satisfied; *see also* Funeral Expenses, above Part III para. 151. For discretionary awards from the Social Fund, *see* below Part X.

Chapter 2. Social Security to Assist with the Costs of Bringing Up Children

189. The cost of bringing up children is substantial.[85] Following very considerable campaigning throughout the first half of the twentieth century, it came to be accepted that the State should bear at least some responsibility for the subsidizing of these costs.[86] A significant percentage of the social security budget is spent on Child Support.

190. One of the major policy challenges of the last thirty-five years relates to the extent to which the State should support the costs of bringing up children where the parents of the child or children have separated. Attempts to ensure that the absent parent (usually the father) pays maintenance regularly through the provision of Child Support have not been successful.

§1. Child Benefit

I. Background

191. The principal social security benefit, designed to subsidize the costs of bringing up children, is Child Benefit. This is a non-means-tested, non-contributory and untaxed benefit that is paid, as of right, to those who are responsible for the upbringing of children, usually in practice to mothers.[87] In 2010, Child Benefit was being paid for over 13 million children in Great Britain (GB).[88] As part of its programme of cuts in public expenditure, the Coalition Government in 2012 decided that, from April 2013, Child Benefit would no longer be paid to higher rate taxpayers or their partners. Further, currently a claimant may have to pay a tax charge if their or their partner's individual income is over GPB 50,000.

192. The history of its introduction in 1975[89] is a long and complex one, though perhaps also very revealing in terms of the assumptions which policymakers and

85. For estimates of this cost, *see*, for example, CPAG Poverty Paper No. 85, N. Oldfield & A.C.S. Yu, *The Cost of a Child* (London: CPAG,1993); S. Middleton, K. Ashworth & I. Braithwaite, *Small Fortunes: Spending on Children, Childhood Poverty and Parental Sacrifice* (York: Joseph Rowntree Foundation, 1997).
86. The detailed history of the creation of Child Benefit is in J. Macnicol, *The Movement for Family Allowances, 1918–1945: A Study in Social Policy Development* (London: Heinemann, 1980); *see also* F. Field, *Poverty and Politics: The Inside Story of the CPAG Campaigns in the 1970s* (London: Heinemann, 1982).
87. SSCBA 1992, Part IX, ss. 141–147; *see also* Child Benefit (General) Regulations, 1976 (as amended) SI 1976 No. 965.
88. *See* www.neighbourhood.statistics.gov.uk/dissemination/datasetList.do;jsessionid=ac1f930d30d556 74349b0b8a4101a6a9d879b81e4136?JSAllowed=true&ph=60& CurrentPageId=60&step=1& datasetFamilyId=215&Next.x=1&Next.y=1&bhcp=1&nsjs=true&nsck=true&nssvg=false&nswid= 1024.
89. Child Benefit Act 1975; it replaced the former Family Allowance and also child allowances which were part of the structure of tax relief for those who paid income tax.

politicians had about the importance of bringing up children. Initially, the then-new benefit was regarded as a major step forward in social policy terms, as it was financed by the abolition of tax allowances for children (which, of course, only benefited families earning sufficient income to be paying tax at all) and family allowances (a modest benefit created in 1948, which was not even paid for the first child of a family).

193. The main advantages of Child Benefit were that *all*[90] families receive the benefit, and the money is paid direct to the mother.[91] A review of Child Benefit by the HC Select Committee dealing with social security[92] in 1999 saw the benefit as serving a wide range of further functions:

- providing horizontal equity between people of similar incomes, reflecting the higher costs of those with children;
- supplementing wages, since they take no account of the costs of rearing a child;
- acting as a work incentive by reducing poverty and unemployment traps on the transition into work;
- providing an element of financial security when a family is otherwise facing insecurity;
- providing the only independent income for some mothers; and
- being money that is more likely to be spent on children because it goes primarily to mothers.

194. In recent years, there has been increasing criticism that the value of Child Benefit is inadequate and, indeed, has declined in that it has either not been uprated fully in line with inflation or, in some years, not been uprated at all. It may be noted that, in recent years, allowances for children in the means-tested assistance scheme have been increased.[93] This led Government spokesmen to argue that, by this means, more resource for children was being better directed to the least well off. This has been used as a justification for not maintaining the value of Child Benefit itself.

195. The New Labour Government in 2000 made clear its commitment to universal Child Benefit as a form of public support for the extra costs involved in bringing up children,[94] and the level of benefit was increased.[95]

---

90. However, the benefit is taken into account in full as income for those on means-tested benefits.
91. On this last point, *see* J. Goode, C. Callendeer & R. Lister, *Purse or Wallet? Gender Inequalities and Income Distribution Within Families on Benefit* (London: DSS, 1998); and the discussions of this issue surrounding the introduction of the WFTC (*see* Part X, Ch. 2).
92. Social Security Committee, 'Fourth Report: Child Benefit', HC No. 114 (London: TSO) 1998–1999 and 'Minutes of Evidence: Taxing Child Benefit', HC No. 114-I (London: TSO, March 1999 and December 1998 respectively) 1998–1999.
93. *See* below Part X.
94. *See* 'New Ambitions for Our Country: A New Contract for Welfare', Cmd 3805 (London: TSO, March 1998), 58.
95. A further 3% real terms increase was announced in the March 99 Budget (HC 1998–1999, 298, para. 5.8) with effect from April 2000, topping up the increase (of GBP 2.95 together with the annual uprating) in the amount payable for the eldest child that took effect following the previous Budget.

196. However, there remained much argument as to whether it could be retained in its original form. While calls for the means-testing of Child Benefit[96] were rebuffed, the later UK Coalition Government has decided to take the benefit away from higher rate taxpayers, a measure which constitutes an alternative means of crudely targeting the benefit but which compromises some of the perceived functions of Child Benefit (such as the achievement of horizontal equity between families with and without children on similar income levels and the channelling of some money to mothers not in paid work).

197. Since April 1991, the rate of benefit has been set at a slightly higher rate for the first child than is payable for other children, reflecting the view that the costs of the first child are regarded by many as being greater than for subsequent children in a family. (Notwithstanding this point, when the benefit was first introduced, the rate was the same for each child.) The rate is currently GBP 20.70 a week for the first or only child and GBP 13.70 a week for the second and other children. However, so long as the children are below the age which establishes entitlement, the rates of benefit remain the same, no matter what their age; they do not increase as the children grow older. Thus, no recognition is given to the fact that the costs associated with the rearing of children increase as they get older. There is no extra compensation for the extra food they consume, nor the more expensive clothes that they wear.[97]

II. Entitlement

198. The benefit is payable to a person who is *responsible* for one or more children. Responsibility is established where either the child lives with that person or the person is contributing to the child at a rate not less than the level of Child Benefit. Where more than one person could be entitled, priority is given to the person

96. Superficially, this might seem an attractive argument; however, it ignores the fact that Child Benefit is actually paid out of general taxation – not on the basis of contributions – and, insofar as such funds are derived from revenue gathered through the income tax system, it has been funded on a 'progressive' basis. It can, therefore, be argued that the better off are already paying, comparatively, more towards the cost of Child Benefit than the lower paid. This particular argument cannot be pursued too far, however, since a greater proportion of Government revenue is today derived from the indirect value added tax which impacts more severely upon the less well-off consumer. There is extensive literature on the matter: *see*, for example, J. Creedy (ed.), *Taxation, Poverty and Income Distribution* (Aldershot: Edward Elgar, 1994).
97. Some doubt has been cast on whether in fact the difference between the costs of younger and older children is as great as had been thought and calls have been heard for an increased rate for younger children to reflect, for example, higher childcare costs, loss of earnings and knock-on costs that follow from the difficulties with travel (e.g., to less local, cheaper shops) that can face those with younger children. (*See* the evidence of Ruth Lister to the Social Security Committee in *Minutes of Evidence: Taxing Child Benefit* (December 1998) at para. 15 and the evidence she cites). IS allowances for children under 11 have been increased in recognition of additional pressures on those with young children: *see* 'New Ambitions for Our Country: A New Contract for Welfare', Cmd 3805 (London: TSO, March 1998), 56, para. 4.

with whom the child lives, and to the wife over the husband and to the mother over the father. In the normal course of events, therefore, the recipient of Child Benefit is the mother.[98]

199. Entitlement can continue, notwithstanding the absence of the child, if the child is away at a boarding school.[99] If the child goes into hospital, entitlement continues for eighty-four consecutive days, though continues even beyond that time limit if the person entitled continues to incur expenditure in respect of the child, for example, as a result of visiting the child.[100] In any other case, absence of the child for up to fifty-six days in any period of sixteen weeks does not remove entitlement to Child Benefit.[101]

200. Although the normal principle of British social security law is that only natural persons are entitled to claim benefit, the Child Benefit Regulations 1976[102] do permit voluntary organizations – such as a children's charity, with whom a child lives – to claim Child Benefit in respect of that child.

201. However, where the child is in the care of a local authority, such authority is not entitled to claim Child Benefit. The mother or other person entitled may continue to receive Child Benefit for eight weeks after the child goes into care and can continue to do so where the child, in fact, stays with that person while subject to an order of the court.[103]

III. Child

202. In order to establish entitlement, there must be a child for whom the claimant is responsible. 'Child' is defined[104] as anyone under the age of 16, or anyone under the age of 19 who is still receiving full-time[105] non-advanced education (i.e., secondary education), or a person under the age of 18 who has ceased full-time education but falls within an 'extension period'.[106]

98. SSCBA 1992, s. 141–s. 143 and Sch. 11.
99. SSCBA 1992, s. 143(3).
100. SSCBA 1992, s. 143(3) and (4) and Child Benefit (General) Regulations, 1976 (as amended) regulation 4.
101. SSCBA 1992, s. 143(2).
102. *See* regulation 17.
103. *Ibid.*, regulation 16. The same regulation deals with the situation where the child is in prison or is detained in custody.
104. SSCBA 1992, s. 142.
105. Defined (in respect of education provided at a recognized educational establishment) as a course of education of more than twelve hours per week: Child Benefit (General) Regulations, 1976 regulation 5. Child Benefit is not available where the child is undertaking an 'advanced course', for example a University level course: *ibid.*, Regulations 1 and 7A. In many such cases the person will be entitled to a student loan.
106. An extension period is where the child is over 16 but under 18; is registered with the Careers Service, Connexions Service or Ministry of Defence as available for work or training scheme; is not in remunerative work for twenty-four hours a week or more; is not receiving IS or income-based JSA; and is not on a training scheme. The 'extension period' has the effect of extending entitlement

IV. Residence and Presence Conditions

203. In general, it is a condition of entitlement to Child Benefit in any given week that both the child and the claimant are present in GB and that either the child or at least one of his/her parents has been in GB for more than 182 days in the fifty-two weeks preceding the relevant week.[107] These rules are however subject to modification. For example, temporary absences abroad for up to twelve weeks do not count; thus, entitlement is not lost by taking a holiday abroad. Longer absences abroad are permitted where the child is being educated[108] in the EEA or is on an educational exchange or visit approved by the child's school or where the child is being treated for an illness, and there are a number of other relaxing provisions relating, for example, to members of the Armed Forces or those working temporarily abroad.[109] There are also further relaxations for those covered by European law which allow resident EEA workers to claim benefits in respect of family members who are abroad[110] and also allow certain former resident EEA workers (broadly those on old age or invalidity pensions) to retain their entitlement to 'family benefits', of which Child Benefit is one, when they move to another EEA State or to have local benefits topped up to the level of the benefits available to those in the first State.[111]

204. A bar was introduced in 1996 preventing any person subject to immigration control from claiming Child Benefit. There are a few exceptions: for refugees, those with exceptional leave to enter or remain in the country, those with unlimited leave to enter or remain, those who were entitled to (and in receipt of) the benefit before 7 October 1996 and for workers from the EEA and their families and workers from other countries with which either the EC or Britain have reached special agreements.[112]

---

to Child Benefit to the parents of children who are waiting to get onto a training scheme (on which *see* below Part VII, Ch. 3) for the equivalent of another school term, even though the child is not actually at school: *ibid.*, Regulations 7-7I.

107. SSCBA 1992, s. 146, and the Child Benefit (Residence and Persons Abroad) Regulations, 1976 (as amended) SI 1976 No. 963.

108. Education in a narrow sense must be the sole purpose of the absence. In Commissioners' Starred Decision 63/97 (CF 7146/95), a child was abroad not only to be educated but also to absorb the local cultural and religious atmosphere. It was held that education was therefore not the sole purpose of the visit, and so there was no ongoing entitlement to Child Benefit.

109. For full details, *see* Child Benefit (Residence and Persons Abroad) Regulations, 1976.

110. *See* EU Regulation 1408/71. *See also Hoever and Zachow v. Land Nordrhein Westfalen*, ECJ joined Cases C254/94 and C-312/94 (10 Oct. 1996).

111. *See* EU Regulation 1408/71 and Commissioner's Decision R(F) 1/95.

112. SSCBA 1992, s. 146A and Child Benefit (General) Regulations, 1976 (as amended) SI 1976 No. 965, regulation 14B.

§2. Lone-Parent Benefit

205. The financial difficulties faced by lone parents bringing up children were analysed in great detail in the early 1970s in the Finer Committee's Report on One-Parent Families.[113] The principal recommendation of the Committee was that a new benefit, the Guaranteed Maintenance Allowance, should be introduced. The Government of the day rejected this proposal on the grounds of cost. One Parent Benefit was the very modest response that was made by Government. Single (lone) parents who had a child living with them were entitled to an additional supplementary payment known as One Parent Benefit. Only one such payment could be made irrespective of the number of children for whom the claimant was responsible.[114]

206. One Parent Benefit was abolished from April 1997 and incorporated into a new higher rate of Child Benefit for the first child of a single parent.[115] This, in turn, was abolished with effect from 6 July 1998, subject to transitional protection for the then-existing claimants, which ended in April 2007. The cut was introduced despite criticisms that it was fiscally unnecessary and not supported by any evidence discrediting the traditional belief that lone parents face relatively greater costs than do couples with children.[116] Government statements aimed to scotch any hopes of a reversal of policy on this issue.[117] The cut was used to fund improvements in support with childcare costs through the new Working Families Tax Credit (WFTC) and the introduction of the New Deal for Lone Parents which aimed to help lone parents to work. While lone parents may still be exempt from the job-seeking requirements of JSA, they are increasingly categorized alongside those who are capable of and expected to work.[118]

207. Further schemes designed to encourage and facilitate the return to work for lone parents were introduced since April 2004 and included In Work Credit, Work Search Premium, Extended Schools Childcare and Childcare Tasters, Quarterly Work-Focused Interviews for lone parents with a child over 12 and who live where a Local Education Authority is operating an Extended Schools Childcare pilot and

113. Cmnd 5629 (1974) (London: HMSO).

114. The regulations did not actually label this additional benefit 'One Parent Benefit', but this is how it was known in practice: *see* Child Benefit and Social Security (Fixing and Adjustment of Rates) Regulations 1976 (as amended) SI 1976 No. 1267.

115. SSA 1998, s. 72 and Child Benefit and Social Security (Fixing and Adjustment of Rates) (Amendment) Regulations 1998 SI 1998/1581.

116. *See* the Third Reading debate on the Social Security Bill Hansard HC debates Vol. 302 (10 Dec. 1997) col. 1033 et seq. during which the Government raised no argument in favour of the change save that it was fiscally necessary and the related report of the Social Security Advisory Committee dealing mainly with the parallel move to remove increased premiums for lone parents in means-tested benefits: 'The Social Security (Amendment) Regulations 1997 SI 1997/ 1790', Cmd 3713 (London: TSO July 1997).

117. *See*, for example, 'New Ambitions for Our Country: A New Contract for Welfare', Cmd 3805 (London: TSO, 1998), 57, Ch. 7 para. 2: 'We believe that additional support should be provided for children in poorer families on the basis of identifiable needs of children, not on whether there happens to be one parent or two.'

118. *See* below Parts VII and X. Information on the numbers of lone parents claiming JSA can be found at http://research.dwp.gov.uk/asd/asd1/jsa/lone_parents/index.php?page=jsalp.

New Deal Plus for Lone Parents. The Coalition Government has been reviewing the extent to which it will sustain its commitment to all these programmes, though it accepts that the Government must continue to support the provision of early learning and childcare, which do help lone parents.[119] Currently GBP 57.90 weekly.

§3. Guardian's Allowance

208. This benefit is payable, in addition to Child Benefit. Guardian's Allowance (GA) is for those who are looking after children who have been orphaned, or who are effectively orphaned. By contrast with the enormous expenditure on Child Benefit, expenditure on GA is tiny: spending averaged between GBP 1 million and GBP 2 million a year since the mid-1990s.[120]

209. For GA to be payable, one of three alternative conditions must be satisfied. Either:

- both the parents of the child must have died;[121] or
- one of the child's parents must have died and the person claiming the benefit must be able to show that he/she did not know of the whereabouts of the other parent at the time of the death of the first parent;[122] or
- one of the child's parents must have died and the other must be serving a prison sentence with more than two years left to run at the date of death or must be detained in hospital by order of a court.[123]

210. GA is a non-contributory benefit and is currently GBP 17.20 a week.

211. In addition to the rule (*see* below, paragraph 212) that the claimant must be in receipt of Child Benefit in respect of the child in question – and thus be subject to the normal conditions of residence in GB – it is also necessary that one of the parents of the child must have been born in the UK, or have been present in GB for at least fifty-two weeks in any period of two years after reaching the age of 16.[124]

119. A summary of current Government thinking is to be found at www.education.gov.uk/childrenandyoungpeople/earlylearningandchildcare.
120. Current data not available.
121. SSCBA 1992, s. 77(1) and (2)(a).
122. *Ibid.*, s. 77(2)(b). The person claiming must also have failed, after making 'all reasonable efforts' to discover the whereabouts of the other parent.
123. *Ibid.*, s. 77(2)(c). The detailed rules about what counts as a prison sentence for these purposes are very complex: for those details, *see* Guardian's Allowance (General) Regulations 2003, SI 495, regulation 7.
124. *Ibid.*, regulation 6.

212. Step-parents do not count as parents for these purposes and so may be able to claim the benefit if the natural parent(s) dies.[125] However, where a child has been legally adopted, the adoptive parents are regarded as the parents of the child, not the natural parent(s).[126]

213. In a situation where the child is born illegitimate, the benefit is payable after the death of the mother only, so long as the paternity of the child has not been clearly established or admitted by the father.[127]

214. Where the child's natural or adoptive parents have been divorced and one parent has died and the other did not have custody of the child and was not maintaining the child nor under a legal duty so to do, the benefit is payable to a claimant, other than, of course, the surviving parent.[128]

215. The person claiming the GA must, as noted, also be receiving Child Benefit (*see* paragraph 198) in relation to the child.[129] In addition, he/she must either have the child living with him/her, or be treated as having the child living with him/her, or be contributing to the maintenance of the child by an amount at least equivalent to the current rate of GA.[130]

§4. Child Tax Credit

216. In addition to the provision of social security benefits to assist with the cost of child rearing, assistance has also been given through the income tax system. In the past, tax allowances were given to provide some compensation for the cost of rearing children through the married couples' allowance (for those married) and an additional personal allowance. Of course, only those earning enough to pay income tax benefited from these allowances.

217. From April 2001, these allowances were withdrawn and were replaced by the CTC. Subsequently renamed the CTC, it applies to individuals with a dependent child or young person on a sufficiently low income who are present and ordinarily resident in the UK and are not subject to immigration control. The claimant must be responsible for a child or young person[131] which means the child must live with them or they have the main responsibility for that child.

---

125. National Insurance Act 1957, s. 6.
126. Social Security (Guardian's Allowance) Regulations 1975, regulation 2. It is therefore theoretically possible for the original natural parents to become entitled to Guardian's Allowance, should the adoptive parents die: *Secretary of State for Social Services v. S* (1983) 1 WLR 1110.
127. *Ibid.*, regulation 3.
128. *Ibid.*, regulation 4.
129. SSCBA 1992, s. 77(1).
130. SSCBA 1992, s. 77(5) and (6).
131. A young person qualifies where he/she is in full-time non-advanced education or approved training and is under 20 years of age, or is under 18, and it is not more than twenty weeks since they ceased full-time education or training. *See* Tax Credits Act 2002 s. 8(4) and Child Tax Credit Regulations 2002 No. 2007 Regulations 2 & 5(1)–(3A).

218. Individuals on IS, income-based Job Seeker's Allowance or PC automatically get the maximum CTC. The entitlement of other claimants is calculated by considering the maximum CTC they could receive, based on a number of 'elements', how much income they receive and the income threshold figure which applies to the claimant.

The 'elements' which make up the amount of CTC are as follows.[132]

CTC Rates for the 2018 to 2019 Tax Year

Element	*Yearly Amount*
The basic amount (this is known as 'the family element')	Up to GBP 545
For each child (this is known as 'the child element')	Up to GBP 2,780
For each disabled child	Up to GBP 3,275 (on top of the child element)

219. When calculating the maximum CTC, each family receives one family element, then one child element per child, plus disability and severe disability elements where relevant.

220. Where claimants earn under the 'income thresholds',[133] they are entitled to the maximum tax credits.

221. The CTC is paid directly to the carer of the child by Her Majesty's Revenue and Customs (HMRC), and it is not dependent on NI contributions. CTCs do not count as income when making an assessment for IS, income-based JSA or PC purposes.

132. The disability element is awarded where there is any child on DLA, or who is registered blind, or who has been taken off the register in the last twenty-eight weeks. The severe disability element covers children receiving the highest rate of the care component of DLA (for DLAs *see* below Part IX).

133. Currently GBP 15,860 for claimants entitled to CTC and not WTCs. *See* www.hmrc.gov.uk/rates/taxcredits.htm for latest rates. Where a claimant is entitled to both CTC and WTCs, the threshold is lower and is currently set at GBP 6,420. For WTCs, *see* below Part X.

Chapter 3. Child Support

222. One of the matters which Beveridge did not anticipate when drawing up his blueprint for the British Welfare State was the growth in the numbers of lone parents bringing up children. Although for the better off, financial arrangements following a divorce usually include the provision of financial maintenance for the children, this was not in practice a sound basis for providing maintenance for the children of poorer families. Furthermore, even where maintenance orders made by the courts as part of the divorce process were in place, they were frequently not obeyed. Thus increasing numbers of lone parents became dependent on means-tested social assistance benefits.

223. As already mentioned, the existence of the problem was officially noted years ago with the establishment of the Finer Committee on One Parent Families in 1972. The main recommendation of the subsequent report was that a new form of social security benefit should be created – the Guaranteed Maintenance Allowance. This was seen by the Committee as providing the best way of taking lone parents – typically mothers – off means-tested benefits (then Supplementary Benefit, now IS). The cost, however, would have been substantial, and – as already noted above, paragraph 208 – the recommendation was not accepted by the then Government.

224. The Government determined in 1991 to enact new legislation which would introduce a new mechanism for providing Child Support. This is not the place to consider the new Child Support scheme in detail, since it is, in effect, a mechanism for replacing social security benefits provided by the State, by the enforced provision of financial support by the absent parent. But any consideration of social security provision relating to children must take the existence of the Child Support scheme into account. Hence, brief mention is made of the scheme in this context.

225. The central idea behind the Child Support scheme is that the biological parents should be responsible for the financial support of their children. However, instead of relying on court orders relating to maintenance, the amount of Child Support would be determined by a statutory formula. Furthermore, assessment of such orders and their enforcement would be carried out, not through the courts but by means of a statutory agency, the Child Support Agency (CSA), operating policies determined by the (then) DSS (now DWP).

226. Once in payment, the intention was that a lone parent's means-tested social security benefits (not Child Benefit or Lone-Parent Benefit) would be reduced by the amount of the Child Support received.[134] To compensate for this loss of benefit from the Government, there were increased incentives given to the lone parent to

134. As a consequence, the majority of lone parents would be no better off as a result; 80% of all lone parents are in receipt of IS: CPAG, *Child Support Handbook*, 1st edn (London: CPAG, 1993), xi.

go out to work by allowing for a 'maintenance disregard'[135] for those receiving the means tested FC and Housing and CTB.[136]

227. Initial reaction to the introduction of the scheme was extremely critical. The operation of the financial formula was criticized for being too rigid and bearing too harshly particularly on those parents who had formed second relationships and were finding they were having to contribute substantial proportions of their income to their former partners; there was also much criticism that the effect of the new scheme was retrospectively to alter agreements endorsed by the courts, particularly relating to the distribution of capital assets on divorce.

228. The political pressures on the former Conservative Government relating to the operation of the Child Support scheme resulted in a substantial package of measures being introduced by the Child Support Act 1995, designed to give more flexibility and discretion to the officials who operate the scheme. In particular, it introduced what was called the 'departures scheme' which allowed for the normal rules for the assessment of Child Support liability to be departed from in order to take account of exceptional circumstances not recognized in the formula-based assessment; this was designed to reduce some of the rigidity of the original mathematical formula. In addition, that Act introduced a Child Maintenance Bonus, intended as an incentive to encourage parents with care to go back into work, by providing additional money if they were in work.

229. The key changes proposed in 2000 to address these issues were: first, simplification of the way in which Child Support liability was assessed by replacing the current complex assessment formula with a simple percentage of the non-resident parent's net income; second, the introduction of a child maintenance premium in IS and income-based JSA that would enable families receiving these benefits to keep up to GBP 10 a week of the maintenance paid for their children; third, strengthening the sanctions regime by building on existing powers contained in the current scheme, and introducing new measures to improve compliance; fourth, reforming the CSA's service by increasing use of the telephone and face-to-face contact, directing a greater proportion of its resources to making sure maintenance is paid on time and sorting out disputes about liability or payment arrangements as soon as possible and, wherever possible, without the need to refer the dispute to an appeal tribunal.

230. The provisions in the Child Support, Pensions and SSA 2000 which replaced the then-existing formula with a simpler system of rates and sought to clarify the responsibilities of parents covered in particular: the processes for applying for Child Support and the way in which Child Support liability was decided; the rates used for calculating maintenance liability, based on 15% of the non-resident parent's income for one child, 20% for two and 25% for three or more; what was to

135. That is to say, in determining their entitlement to benefit, a part of the maintenance actually received by the parent would be disregarded in working out their means.

136. Child Support Act 1991, s. 1.

count as income; penalties for parents who deliberately misrepresented their circumstances to the CSA – and for those who refuse to provide the information needed to calculate liability and collect maintenance; the variation of the normal rate of maintenance liability to recognize certain exceptional costs and sources of income; rights to dispute and appeal decisions on Child Support liability and the processes by which liability would be kept up to date; the formation of a complete and comprehensive collection scheme with financial and other penalties for late and non-payment; improvements to the provisions for establishing paternity; transitional provisions and phasing processes to allow movement from the existing scheme to the new scheme. The Act also dealt with other matters such as the relationship between court orders for child maintenance and the Child Support system; liability for certain non-resident parents living abroad; the introduction of fees for Child Support services when these reached an acceptable standard; and benefit penalties when a parent with care who is in receipt of IS opted out of Child Support arrangements without good cause.

231. Notwithstanding these reforms, the Child Support system continued to operate in an extremely inefficient and unsatisfactory way. It has been bedevilled by major computer problems and has been subject to continuing political pressure for change. The latest attempts to create a workable scheme are found in the Child Maintenance and Other Payments Act 2008. This created a new agency, the Child Maintenance Enforcement Commission (CMEC),[137] which started work in 2008 (cf. https://www.gov.uk/child-maintenance/overview).

232. The stated objective of the CMEC is to maximize the number of children living apart from one or both of their parents for whom effective maintenance arrangements are in place. This objective is to be supported by the following subsidiary objectives: to encourage and support the making and keeping by parents of appropriate voluntary maintenance arrangements for their children; and to support the making of applications for Child Support maintenance under the Child Support Act 1991 and to secure compliance when appropriate with parental obligations under the Act. In addition, the CMEC has further responsibilities for raising awareness among parents of the importance of taking responsibility for the maintenance of their children and making appropriate arrangements for the maintenance of children of theirs who live apart from them. To support this process, the CMEC is required to provide a service that provides information and guidance to both parents for the purpose of helping to secure the existence of effective maintenance arrangements. This is called the Child Maintenance Options Service. While the CSA was able to commission external service providers to help enforce maintenance payments, the CMEC has more flexibility to commission external providers to carry out its functions in order to deliver services in the most efficient and effective way.

233. Further changes to the operation of the Child Support scheme were enacted in 2012, and these included:

137. For further information about CMEC *see* www.childmaintenance.org/.

- allowing caseworkers from the Child Maintenance Service to request current income information from the non-resident parent at the application and annual review application stages;
- basing a non-resident parent's income on historical income provided by HM Revenue and Customs even where that figure is nil; and
- making parents responsible for reporting relevant changes in circumstances relating to a variation in their maintenance calculation.

234. Child Support (miscellaneous amendments) Regulations 2013[138] enacted these changes and introduced a number of measures designed to improve the efficiency and effectiveness of the new child maintenance scheme following the experience gained thus far in the handling of a small number of cases under the new scheme. The measures came into force from September 2013. The main measures:

- allow current income information to be sought from a non-resident parent if historical income information cannot be requested or obtained from HMRC for the purposes of making a maintenance calculation;
- allow a 'nil' historic income figure from HMRC to be used as the gross weekly income figure for a non-resident parent for the purposes of a maintenance calculation;
- allow previously agreed variations to child maintenance liability to be reinstated automatically in appropriate circumstances; and
- make minor supplemental amendments which clarify that the DWP will treat parents who elect to not receive Child Benefit payments as the same as those who continue to receive the payments (this applies to all three-child maintenance schemes).
- enforcement charges;
- The Child Maintenance Service introduced enforcement charges for non-payment on 30 June 2014.

Action Taken by Child Maintenance Service	*Charge*
Liability order	GBP 300
Lump sum deduction order	GBP 200
Regular deduction order	GBP 50
Deduction from earnings request or order	GBP 50

138. *See*: *CH v. Secretary of State for Work and Pensions & Anor (Child Support: Maintenance Assessments/Calculations) [2015] UKUT 381 (AAC)*, for recent guidance.

Part V. Incapacity to Work

Introduction

§1. The Scope of This Part

235. The British system of sickness and disability benefits has, in overall terms, been subject to much controversy over the last two decades and continues to do so. Generally, these criticisms focus on the current system disregarding living standards in assessing actual disability benefit levels, as well as taking little, if any, account of the problems faced by claimants. On a more practical level, much criticism is centred on the complexity surrounding disability benefits.

236. There are many situations in which a person may find himself/herself with reduced capacity for work, for example as the result of industrial accident or disease, the effects of physical disability, the demands of childbirth or the limitations of old age. Separate Parts in this volume discuss the social security benefits available in these contexts.[139] This Part looks specifically at social security benefits which relate to incapacity or reduced capacity for work resulting from sickness and which, therefore, provide some measure of compensation for such incapacity/reduced capacity.

237. In this Part, after commenting on the background to the development of policy in this area, we consider:

- *SSP*, which is now the principal type of payment for those suffering from short-term illness; and
- *ESA*, which is now the principal benefit for those with long-term reduced capacity for work. This has largely replaced *IB* which used to be the main benefit for the long-term sick.

§2. Background

238. To understand how the present structure has evolved, it is necessary to set out the context of the development of policy in this area.

139. *See*, respectively: Part VI on benefits for industrial accidents; Part IX on benefits for the handicapped and the disabled; Part IV on benefits for pregnancy; and Part VII on pensions for the aged.

239. Before the Beveridge proposals for the restructuring of social security provision were introduced by the National Insurance Act 1946, there had existed a system of cash benefits for the sick which were administered by private bodies known as 'approved societies'. These were swept away by the National Insurance Act 1946, which introduced a new *Sickness Benefit*, a contributory benefit which was payable as a form of income replacement for those incapable of work through sickness. Initially this benefit was paid at a single flat rate; it was not related to the earnings of the claimant when in work.

240. Two issues emerged during the 1950s and 1960s. First, it came to be realized that there was a sharp distinction to be drawn between the income replacement needs of those sick for only a short period of time and those who were sick for a longer term. Second, as a result of successful collective bargaining in the workplace, many employers in fact began to provide their own sick pay for their employees.

241. The response to the first issue was that from 1971 a distinction was drawn between *Sickness Benefit*, which became a short-term benefit payable only for up to six months' incapacity for work, and *invalidity benefit*, a substantially more generous benefit payable on a long-term basis for those who were incapable of work for more than six months.

242. The response to the second was that in 1980, and it was decided that the principle of sick pay should be statutorily extended to all employees – whether or not they were a beneficiary of a company sick pay scheme. Thus SSP was introduced in 1982 to cover the first twenty-eight weeks of a period of incapacity. Although a statutory scheme, it was to be paid to employees by their employers. Sickness Benefit, paid directly by the State, remained in place as a residual benefit for those who for whatever reason could not qualify for SSP (principally the self-employed). Where employees had negotiated an *occupational sick pay scheme* that was more generous than SSP, the occupational scheme remained effective and in such situations, employers would not pay SSP. The SSP scheme provided a benchmark, below which occupational schemes were not permitted to fall.

243. Whatever the true explanation, the former Conservative Government from 1992–1997 determined that new measures were needed to curb expenditure on this area of the social security budget. Two principal measures were taken.

First, the costs of SSP, which initially had been met in full by the Government were, with limited exceptions, transferred to employers.[140] Second, a new benefit, *IB*, was introduced to replace Sickness Benefit and invalidity benefit.[141]

244. Despite these changes, spending on earnings replacement benefits for those found incapable of work remained substantial. The Blair Labour Governments from

140. SSP Act 1994.

141. Social Security (Incapacity for Work) Act 1994, which had the effect of amending the relevant provisions of the SSCBA 1992.

1997 believed that levels of unemployment among the disabled were too high. A package of measures was proposed to address this issue.[142]

245. The test of incapacity used in the benefits system also came in for specific criticism. Entitlement to IB, or IS on the grounds of ill health or disability, was dependent in the longer term on being adjudged incapable of any work. The Government felt that this label promoted an inappropriate self-image among claimants and could detract from the desired aspiration to independence. A new 'personal capacity assessment' was introduced, incorporating the existing test but also identifying what the claimant could do rather than what he/she could not do.[143]

246. The Government also believed that the rules whereby claimants became entitled to higher rates of IB after two separate qualifying periods of incapacity did not make sufficient allowance for those who take jobs on trial. They therefore allowed those who returned to benefit after interruptions to a claim of in some cases up to a year to requalify for benefit as if their claim had remained unbroken. The aim was to make people more willing to try working. They also removed limits on the amount of voluntary work which a claimant of IB could do without losing entitlement to benefit and introduced pilot schemes relaxing the rule that bars those carrying out work from eligibility for benefit.

247. The pressure to reduce spending on benefit also led to the proposal to exclude those who had been out of work for *any* length of time before making a claim for IB from eligibility for IB.[144] It also saw the Government introduce legislation to reduce the possibility of using IB to top up occupational or personal pensions for those who had taken early retirement, by introducing a means-test. Now certain sums paid by way of occupational pension lead to reductions in the level of payment of IB.[145] These moves were said to restore the benefit to its core purpose and to stop its abuse as a means of support for the long-term unemployed or those who have taken early retirement.

248. In the result, the New Labour Government in 2005 decided that these changes had still not gone far enough. They argued that there were still too many people who were in receipt of IB who could enter the labour market. This led to further reforms which were introduced in the WRA 2007.

249. Consequently, from October 2008, a new ESA replaced the then-existing system of payments of IB and IS on the grounds of incapacity for work or disability. A person could be entitled to an ESA by satisfying either an NI contribution test (similar to IB) or an income-related test (similar to IS) and also being assessed as having a reduced capacity for work because of their physical or mental condition

142. *See* 'A New Contract for Welfare: Support for Disabled People', Cmd 4103 (London: TSO, 1998), 3–4 and 15 et seq.
143. WRPA 1999, s. 61.
144. WRPA 1999, s. 62.
145. WRPA 1999, s. 63.

and satisfying certain other conditions. The Act also provided for the introduction of conditionality to some claimants receiving the benefit. This means that entitlement to ESA is conditional upon certain classes of claimant trying to find work or in other ways becoming engaged in the labour market. It brought into effect proposals discussed in the Welfare Reform Green Paper published in January 2006.[146] Similarly, the current UK Conservative Government, since 2015, has controversially determined that its Welfare Reform programme, under its WRA 2016, shall limit disability benefits.

146. *See*: https://www.gov.uk/government/uploads/system/uploads/attachment_data/file/272235/6730.pdf.

Chapter 1. Statutory Sick Pay

250. SSP was introduced in 1982. Before that date, short-term *Sickness Benefit* was payable to those who became incapable of work through illness. However by 1981, it was thought that about 90% of all workers were additionally protected by some form of private occupational sick pay scheme. Entitlement to Sickness Benefit was not affected by receipt of occupational sick pay, though amounts payable under occupational schemes usually assumed that the statutory benefit was in payment as well.[147]

251. The Government took the view that there might be some public expenditure savings to be achieved, if employers were to be required to take over responsibility for paying the short-term sick. In addition, the idea of transferring administrative responsibility to employers would enable the then Thatcher Governments of the 1980s to achieve another objective, namely a reduction in the numbers of civil servants employed in the then DSS (now DWP).

252. The Government, therefore, decided that employers would take over the vast bulk of payments to the short-term sick through SSP. Initially the Government accepted arguments from industry that the full cost of payment under the SSP scheme should be met by the Government; employers recouped these amounts from sums they would otherwise have paid to the Government under the PAYE Income Tax scheme and NI contributions out of the NI Fund, thus reducing the scope for reducing public expenditure.

253. However, in recent years, this funding situation has been radically altered. From April 1991, new financial arrangements were introduced, as a result of which employers[148] were able to claim only 80% of the sums paid as SSP.[149] From 1994, this process was taken a step further; employers other than 'small employers' have been obliged to bear 100% of the cost of SSP.[150] It should be noted that this decision was taken, at least in part, to give a financial incentive to employers to look more closely at the health records of their employees.

254. In cases where an employer has become insolvent, liability to pay SSP is transferred to the Secretary of State.[151]

255. When first introduced, the period of entitlement to SSP was limited to six weeks. From 1985, the maximum period of entitlement was extended to twenty-eight weeks, thereby enabling the long-term sick to transfer direct to IB, now ESA (*see* paragraphs 269 et seq).

---

147. SSCBA 1992, Part XI, ss 151–163.
148. 'Small' employers – those whose National Insurance Contributions the previous year did not exceed GBP 15,000 – can still receive 100% reimbursement.
149. SSCBA 1992, s. 158.
150. SSP Act 1994.
151. SSCBA 1992, s. 151(6); SSP (General) Regulations, regulations 9A, 9B and 9C (which came into force in 1987).

§1. THE RULES OF ENTITLEMENT

I. Persons Entitled

256. In order to be entitled to SSP, the claimant must be an 'employee'.[152] Thus the self-employed and (in most cases) the unemployed cannot claim SSP; they will remain entitled to IB (below). It is the *fact* of employment that is the crucial test, not, for example, whether a person has properly signed a contract of employment. It is not possible to contract out of entitlement to SSP.[153]

257. The following groups of employees are not entitled to SSP:

- those whose employers are not resident or present in GB;
- those whose employers are exempt under an international treaty;[154]
- people with gross earnings below the lower NI limit GBP 228 per week;[155]
- pregnant women;[156]
- prisoners;
- persons involved in trade disputes;[157]
- those employed outside the EEA area,[158] unless their employer is liable to pay UK NI contributions;[159]
- those who have not yet started work under a contract of employment;
- 'welfare to work' beneficiaries who are in the two-year 'linking period,' who are entitled to IB or Severe Disablement Allowance (SDA) (now replaced by ESA).

Prior to October 2006, those under 16 and over 65 were excluded, but there is now no upper or lower age limit for SSP.

II. Incapacity for Work

258. To be entitled to SSP, a claimant must be 'incapable of work'. For the purposes of SSP, this means either:

152. SSCBA 1992, s. 163, and SSP (General) Regulations, 1982 – regulation 16. The issue is very similar to the issue of whether a person is an 'employed earner' for the purposes of the industrial injuries scheme: *see* Part VI.
153. SSCBA 1992, s. 151(2).
154. SSP (General) Regulations, regulation 16(2)(b).
155. *See* Part II.
156. They will usually be entitled to SMP or Maternity Allowance: Part III. If not, they still cannot receive SSP within the period of eighteen weeks from either the week of birth or the week in which she is incapable of work due to pregnancy. If SSP is being paid, it will cease at the first of these dates.
157. This rule applies so that SSP cannot be claimed throughout the period of sickness even though the strike may have ended the day after the sickness began.
158. If employed outside the UK, those in the EEA will only qualify if it is UK benefits that are payable under the rules that apportion responsibility between EEA States.
159. There are special rules for mariners, airmen and oil workers.

- the person is incapable of doing work they might reasonably be expected to do under the terms of his/her contract of employment, because of a specific disease, or because of physical or mental disablement; or
- the person is 'treated as incapable' of such work.

259. A person is 'treated as incapable' of work where he/she has been excluded from work because they have been in contact with a person suffering from a serious infectious disease that must be notified to the public health authorities, or because, although no longer suffering from a disease or disablement, the doctor has ordered the person to *convalesce and not return to work.*

III. Conditions of Entitlement

260. There are three conditions of entitlement to SSP.

261. First, there must be a day of incapacity for work which must form part of a period of incapacity for work.[160] A 'period' is any period of four or more consecutive days (including Sundays), each of which is a day of incapacity. Any two periods separated by less than eight weeks can be treated as a single period.[161] (Thus, there is no payment for the first three days of sickness.).

262. Second, the day of incapacity must fall within a 'period of entitlement'.[162] This is the period starting with the commencement of a period of incapacity and ending when either:

- the illness or any period of convalescence is over; or
- the employee reaches his/her maximum entitlement[163] as against that employer; or
- the contract of employment ends (unless it has been ended solely or mainly to avoid liability for SSP);[164] or
- the day before the claimant is disqualified on the ground of pregnancy;[165] or
- three years have elapsed since the start of the period.[166]

263. If the period of entitlement ends before the period of incapacity ends, then entitlement to SSP ceases and cannot be re-established until the claimant has worked for another eight weeks.

160. SSCBA 1992, s. 152(1).
161. *Ibid.*, s. 152(2) and (3). This removes the need for the three 'waiting days' to be served again.
162. SSCBA 1992, s. 153.
163. That is, up to twenty-eight weeks: SSCBA 1992, s. 155(4).
164. SSP (General) Regulations, 1982 regulation 4.
165. This rule does not apply if the pregnancy has been terminated other than by a confinement: SSCBA 1992, s. 153(11) and s. 171(1).
166. SSP (General) Regulations, 1982 regulation 3(3).

264. Third, the day must be a 'qualifying day', that is a day on which the claimant is required by his/her contract of service to be available for work.[167]

265. Waiting days: SSP is not payable for the first three days in any period of entitlement.[168]

266. Notification: There are rules relating to the ways in which the employee is to notify the employer that he/she is sick, but in effect, these leave considerable freedom to employers and employees to negotiate the details.[169]

267. Rates of benefit: Until 1995, there were two rates of SSP, a higher and a lower rate,[170] the level which the claimant received depending on his/her earnings.[171] Currently, there is now just a standard rate of SSP – currently GBP 92.05 a week. This statutory rate is only a minimum; employers are at liberty to be more generous through occupational sick pay schemes than the SSP scheme requires but cannot be less generous.

268. Adjudication: Although SSP is administered by employers, the fact that the scheme is statutory means that there are mechanisms for resolving disputes within HM Revenue and Customs. There are therefore procedures for referring disputed issues to HMRC Officials and thence to the Tribunals Service.[172]

---

167. SSCBA 1992, s. 154. The rules allow some flexibility to employers and employees to determine which those days are; there must be at least one such day per week. *See also* SSP (General) Regulations, 1982 regulation 5(3).
168. SSCBA 1992, s. 155.
169. SSCBA 1992, s. 156; SSP (General) Regulations, regulation 7.
170. Originally there were three rates.
171. Defined in SSP (General) Regulations, 1982 (as amended) regulation 17.
172. *See* generally Part XI.

Chapter 2. Employment and Support Allowance

269. ESA was introduced on 27 October 2008. It is a benefit for people who have 'limited capability for work' – where it is unreasonable to require them to work because of illness or disability – and who are not entitled to SSP. The policy objective is to continue to provide the very ill with some financial support while encouraging those who could do some work to move towards re-engagement in the labour market.[173]

270. The former Coalition Government, 2010–2015, sought to introduce a 'claimant commitment' which recorded the responsibilities that the claimant has accepted by receiving an award of ESA; this includes requirements to attend work-focused interviews and to undertake work-related activity. ESA replaced IB and also IS 'on the grounds of disability'.

271. There are two sorts of ESA: *contributory ESA* and *income-related ESA*.

272. Contributory ESA is payable to those who have limited capability for work and who satisfy the relevant NIC conditions.[174] Some young people who are not in full-time education but who have not been in work long enough to build up the requisite contribution record are currently still eligible for contributory ESA – referred to as *ESA in youth.* The Coalition Government decided that ESA in youth should be abolished; it has also decided that payment of contributory ESA to those receiving the 'work-related activity component' – defined below – should be limited to one year. These new rules were introduced in the WRA 2012.

273. Income-related ESA is payable to those who have limited capability for work and who satisfy the relevant means-test; there are no NI contribution conditions to be satisfied. It is possible for income-related ESA to be paid as a supplement to contributory ESA.

§1. Limited Capability for Work

274. Unlike IB, where the core qualifying test was a claimant's incapacity to work, entitlement to ESA arises where the claimant is able to show that he/she has 'limited capability for work'. Having limited capability for work means that it would be unreasonable to require that person to work. Underpinning this formulation is the idea that claimants, other than the most severely ill or disabled, should have their employability assessed and where possible should be moved towards doing things in the labour market that they are capable of doing – even if they are

173. *See* generally Welfare Reform Act 2007, Part 1; *see also* Welfare Reform Bill 2011, Part 2, Ch. 2. The detailed regulations relating to ESA are to be found in the Employment and Support Allowance Regulations 2008 SI 2008 No. 794, the text of which can be found at www.legislation.gov.uk /uksi/2008/794/contents/made.

174. Contribution conditions are discussed above at paras 74–81.

no longer fit enough to do the job they were originally doing. It is intended that the claimant will work with officials in JobCentre Plus (who administer the benefit) to explore these issues.

275. When a claim for ESA is made, the claimant must usually undergo an assessment as to the extent, if any, that he/she has a limited capability for work. During the assessment phase, which usually lasts for thirteen weeks, and where the claimant has a sufficient NI contributions record to entitle him/her to contributory ESA, the claimant is paid a 'basic allowance'. This is GBP 57.90 for those aged under 25 and GBP 73.10 for those over that age but under the statutory pension age. (No entitlement to ESA arises once a claimant is over the statutory pension age.) For those without entitlement to contributory ESA, they are subjected to a means-test to determine whether they are entitled to income-related ESA. Again, there are lower amounts payable to those under 25 during the assessment phase.

276. After the assessment period is over, the claimant moves from the 'assessment phase' to the 'main phase'. Assuming that the assessment is that the claimant has a limited capability for work, the contributory ESA is then payable at the same rate – GBP 73.10 – to all; thus claimants under the age of 25 are brought up to the same level as other claimants. Similarly, those entitled to income-related ESA are paid at the same rate, irrespective of age.

Financial Support

Claimants receive the assessment rate for 13 weeks after your claim. This will be:

- up to GBP 57.90 a week if you are aged under 25;
- up to GBP 73.10 a week if you are aged 25 or over.

After that, if the claimant is entitled to ESA, the claimant will be placed in one of two groups and will receive:

- up to GBP 73.10 a week if you are in the work-related activity group;
- up to GBP 110.75 a week if you are in the support group.

They may also qualify for the severe disability premium at GBP 64.30 per week.

277. Where a claimant is assessed as having a limited capability for work, there are two possible outcomes: either assessment as having limited capability for work-related activity or assessment as being capable of work-related activity. The first group, who are in effect the most seriously ill, are placed in what is called the 'support group'. This means that they receive both the main allowance plus an additional support allowance, currently GBP 36.20 a week. A claimant is placed in this group if they are assessed as being of limited capability for work-related activity. A claimant automatically qualifies for the support group and does not have to wait until the end of the assessment phase, if he/she:

- has a terminal illness and has claimed ESA expressly on that ground;

- is claiming following an earlier period of entitlement to ESA for which the claimant received support allowance, and the new claim can be linked to the earlier claim.

278. Following the assessment process, other claimants will automatically be placed in the support group:

- those who are terminally ill but who have not claimed ESA expressly on that ground;
- those receiving chemotherapy or recovering from chemotherapy;
- those suffering from a specific disease or disablement that would be a substantial risk to the claimant or another person if they were not found to have limited capability for work-related activity; or
- those who are pregnant where there would be serious risk of damage to health of either the claimant or the baby if they did not refrain from work-related activity.

279. Those not so assessed are placed in the 'work-related activity group'. This means that they will be required to attend for work-focused interviews and possibly undertake some work-related activity. Those in this group receive an additional 'work-related activity component', currently GBP 29.05 a week. Refusal to engage in the required work-related activity will lead first to a reduction, finally to the withdrawal of the work-related activity component.

§2. The Assessment Process

280. It is quite clear that the claimant has the responsibility of demonstrating the factual evidence from which a conclusion may be drawn that she/he is incapable of work because she/he is suffering from a disease or disablement. The starting point for the provision of such evidence is by the use of medical certificates, known colloquially as 'sick notes'/'fit notes'.[175]

281. The first seven days of a claim for ESA may be covered by a simple self-certificate, signed by the claimant, that he/she has reduced capability for work. After seven days, a doctor's certificate is almost always required.[176] The certificate may be a 'closed' one, that is one which defines in advance a period of time during which the person will be unfit for work but also stating that at the end of that period he/she will be able to return to work; or an 'open' one, that is, a certificate stating that the person will be unfit for a period of up to six months but leaving open (vague or undetermined) the actual date on which a return to work may take place. (It will be

175. A detailed statement of how the assessment process is supposed to work is to be found at www.direct.gov.uk/prod_consum_dg/groups/dg_digitalassets/@dg/@en/@disabled/documents/digitalasset/dg_177366.pdf.

176. *See* Social Security (Medical Evidence) Regulations, SI 1976 No. 615 (as amended); alternatives are permitted in the case of those, such as Christian Scientists, who will not go to see doctors.

remembered that most people will receive SSP for shorter periods of sickness; thus, claims for ESA will usually be from those who have been ill for longer than the period of entitlement for SSP.)

282. For the first thirteen weeks after a claim for ESA is made, and assuming that the required medical certificates have been submitted, the claimant is treated as having limited capability for work and receives the 'assessment phase' level of ESA (*see* paragraph 280).

283. The assessment itself is designed to establish the answers to two different questions which are quite hard to distinguish but need to be kept distinct. The first question is whether the claimant's capability for work is limited by his/her physical or mental condition. If the claimant does not satisfy this test, the claim for ESA fails. If the claimant passes this test, the second question is whether the limitation is so great that it is not reasonable to require the claimant to work. Those who are so ill that it is not reasonable to require them to work are placed in the 'support group'; the rest are placed in the 'work-related activity group' – *see* paragraph 274.

284. The assessment is based on two key elements: first, the claimant will usually be required to complete a detailed questionnaire setting out how his/her physical and/or mental condition affects their capability for work;[177] and, second, in most cases the claimant will be required to attend an interview with a specially appointed health care professional.[178]

285. An assessment does not always mean that the approved health care professional undertakes a physical examination. They may just talk to the claimant about how their health condition or disability affects their everyday activities. The claimant has an opportunity to give any other information relevant to their assessment. The approved health care professional considers all the information and exercises clinical judgment to reach an opinion on the nature and severity of the effects of the disabling condition. They are also required to take full account of factors such as pain, fatigue, stress and of the possible variability of the condition. For example, if the claimant can perform a particular activity only by incurring a considerable degree of pain, they are classed as being incapable of performing that activity. The approved health care professional also considers the effects of the condition on the claimant for the majority of the time so that the opinion is not based on a snapshot of their condition on the day of the medical assessment.

286. It should be noted that the approved health care professional does not actually decide the question whether the claimant is entitled to ESA; he/she simply provides advice to the benefit decision-maker (who is an official working within JobCentre Plus, the Government Agency that determines ESA claims). The

177. The questionnaire is quite long and complex. The form can be found at www.direct.gov.uk/prod_consum_dg/groups/dg_digitalassets/@dg/@en/@money/documents/digitalasset/dg_195544.pdf.

178. These are medical professionals who work for a private company to which the Government has contracted this assessment work.

approved health care professional should also provide a full explanation for their advice particularly where the opinion is different from the claimant's own perception of their functional limitations. The benefit decision-maker will also consider the evidence in the completed questionnaire and any other evidence, for example evidence from the claimant's own doctor. The policy reason for this is that while health care professionals are trained to make a diagnosis of whether a person is suffering from a disease or bodily or mental disablement, they are not specifically trained to decide whether this means that a claimant can or cannot perform one of the specific activities defined for the purpose of the 'all work' test. In practice, official decision-makers rely very heavily on the judgments of the health care professional.

287. Consequently, there are two types of assessments:

(1) Assessment of whether a claimant has 'limited capability for work'. The 'limited capability for work' assessment considers activities. Points are awarded as listed below. The higher the points awarded, the more limited the capability for work. The fewer the points awarded, the more capable the claimant is for work and the more likely the claimant will be refused ESA, or if in receipt of ESA, any ESA payment will cease.
(2) Assessment of whether a claimant has 'limited capability for work-related activity'. The 'limited capability for work-related activity' assessment considers capability in undertaking activities and results in either the claimant being placed in the 'Support Group' or the claimant being placed in the 'work-related activity group'.

If the claimant is placed in the 'Support Group', the claimant is not required to work or attend 'work-focused interviews'.

If the claimant is placed in the 'work-related activity group', the claimant has to attend six 'work-focused interviews'. Each interview is usually set at monthly interviews and a 'work action plan' is imposed on the claimant.

288. In order to try to bring some rigour and consistency to the assessment, the Government has set down a list of activities – for example, the ability to move about. Against each activity, there is a further list of 'descriptors' – for example, in the context of the mobility activity, can the claimant climb up or down two stairs unaided? The Government also sets a numerical score against each descriptor. In order to qualify for ESA, the claimant must achieve a score of at least fifteen points. (The point score for the stair-climbing descriptor is nine.) The total points may be achieved either by a single very serious failure to perform a descriptor which scores fifteen or by a combination of descriptor scores which aggregate to at least fifteen. Both mental and physical capabilities are assessed.

Assessment of whether a claimant has 'limited capability for work': The assessment defines activities, descriptors and points. If the claimant obtains less than fifteen points, then the claimant is not eligible for ESA. If the claimant obtains fifteen points or more, then the claimant is likely to be subject to the 'limited capability for work-related activity' assessment.

Part 1 Physical Disabilities

Activity			*Descriptors*	*Points*
1.	**Mobilizing unaided by another person with or without a walking stick, manual wheelchair or other aid if such aid can reasonably be used**			
	1	(a)	Cannot either: (i) mobilize more than 50 metres on level ground without stopping in order to avoid significant discomfort or exhaustion; or (ii) repeatedly mobilize 50 metres within a reasonable timescale because of significant discomfort or exhaustion.	15
		(b)	Cannot mount or descend 2 steps unaided by another person even with the support of a handrail.	9
		(c)	Cannot either: (i) mobilize more than 100 metres on level ground without stopping in order to avoid significant discomfort or exhaustion; or (ii) repeatedly mobilize 100 metres within a reasonable timescale because of significant discomfort or exhaustion.	9
		(d)	Cannot either: (i) mobilize more than 200 metres on level ground without stopping in order to avoid significant discomfort or exhaustion; or (ii) repeatedly mobilize 200 metres within a reasonable timescale because of significant discomfort or exhaustion.	6
		(e)	None of the above applies.	0
2.	**Standing and sitting**			
	2	(a)	Cannot move between one seated position and another seated position located next to one another without receiving physical assistance from another person.	15

Activity			*Descriptors*	*Points*
		(b)	Cannot, for the majority of the time, remain at a work station, either: (i) standing unassisted by another person (even if free to move around); or (ii) sitting (even in an adjustable chair) for more than 30 minutes, before needing to move away in order to avoid significant discomfort or exhaustion.	9
		(c)	Cannot, for the majority of the time, remain at a work station, either: (i) standing unassisted by another person (even if free to move around); or (ii) sitting (even in an adjustable chair) for more than an hour before needing to move away in order to avoid significant discomfort or exhaustion.	6
		(d)	None of the above applies.	0
3.	**Reaching**			
	3	(a)	Cannot raise either arm as if to put something in the top pocket of a coat or jacket.	15
		(b)	Cannot raise either arm to the top of the head as if to put on a hat.	9
		(c)	Cannot raise either arm above head height as if to reach for something.	6
		(d)	None of the above applies.	0
4.	**Picking up and moving or transferring by the use of the upper body and arms**			
	4	(a)	Cannot pick up and move a 0.5-litre carton full of liquid.	15
		(b)	Cannot pick up and move a 1-litre carton full of liquid.	9
		(c)	Cannot transfer a light but bulky object such as an empty cardboard box.	6
		(d)	None of the above applies.	0
5.	**Manual dexterity**			
	5	(a)	Cannot either: (i) press a button, such as a telephone keypad; or (ii) turn the pages of a book with either hand.	15

Activity			*Descriptors*	*Points*
		(b)	Cannot pick up a GBP 1 coin or equivalent with either hand.	15
		(c)	Cannot use a pen or pencil to make a meaningful mark.	9
		(d)	Cannot use a suitable keyboard or mouse.	9
		(e)	None of the above applies.	0
6.	**Making self understood through speaking, writing, typing or other means normally used unaided by another person**			
	6	(a)	Cannot convey a simple message such as the presence of a hazard.	15
		(b)	Has significant difficulty conveying a simple message to strangers.	15
		(c)	Has some difficulty conveying a simple message to strangers.	6
		(d)	None of the above applies.	0
7.	**Understanding communication by both verbal means (such as hearing or lip reading) and non-verbal means (such as reading 16-point print) using any aid it is reasonable to expect them to use, unaided by another person**			
	7	(a)	Cannot understand a simple message due to sensory impairment, such as the location of a fire escape.	15
		(b)	Has significant difficulty understanding a simple message from a stranger due to sensory impairment.	15
		(c)	Has some difficulty understanding a simple message from a stranger due to sensory impairment.	6
		(d)	None of the above applies.	0
8.	**Navigation and maintaining safety using a guide dog or other aid if normally used**			
	8	(a)	Unable to navigate around familiar surroundings, without being accompanied by another person, due to sensory impairment.	15
		(b)	Cannot safely complete a potentially hazardous task such as crossing the road, without being accompanied by another person, due to sensory impairment.	15

Activity			*Descriptors*	*Points*
		(c)	Unable to navigate around unfamiliar surroundings, without being accompanied by another person due to sensory impairment.	9
		(d)	None of the above applies.	0
9.	**Absence or loss of control leading to extensive evacuation of the bowel and/or bladder, other than enuresis (bed-wetting) despite the presence of any aids or adaptations normally used**			
	9	(a)	At least once a month experiences: (i) loss of control leading to extensive evacuation of the bowel and/or voiding of the bladder; or (ii) substantial leakage of the contents of a collecting device sufficient to require cleaning and a change in clothing.	15
		(b)	At risk of loss of control leading to extensive evacuation of the bowel and/or voiding of the bladder, sufficient to require cleaning and a change in clothing, if not able to reach a toilet quickly.	6
		(c)	None of the above applies.	0
10.	**Consciousness during waking moments**			
	10	(a)	At least once a week, has an involuntary episode of lost or altered consciousness resulting in significantly disrupted awareness or concentration.	15
		(b)	At least once a month, has an involuntary episode of lost or altered consciousness resulting in significantly disrupted awareness or concentration.	6
		(c)	None of the above applies.	0

Part 2 Mental, Cognitive and Intellectual Function Assessment

Activity			*Descriptors*	*Points*
11.	**Learning tasks.**			
	11	(a)	Cannot learn how to complete a simple task, such as setting an alarm clock.	15
		(b)	Cannot learn anything beyond a simple task, such as setting an alarm clock.	9

Activity			*Descriptors*	*Points*
		(c)	Cannot learn anything beyond a moderately complex task, such as the steps involved in operating a washing machine to clean clothes.	6
		(d)	None of the above applies.	0
12.	**Awareness of everyday hazards (such as boiling water or sharp objects)**			
	12	(a)	Reduced awareness of everyday hazards leads to a significant risk of: (i) injury to self or others; or (ii) damage to property or possessions such that they require supervision for the majority of the time to maintain safety.	15
		(b)	Reduced awareness of everyday hazards leads to a significant risk of: (i) injury to self or others; or (ii) damage to property or possessions such that they frequently require supervision to maintain safety.	9
		(c)	Reduced awareness of everyday hazards leads to a significant risk of: (i) injury to self or others; or (ii) damage to property or possessions such that they occasionally require supervision to maintain safety.	6
		(d)	None of the above applies.	0
13.	**Initiating and completing personal action (which means planning, organization, problem-solving, prioritizing or switching tasks)**			
	13	(a)	Cannot, due to impaired mental function, reliably initiate or complete at least 2 sequential personal actions.	15
		(b)	Cannot, due to impaired mental function, reliably initiate or complete at least 2 personal actions for the majority of time.	9
		(c)	Frequently cannot, due to impaired mental function, reliably initiate or complete at least 2 personal actions.	6
		(d)	None of the above applies.	0
14.	**Coping with change**			
	14	(a)	Cannot cope with any change to the extent that day-to-day life cannot be managed.	15

Activity			*Descriptors*	*Points*
		(b)	Cannot cope with minor planned change (such as a prearranged change to the routine time scheduled for a lunch break), to the extent that overall day-to-day life is made significantly more difficult.	9
		(c)	Cannot cope with minor unplanned change (such as the timing of an appointment on the day it is due to occur), to the extent that overall day-to-day life is made significantly more difficult.	6
		(d)	None of the above applies.	0
15.	**Getting about**			
	15	(a)	Cannot get to any specified place with which the claimant is familiar.	15
		(b)	Is unable to get to a specified place with which the claimant is familiar, without being accompanied by another person.	9
		(c)	Is unable to get to a specified place with which the claimant is unfamiliar without being accompanied by another person.	6
		(d)	None of the above applies.	0
16.	**Coping with social engagement due to cognitive impairment or mental disorder**			
	16	(a)	Engagement in social contact is always precluded due to difficulty relating to others or significant distress experienced by the individual.	15
		(b)	Engagement in social contact with someone unfamiliar to the claimant is always precluded due to difficulty relating to others or significant distress experienced by the individual.	9
		(c)	Engagement in social contact with someone unfamiliar to the claimant is not possible for the majority of the time due to difficulty relating to others or significant distress experienced by the individual.	6
		(d)	None of the above applies.	0
17.	**Appropriateness of behaviour with other people, due to cognitive impairment or mental disorder**			
	17	(a)	Has, on a daily basis, uncontrollable episodes of aggressive or disinhibited behaviour that would be unreasonable in any workplace.	15

Activity			*Descriptors*	*Points*
		(b)	Frequently has uncontrollable episodes of aggressive or disinhibited behaviour that would be unreasonable in any workplace.	15
		(c)	Occasionally has uncontrollable episodes of aggressive or disinhibited behaviour that would be unreasonable in any workplace.	9
		(d)	None of the above applies.	0

Assessment of Whether a Claimant Has 'Limited Capability for Work-Related Activity'.

Activity			*Descriptors*
1.	**Mobilizing unaided by another person with or without a walking stick, manual wheelchair or other aid if such aid can reasonably be used**		
			Cannot either: (a) mobilize more than 50 metres on level ground without stopping in order to avoid significant discomfort or exhaustion; or (b) repeatedly mobilize 50 metres within a reasonable timescale because of significant discomfort or exhaustion.
2.	**Transferring from one seated position to another**		
			Cannot move between one seated position and another seated position located next to one another without receiving physical assistance from another person.
3.	**Reaching**		
			Cannot raise either arm as if to put something in the top pocket of a coat or jacket.
4.	**Picking up and moving or transferring by the use of the upper body and arms (excluding standing, sitting, bending or kneeling and all other activities specified in this Schedule).**		
			Cannot pick up and move a 0.5-litre carton full of liquid.
5.	**Manual dexterity**		
			Cannot either: (a) press a button, such as a telephone keypad; or (b) turn the pages of a book with either hand.
6.	**Making self understood through speaking, writing, typing or other means normally used**		

Activity			*Descriptors*
			Cannot convey a simple message, such as the presence of a hazard.
7.	**Understanding communication by hearing, lip reading, reading 16-point print or using any aid if reasonably used**		
			Cannot understand a simple message due to sensory impairment, such as the location of a fire escape.
8.	**Absence or loss of control over extensive evacuation of the bowel and/or voiding of the bladder, other than enuresis (bed-wetting), despite the presence of any aids or adaptations normally used**		
			At least once a week experiences: (a) loss of control leading to extensive evacuation of the bowel and/or voiding of the bladder; or (b) substantial leakage of the contents of a collecting device sufficient to require the individual to clean themselves and change clothing.
9.	**Learning tasks**		
			Cannot learn how to complete a simple task, such as setting an alarm clock, due to cognitive impairment or mental disorder.
10.	**Awareness of hazard**		
			Reduced awareness of everyday hazards, due to cognitive impairment or mental disorder, leads to a significant risk of: (a) injury to self or others; or (b) damage to property or possessions such that they require supervision for the majority of the time to maintain safety.
11.	**Initiating and completing personal action (which means planning, organization, problem-solving, prioritizing or switching tasks)**		
			Cannot, due to impaired mental function, reliably initiate or complete at least two sequential personal actions.
12.	**Coping with change**		
			Cannot cope with any change, due to cognitive impairment or mental disorder, the extent that day-to-day life cannot be managed.
13.	**Coping with social engagement, due to cognitive impairment or mental disorder**		
			Engagement in social contact is always precluded due to difficulty relating to others or significant distress experienced by the individual.
14.	**Appropriateness of behaviour with other people, due to cognitive impairment or mental disorder**		

Activity		*Descriptors*
		Has, on a daily basis, uncontrollable episodes of aggressive or disinhibited behaviour that would be unreasonable in any workplace.
15.	**Conveying food or drink to the mouth**	
		(a) Cannot convey food or drink to the claimant's own mouth without receiving physical assistance from someone else; (b) Cannot convey food or drink to the claimant's own mouth without repeatedly stopping, experiencing breathlessness or severe discomfort; (c) Cannot convey food or drink to the claimant's own mouth without receiving regular prompting given by someone else in the claimant's physical presence; or (d) Owing to a severe disorder of mood or behaviour fails to convey food or drink to the claimant's own mouth without receiving: (i) physical assistance from someone else; or (ii) regular prompting given by someone else in the claimant's presence.
16.	**Chewing or swallowing food or drink**	
		(a) Cannot chew or swallow food or drink; (b) Cannot chew or swallow food or drink without repeatedly stopping, experiencing breathlessness or severe discomfort; (c) Cannot chew or swallow food or drink without repeatedly receiving regular prompting given by someone else in the claimant's presence; or (d) Owing to a severe disorder of mood or behaviour fails to: (i) chew or swallow food or drink; or (ii) chew or swallow food or drink without regular prompting given by someone else in the claimant's presence.

289. Notwithstanding the apparent rigidity of the assessment and scoring process, there are circumstances in which a claimant who does not score a total of fifteen may still be entitled to ESA. These are:

(1) where the claimant has an uncontrolled or uncontrollable life-threatening disease, for which there is medical evidence and which cannot be controlled by a recognized therapeutic process;
(2) where because of the claimant's illness, there would be a substantial risk to the mental or physical health of another person, were the claimant to be found not to have limited capability for work.

In such cases, the claimant will still be entitled to ESA.

290. There are also circumstances in which the regulation provides that a claimant has limited capability for work, without the need for any specific assessment. This is where a 'special circumstance' applies to the claimant. These include:[179]

(1) the claimant is terminally ill;
(2) the claimant is receiving treatment by way of intravenous, intraperitoneal or intrathecal chemotherapy or recovering from that treatment and the Secretary of State is satisfied the claimant should be treated as having limited capability for work;
(3) the claimant is excluded or abstains from work, or is otherwise prevented from working by reason of the claimant being a carrier, or having been in contact with a case, of a relevant disease;
(4) in the case of a pregnant woman, there is a serious risk of damage to her health or the health of her unborn child if she does not refrain from work;
(5) the claimant is in hospital;
(6) the claimant is receiving regular weekly treatment by way of haemodialysis for chronic renal failure; or treatment by way of plasmapheresis or by way of radiotherapy; or regular weekly treatment by way of total parenteral nutrition for gross impairment of enteric function.

291. Furthermore, the 'exceptional circumstances' under Regulations 29 and 35 will apply if a claimant has:

- an uncontrolled or uncontrollable illness, or '… suffers from some specific disease or bodily or mental disablement'; and
- by reason of such disease or disablement, there would be a substantial risk to the mental or physical health of any person if they were found not to have limited capability for work/work-related activity.

292. Reassessment: One of the features of the new scheme is that most claimants who received ESA will be reassessed from time to time to make sure that they still satisfy the conditions of entitlement.

§3. Doing Work

293. Although the Government is anxious to 'encourage' those in receipt of ESA who are capable of work back into the labour market, it remains a general principle that if a claimant in receipt of ESA does do work, he/she loses entitlement to ESA. This general principle is, however, subject to some important exceptions. The claimant may:[180]

(a) work as a local Government councillor;
(b) undertake duties on either one full day or two half days a week as:

179. ESA Regulations 2008, Regulations 20, 25 and 26.
180. ESA Regulations 2008, Regulation 40.

(i) a member of the DLA Advisory Board; or
(ii) a member with a disability qualification of the First-Tier Social Entitlement Tribunal.

(c) carry out domestic tasks in the claimant's own home or the care of a relative;
(d) undertake duties in caring for another person who is accommodated with the claimant and where the claimant is in receipt of a payment (e.g., foster parent);
(e) undertake any activity during an emergency to protect another person or to prevent serious damage to property or livestock.

§4. Appealing Adverse Decisions

294. Appeals by claimants against adverse decisions are dealt with by the First-Tier Tribunal (Social Entitlement Chamber).[181]

295. For an appeal to have any chance of success,[182] it is very important in practice for the claimant to be able to present evidence from other professional sources (e.g., from his/her own general practitioner (family doctor) or a hospital consultant) and which relates to the extent of incapacity of the claimant.

§5. Disqualifications

296. There are a number of circumstances in which it is possible for a claimant to be disqualified from ESA. It is perhaps significant that the maximum period of disqualification in this context has remained at a relatively modest level of six weeks.[183]

297. The *grounds* for disqualification[184] are:

(1) becoming incapable of work as a result of the claimant's own misconduct (though not where incapacity is due to venereal disease or pregnancy); or
(2) failing without good cause to accept medical treatment recommended by a doctor which would be likely to overcome the limited capability for work; or
(3) failing without good cause to refrain from behaviour calculated to retard recovery;
(4) without good cause being absent from home without telling the DWP where he/she may be found.[185]

181. *See* Part XI for further discussion.
182. Statistical information about appeal success rates is provided in the Annual Reports of the Tribunal Service. *See* www.tribunals.gov.uk for more information.
183. *See* Part VII.
184. Social Employment and Support Regulations 2008 (SI 794, 2008) regulation 157.
185. This is designed to catch those who deliberately seek to evade visiting officers from the Department. Claimants of no fixed abode cannot be caught by this rule, since it does not impose an obligation to have a residence.

298. Although these rules do not appear to be widely applied in practice, they nonetheless signify a Government view that entitlement to social security benefits in this area – just as much as in the area of unemployment – should be at least in part determined by the imposition of a sense of responsibility and appropriate behaviour onto the claimant. In 2017, the DWP was found to have unlawfully stopped people appealing their benefits decisions. The Upper Tribunal found it was wrong for the DWP to refuse claimants the right to appeal if they took more than a month to ask for a review of the benefit decision. The DWP system was challenged by the Child Poverty Action Group (CPAG) and two claimants with serious mental health problems who were refused disability benefits and then failed to ask for an internal review within the one-month time limit. They made late applications for an internal review, called 'mandatory reconsideration', of their benefit decisions, but the DWP initially refused to change the decision or let a tribunal consider whether that was correct. The court held that 'The reality is that many claimants will be vulnerable for reasons including issues relating to their mental health or learning disabilities. It is obvious that there is a high risk that many of them with good claims on the merits will miss time limits. This risk has been exacerbated over recent years by changes in the scope of legal aid and local authority and advice sector provision, and hence the reduction in the numbers of welfare rights officers and others who are readily available to assist claimants with their benefits claims and appeals'.

They concluded: 'We are concerned with the situation where a claimant sends the secretary of state a request for a mandatory reconsideration to which the secretary of state responds by stating that the application is late and does not meet the criteria for extending time. We have concluded that as a matter of statutory interpretation a claimant in such circumstances has a statutory right of appeal to the first-tier tribunal.'

The UK Government had argued that claimants had recourse to judicial review if their right to go to tribunal was refused, but the judges observed that out of 1,544,805 mandatory reconsideration decisions made by the Government between 2013 and 2017, there had not been a single example of a claimant taking this legal path.

Chapter 3. Incapacity Benefit

299. As already noted, this benefit came into operation in April 1995 and replaced both sickness benefit and invalidity benefit. From October 2008, IB and IS which were paid on the basis of incapacity for work were replaced by the new ESA, which is paid to new claimants. Previous claimants of IB/IS are likely to be transferred to ESA later and will then have to participate in work-focused interviews and prepare action plans with the eventual aim of getting into work. Given the changes set out in the previous Chapter, it is not proposed to discuss IB or IS on the ground of incapacity further here.

Chapter 4. The Macfarlane Trust Funds

300. The Macfarlane Trust is one of a number of funds which have been established in recent years[186] to provide additional help for specific groups outside the treatment provided by the health service and in addition to the cash allowances paid through the social security system.

301. The Macfarlane Trust makes payments, either by way of single grants or more regular payments for living expenses, to those who are haemophiliac and who have been diagnosed as Human Immunodeficiency Virus (HIV) positive. The distinctive feature of this Trust is that its funds derive not from charitable donations but from a special grant provided by the Government. Other trusts have been subsequently set up using the same model. These include the Eileen Trust, which provides support to individuals who have become HIV positive through NHS treatment, and the Skipton Fund, which does the same for individuals who have contracted Hepatitis C through NHS treatment. For this reason, it is right that these Trusts and Funds should be seen as a modest extension of the British social security system.

186. Two others are the Family Fund, administered by the Joseph Rowntree Charitable Trust, and the Independent Living Fund: these are discussed further below, *see* Part IX.

Part VI. Industrial Accidents and Occupational Diseases

Introduction

302. Industrial injury schemes have a long history in the UK legal system. The first scheme for compensating those injured at work was provided by the Workmen's Compensation Act of 1897. That scheme required the employer to pay benefits to those who suffered injury at work. In fact, the present scheme dates from 1948.

303. When the modern Welfare State was created in Britain after the end of the Second World War, particular attention was given to benefits for those injured in industrial accidents. Industrial injuries benefits were the subject of separate legislation;[187] they were not brought into the mainstream legislative provisions until 1975.[188] The rates of benefit were set at more generous levels than those established for comparable benefits under the NI Scheme. Partly this reflected the special history of these benefits, going back to the Workmen's Compensation legislation of the late nineteenth century; partly this reflected public sentiment that there should be an 'industrial preference' for those injured while labouring for the general economic good.[189]

304. Whatever merits these arguments may have had historically, the past decades have seen an erosion by Government of nearly all the special privileges that used to attach to Industrial Injury Benefits. Much of the justification for these changes is that resulting savings on the Industrial Injuries Benefits budget have been utilized to make more generous provision for the disabled in general, whether or not their condition was work-related.[190]

187. National Insurance (Industrial Injuries) Act 1946.
188. They are now to be found in SSCBA 1992, Part V, ss 94–110.
189. For an introduction to the extensive literature on this matter, *see* A.I. Ogus, E. Barendt & N. Wikeley, *The Law of Social Security,* 5th edn (London: Butterworths, 2002).
190. *See* below Part IX. Indeed, one of the practical difficulties that now faces those disabled as a result of work injury is knowing whether they would be better off claiming the disablement benefit analysed in this Part or the general benefits for the disabled analysed in Part IX.

305. As originally conceived, the industrial injuries scheme is of fundamental importance to the UK's social security law. For instance, it continues to protect some 20 million claimants.

306. In this Part, we consider the current structure of industrial injuries benefits in Britain and also note briefly the existence of health and safety at work legislation.

Chapter 1. The Industrial Injuries Scheme

307. The industrial injuries scheme provides cash benefits for two distinct situations:[191]

(1) where people have been injured at work and as a result are disabled; and
(2) where people have contracted a disease which was caused by their work.

308. The main benefit is *industrial injuries disablement benefit.*[192] This comprises three possible components: a basic *Disablement Pension*[193] which in very serious cases may be supplemented by *constant attendance allowance* and *severe disablement allowance.*[194]

309. To establish entitlement to industrial injuries disablement benefit, four basic conditions must be satisfied:

(1) the claimant must have suffered a personal injury[195] caused by an industrial accident[196] arising out of or in course of employment, or be suffering from a prescribed[197] industrial disease;[198]
(2) the claimant must have suffered a loss of faculty *as a result of* the accident or disease; that is, there must be a causal link between the industrial accident/disease and the claimant's present condition;
(3) the claimant must be *disabled* as a result of the loss of faculty; and
(4) the claimant must be an employed earner.

Each of these conditions is now discussed.

191. *See*, for the present statutory basis, SSCBA 1992, Part V, ss. 94–111.
192. SSCBA 1992, ss 103–105 and Sch. 7 paras 2 and 3 and Parts II and III.
193. *Ibid.*, s. 103.
194. *Ibid.*, ss. 104 and 105. Unusually, no appeals against adverse determinations on entitlement in relation to these benefits are possible; *see* Social Security and Child Support (Decisions and Appeals) Regulations 1999, Sch. 2, para. 14.
195. It is essential that there should have been a personal injury arising by accident. Personal injury, however, includes psychological injury, just as much as more obvious physical injuries such as broken bones.
196. Despite the label, the scheme does not only apply to industrial workers; it includes other categories, for example office workers, as well.
197. These are the diseases prescribed in the Social Security (Industrial Injuries) (Prescribed Diseases) Regulations 1985, as amended, Sch. 1, which are known to be linked to particular occupations. The list is kept under review by the Industrial Injuries Advisory Council, and as scientific and medical knowledge develops, new diseases are added from time to time. It is still necessary for a claimant to prove a causal link between the occupation and the disease, but this will usually be done where the disease manifests itself within one month of the person last working in the job. In special cases – pneumoconiosis, byssinosis or diffuse mesothelioma – where it is known that the disease takes a long time to manifest itself, there is a separate scheme whereby a lump sum may be paid to those disabled by these diseases or their dependants, if they have died; The Pneumoconiosis etc. (Workers' Compensation) Act 1979.
198. SSCBA 1992, s. 94. *See* generally, N.J. Wikeley, *Compensation for Industrial Disease* (Aldershot: Dartmouth Publishing, 1993).

§1. INDUSTRIAL ACCIDENT OR DISEASE

I. Accident

310. It is a requirement of eligibility that the claimant suffered an injury caused '*by accident* arising out of and in the course of employment'. It has been held judicially that the phrase 'by accident' should be understood in the usual adverbial sense: the event should be something that happens 'though not designed or planned to happen'. It was stressed that it is irrelevant that the accident was foreseeable or even of a kind which might be expected to be encountered by a person routinely carrying out hazardous duties as part of his/her job. Further, there need be no hard and fast distinction between the suffering of injury and the occurrence of an accident; if the injury is the unintended consequence of an otherwise normal event, the suffering of the injury can itself constitute an accident.[199] This confirms the earlier understanding that an individual falls within the scheme even though the injury he/she suffers might in fact have been expected, for example where a person injures himself/herself as a result of heavy exertion.

311. The accident itself must arise *out of and in the course of employment.* This statutory phrase, which was brought into the industrial injuries scheme from the former Workmen's Compensation Scheme, has been the subject of considerable litigation and much interpretation. In determining whether or not the injury can be said to arise in the course of employment, two issues are to be considered: first, the nature of the contractual duties of the employee, and, second, whether or not what he/she was doing at the time of the accident can be held to constitute part of those duties. Whether the test is satisfied will, in the individual case, be very much a question of judgment, based on an analysis of all the evidence surrounding the accident and the findings of fact made therefrom. Indeed it has been judicially decided that so long as all the relevant circumstances have been taken into account, the question whether an accident has arisen which falls within the statutory formula is itself a question of fact.[200]

312. It has also been said judicially that the accident must occur 'while (the claimant) is doing what a man so employed may reasonably do within a time during which he is employed, and at a place where he may reasonably be during that time to do that thing',[201] or while 'doing something he was employed to do'.[202]

199. *See Chief Adjudication Officer v. Faulds* (Extra Division of Court of Session) (1998) ((33) Scots Law Times 1203), where it was held that a senior fireman who suffered (unintended) post-traumatic stress disorder as a result of attending at a sequence of fatal incidents (as was to be expected of someone doing his job) could claim on the basis that the occasion of his suffering injury in itself constituted an accident.

200. *Nancollas v. Insurance Officer* (1985) 2 All ER 833 (CA); *see also Faulkner v. Chief Adjudication Officer* (1994) The Times 8 April (CA); and *Chief Adjudication Officer v. Rhodes* (1998) The Times Law Reports 525 (CA).

201. *Moore v. Manchester Liners Ltd* (1910) AC 498 at 500 (HL).

202. Lord Atkinson in *St. Helens Colliery Co Ltd v. Hewitson* (1924) AC 292 (HL).

313. However, while this may work as a test for those who work regular hours in a single place of work, it is less satisfactory as a test for those who do not work in a regular job pattern, or who do not have a single place of work or who are misbehaving at work. It is not difficult to think of examples which do not fit easily into these categories and where, therefore, individual judgment will be called for before a decision can be made.

314. For example, it is clear that a person is not usually in the *course* of employment before he/she gets to work but is still travelling to the workplace, but a person will be in course of employment if he/she has started work for the day and, as part of the job, is travelling from one job to another.[203] There may be problems where a person works a split shift: are they still at work if they leave the work premises during that part of the day when they are not actually working, but, for example, are still on call? The outcome of such cases is not easy to determine in advance and may well turn on some specific aspect of the factual background, including, for example, whether the employee receives wages for travelling.

315. The *scope* of the employment may cause difficulty as well. Is a policeman who is injured while playing a game of football with a local youth team still acting in course of employment? He is not paid to play football but may argue that such games help his credibility in the community and thus improve his chances of being a successful policeman. The decided cases turn at least to some extent on whether what the claimant was doing at the time was compulsory or voluntary.[204]

316. The case law that has been developed by the Social Security Commissioners[205] shows a wide variety of decisions on these and other analogous situations; it reinforces the point that the precise decision will turn very much on the individual facts.

317. A number of statutory rules supplement the case law. For example, certain accidents happening when the claimant is meeting an emergency are deemed to have arisen out of and in course of employment.[206] And the Secretary of State is given the power to rule that certain accidents occurring during an illegal employment or where the claimant was acting in breach of regulations are nonetheless within the scheme.[207]

203. There is a special rule that accidents occurring while the claimant is travelling in transport provided by the employer are to be taken as arising out of and in the course of employment: SSCBA 1992, s. 99.
204. *See*, for example, *R. v. N.I. Commissioner Ex Parte Michaels* (1977) 1 WLR 109: policeman playing football (voluntarily) for his force was held by the court not to be covered by the statutory formula.
205. Now the Upper Tier Tribunal. *See* further, Part XI.
206. SSCBA 1992, s. 100.
207. SSCBA 1992, ss 97 and 98.

318. It must also be shown that the accident arose *out of* the employment. There is a statutory presumption that, in the absence of evidence to the contrary, an accident arising *in the course of* employment shall be taken to have arisen *out of* the employment.[208] However, particular problems, with conflicting results, have arisen where a claimant has been injured during the course of employment by something that could happen to anyone, at any time, for example, getting a piece of grit in one's eye while driving.

319. As a result of statutory amendment in 1961, it is provided that accidents caused by another's misconduct, skylarking or negligence, or by the behaviour or presence of an animal or where the claimant is struck by any object or lightning, shall be deemed to have arisen out of the employment so long as they occurred in the course of the employment.[209]

320. Where a claimant has suffered a personal injury at work because of his own misconduct, the adjudicating authorities may well determine that the accident did not arise 'in the course of' his employment, since – by definition – an employee is employed to work according to the rules of the employer, not in contravention of or outside them. Thus, while there are no formal rules which disqualify a claimant from benefit, as there are, for example, with Unemployment Benefit/UC/JSA[210] or ESA,[211] the practical effect of the application of the statutory test is similar.

II. Diseases

321. Only diseases that have been statutorily prescribed as industrial diseases fall within the scope of the industrial injuries scheme.[212] In addition, the claimant must prove that the disease was linked to the occupation. With advances in medical knowledge or changes in the materials used in employment, new conditions can arise which should be included in the list of diseases.

322. The whole question of what diseases should be regarded as industrial diseases, and their links to particular industries, is kept under review by a special Government Committee, the Industrial Injuries Advisory Council (*see*: https://www.gov.uk/government/organisations/industrial-injuries-advisory-council), which from time to time issues a report recommending to Ministers that a new disease is added to the list.[213] Their advice is usually adopted.

208. SSCBA 1992, s. 94(3).
209. SSCBA 1992, s. 101.
210. *See* below Part VII.
211. *See* above Part V.
212. *See* https://www.gov.uk/government/publications/industrial-injuries-disablement-benefits-technical-guidance/industrial-injuries-disablement-benefits-technical-guidance.
213. *See* Social Security (Industrial Injuries) (Prescribed Diseases) Regulations, 1985 regulations 20–24. J.M. Harrington, 'The Industrial Injuries Advisory Council: Its Role in the Benefits System', *Journal of Social Security Law* 70 (1994). *See also* http://iiac.independent.gov.uk/.

A. Pneumoconiosis, Byssinosis and Diffuse Mesothelioma

323. Special provisions apply to those – principally coal miners – who suffer from the above diseases. In particular, their extent of disability has to be only 1% in order to qualify for disablement benefit not the 14% that applies normally.[214]

§2. Loss of Faculty

324. In order to establish entitlement to benefit, a claimant must be able to demonstrate that, in addition to experiencing an industrial accident or suffering an industrial disease, this has led to a loss of physical or mental faculty, such as impaired limb function. The scheme will therefore not cover trivial incidents. It is statutorily provided that disfigurement is to be regarded as a loss of faculty.[215]

§3. Disablement

325. As a separate issue, the claimant must demonstrate that, as a result of the loss of faculty, he/she is now disabled, either physically or mentally. Disability is for these purposes measured in percentage terms. Certain disabilities have their percentage degree of disablement laid down in the regulations.[216] For example, loss of both hands is assessed at 100%; loss of one eye, without complications and the other eye normal, 40%; partial loss of the great toe, with some loss of bone, 3%.

326. Where there is no prescribed percentage figure, the adjudicating authorities[217] must use their own experience and draw on the figures set out in the regulations to provide analogous starting points for the assessment which they have to determine.

327. In assessing disablement, complex matters can arise in practice where there is a disablement arising from a pre-existing condition which had also caused disablement but which was not the result of an industrial injury. In such cases, the degree of the previously existing disablement must be 'offset' against the degree of disablement now presenting. If the previous degree of disablement was also the result of an industrial injury, then the offsetting exercise does not need to be done. Indeed in some cases, there may be an *aggregation* of the degrees of disablement.

---

214. *See* above para. 313 n. 197.
215. SSCBA 1992, s. 122(1): 'loss of physical faculty' includes disfigurement whether or not accompanied by any loss of physical faculty.
216. *See* Social Security (General Benefit) Regulations 1982 Sch. 2; for occupational deafness *see* Social Security (Industrial Injuries) (Prescribed Diseases) Regulations 1985 (as amended) regulation 34 and Sch. 3.
217. These used to be doctors employed by the DSS who were known as Adjudicating Medical Practitioners working either singly or in pairs; SSAA 1992, s. 45(2). For further details *see* below Part XI, para. 692.

328. For example, one industrial accident may have led to a loss of faculty, for example, loss of the middle finger, where the degree of disablement is prescribed as 12%; a later industrial accident may result in loss of a little finger, however, where the degree of disablement is 7%. After the second accident, the degree of disablement is 19%. This will be important since disablement benefit is not payable unless the degree of disablement is in excess of 14%. So neither injury on its own would have come within the scheme; taken together, they do. The aggregate cannot however exceed 100%.

329. Once a percentage figure is determined, that figure itself is then rounded. A total 14%–19% is rounded to 20%; all other figures are rounded to the nearest 10%. Multiples of five are rounded up, not down.[218]

§4. Employed Earners Employment

330. Only those in employed earners employment are entitled to disablement benefit. This is the same concept as is used for determining liability to pay Class 1 contributions.[219] However, it is not necessary that the claimant has a contribution record of any particular size and indeed will still be covered even though her/his earnings are below the contribution's threshold. To that extent, entitlement to disablement benefit is easier to establish than, for example, contributory ESA.

331. As a result of this definition, there is a very important exclusion from coverage by the scheme, namely those who are self-employed. This is a limitation in the British scheme of compensation for industrial accidents and injuries that is not found in some other countries.[220]

§5. Period of Assessment

332. In every case where entitlement is established, the adjudicating authorities also have to decide for what period their decision will operate. If they think a claimant's condition will not change, they may make an award of benefit for life. If they think it will get better, they may award for a more limited, fixed period. Such awards may be provisional, in which case they will be automatically reviewed by the Department, or final, in which case they will not be reviewed unless the claimant can demonstrate that there has been an 'unforeseen aggravation' of the condition.[221]

218. Details are in SSCBA 1992, s. 103.

219. *See* above Part II. The categories of employment have been extended by regulation: SSCBA 1992, s. 95 and the Social Security (Employed Earners. Employments for Industrial Injuries Purposes) Regulations, 1975 SI 1975 No. 467.

220. *See*, A.I. Ogus, E. Barendt & N. Wikeley, *The Law of Social Security* 5th edn (London: Butterworths, 2002).

221. *See* SSCBA 1992, Sch. 6, paras 6 and 7, and SSAA 1992, s. 47(4). Cases involving unforeseen aggravation are often very hard to decide in practice, since it can be very hard to distinguish

§6. INDUSTRIAL INJURIES DISABLEMENT BENEFIT: ENTITLEMENT

333. If the conditions of entitlement discussed above are satisfied, entitlement to disablement benefit arises where: (i) the claimant's disability has been assessed at least 14%; and (ii) ninety days, excluding Sundays, have elapsed between the date of the industrial accident or the onset of the industrial disease.[222]

Normally, you must be assessed as 14% disabled or more to get the benefit.

Assessed Level of Disablement (Weekly Amount)

Assessed Level of Disablement	*Weekly Amount*
100%	GBP 174.80
90%	GBP 157.32
80%	GBP 139.84
70%	GBP 122.36
60%	GBP 104.88
50%	GBP 87.40
40%	GBP 69.92
30%	GBP 52.44
20%	GBP 34.96

334. The precise sum payable weekly will depend on the percentage figure determined after the appropriate rounding. Claimants aged under 18 without dependants receive a lower rate than other claimants.[223] The current maximum rate, for an assessment of 100% disablement is GBP 174.80 per week.

§7. CONSTANT ATTENDANCE SUPPLEMENT

335. The constant attendance supplement is payable to those assessed as 100% disabled who are also in need of constant attendance. This is paid:

(1) at an exceptional (higher) rate (currently GBP 1139.84 a week) for those 'entirely or almost entirely dependent on (constant) attendance for the necessities of life, and likely to remain so dependent for a prolonged period and the attendance so required is whole-time'; and

between a deterioration in a person's condition related to the industrial accident and deterioration relating to constitutional change in a person, for example as the result of the ageing process.

222. Disablement benefit is not designed to compensate for the short-term consequences of industrial accident or disease. Where relevant, sickness benefits will be payable: *see* above Part V.

223. The rates of benefit are set out in detail in SSCBA 1992, Sch. 4, as amended annually to take into account changes in benefit levels. For the specific provision relating to those under 18 without dependants, *see* Sch. 4 para. 4(b). *See* www.direct.gov.uk for latest figures.

(2) at a normal (maximum) rate (currently GBP 69.92 a week) to those who 'to a substantial extent [are] dependent on [constant] attendance for the necessities of life and is likely to remain so for a prolonged period'.[224]

§8. Exceptionally SDA

336. The exceptionally SDA is a further supplement (currently GBP 69.92 a week) which is paid to those in receipt of the higher rate of constant attendance allowance if they are likely to be in receipt of that supplement permanently.[225]

224. SSCBA 1992, s. 104. This rate may itself be increased up to GBP 66.70 a week if the extent of the attendance 'is greater by reason of the beneficiary's exceptionally severe disablement'.
225. SSCBA 1992, s. 105.

Chapter 2. Former (Abolished) Additional Benefits

337. As was mentioned at the outset of this Part, a number of additional benefits associated with disablement benefit have been abolished save for those who had established entitlement as at the date of abolition. It is the removal of these additions that has largely eliminated the 'industrial preference' considered above. Only a brief mention of these former benefits is made here.

338. They included:

(1) *Unemployability Supplement*, which was *abolished in April 1987* except for existing claimants;
(2) *Hospital Treatment Allowance*, also *abolished in April 1987* except for existing claimants;
(3) *Reduced Earnings Allowance* (formerly known as the *Special Hardship Allowance*), except for those who can show continuous entitlement to the allowance since 1 October 1990;
(4) *Retirement Allowance*, except for those who had been getting Reduced Earnings Allowance; and
(5) *Industrial Death Benefit* except for deaths occurring as a result of industrial accidents or diseases *before 11 April 1988*.

Chapter 3. Prevention of Industrial Accidents and Occupational Disease: Health and Safety at Work

339. To an extent, the existence of the industrial injuries scheme is evidence of failure – the failure of employers to provide their employees with a safe working environment. Although not strictly part of the British system of social security, the industrial injuries scheme is complemented by a reasonably comprehensive system for the creation of systems of health and safety at work. Policy in this area derives from an important Government report, published in 1974, which called for health and safety measures to be built on a partnership between employers, employees and the Government.[226]

340. Responsibility for enforcement of health and safety legislation lies primarily with the Health and Safety Executive,[227] though local authorities do also have some powers in this area as well.

341. Standards of safety at work are not easy to determine. Practical considerations mean that a balance has to be struck between the need to protect workers and the need for employers to carry on their businesses. Thus there will always be questions of where the balance of risk should lie. Wholly safe systems of work may be prohibitively expensive or even in some cases prevent some industrial processes from being carried on at all.

342. Given the pragmatic limitations on the ability of health and safety legislation to create a totally safe working environment, there will still be cases of accidents and industrial disease. It has been accepted that the State retains a responsibility to provide some measure of compensation for those who have the misfortune to be injured at work or to contract industrial diseases.

226. 'Committee on Health and Safety at Work', Chairman: Lord Robens, 'Safety and Health at Work: Report of the Committee, 1970–1972', Cmnd 5034 (London: HMSO, 1972).
227. Large amounts of information about the work of the Health and Safety Executive can be found at www.hse.gov.uk/.

Part VII. Unemployment

Introduction

343. Protection for people suffering loss of income resulting from loss of employment was one of the first risks to be protected from the earliest days of the development of the scheme of social insurance in 1911.[228] When Sir William Beveridge first pressed for the introduction of unemployment insurance, however, he clearly linked this initiative with the complementary provision of services designed to enable and encourage those out of work to get back into employment. Unemployment was to be regarded as a temporary experience only.

344. Initially this was done through the work of the employment exchanges. Although these offices – now known as job centres – are still important, there is today a much more complex network of training schemes and other measures designed to facilitate the return to work of those who are out of work and to encourage those who have never been in the workforce – particularly the young school-leavers – to take employment. Nevertheless, current levels of unemployment in the UK are estimated at around 5.1% in the three months to January of 2016, staying at the lowest in nearly ten years. Unemployment rate in the UK averaged 7.17% from 1971 until 2016, reaching an all-time high of 12% in February of 1984 and a record low of 3.40% in November of 1973. Unemployment rates in the UK are recorded and reported by the Office for National Statistics (https://www.ons.gov.uk/).

345. It is hard to understand the place of Unemployment Benefit in the British social security system without a broader appreciation of general Government policy on employment.

§1. Employment Policy

346. Shortly before the Beveridge scheme of social insurance was first introduced after the end of Second World War, the Government had, in 1944, published a famous White Paper *Employment Policy*[229] setting out a commitment to a 'high

228. There are a number of excellent books on the history of unemployment insurance: *see*, for example, J. Harris, *William Beveridge: A Biography* (Oxford: Clarendon Press, 1977); J. Fulbrook, *Administrative Justice and the Unemployed* (London: Mansell, 1978).
229. 'Ministry of Reconstruction', Cmd 6527 (London: HMSO, 1944).

and stable level of employment'. This was to be the bedrock for the provision of Unemployment Benefit which, in Beveridge's view, should enable the unemployed 'to subsist without demoralization till they can be reabsorbed again after industrial transformations'.[230]

347. For the first forty years after the war, political rhetoric suggested – often in the teeth of all the empirical evidence – that this fundamental commitment to high levels of employment should remain.

348. However, the context within which the labour market operated was subject to profound change. The driving forces in the economy were under considerable pressure. In particular, reliance on heavy manufacturing industry, which in the years immediately after the war had been at the heart of British economic activity, became, during the 1970s, increasingly hard to maintain. During the 1980s, the British economy underwent a period of substantial restructuring, in which many traditional industries closed, to be replaced by new ones. Particularly noticeable was a shift from manufacturing to service industries.

349. In 1985, there was a significant change of emphasis in Government statements on employment. The White Paper *Employment: The Challenge for the Nation*[231] identified the foci of employment policy as 'bringing inflation under control; (…) restraining public expenditure; (…) breaking up monopolies; (…) and providing a surer and better-balanced framework of law for responsible and constructive industrial relations'. Three months later, a Green Paper on the reform of social security observed that the social security system should not create barriers to the creation of jobs, but rather should encourage job mobility, and enable people to rejoin the labour force.[232]

350. Such statements signalled that, in future, there would be less reliance on job protection than had been the case in the past, and more reliance on the operation of a free labour market. These sentiments were accompanied by other developments in the labour market. There was a considerable reduction in the power and influence of the trade unions. Changes to employment protection legislation sought, for example, to further encourage job mobility by reducing the scope of employment protection. There was a substantial rise in the numbers of short-term and part-time employment contracts. The 1990s Conservative Governments also sought to encourage people, so far as possible, to take work at the lowest possible levels of pay. Wages councils – that used to determine nationally the rates of pay in a number of traditionally low-waged employments, for example agricultural labour – were abolished by the Conservative Government in 1993. In short, there was a shift from an employment policy which accepted that the primary aim was to ensure that all (mainly men) should be in permanent employment, to one in which the vagaries of

---

230. W. Beveridge, *Unemployment: A Problem of Industry (1909)* (New York: AMS Press, reprinted, 1969), 236.
231. Cmnd 9474 (London: HMSO, 1985).
232. Cmnd 9517 (London: HMSO, 1985).

the market were more predominant. The reluctance of the Conservative Government in 1992 to return to the earlier policy was evidenced in their hostility to the Social Chapter contained in the Maastricht Treaty.

351. When elected in 1997, the Blairite 'New' Labour Government did not return[233] to a simple commitment to full employment, but it set as its goals the pursuit of 'high and stable levels of employment' and the promotion of employment opportunities for those who had been excluded from the labour market. It also committed itself to increasing the proportion of the working age population that are in work and decreasing the number of households in which no one is in work. It aims thereby not only to 'enhance growth and productivity' but also to 'decreas[e] (…) poverty and benefit dependency'. The reduction of levels of unemployment was the cornerstone of the Government's social security policy; it saw unemployment as a prime cause of social exclusion and believed the way to tackle that for those who are capable of work was not just to enhance benefit levels but rather to help them to work. They sought to do this by providing an appropriate macroeconomic framework, through the mixture of compulsion and opportunity that made up the New Deal,[234] by reforming the tax and benefits system 'to fulfil the objectives of [inter alia] promoting work incentives and reducing poverty and welfare dependency (…)',[235] and by placing a renewed emphasis on training and the enhancement of employability.

352. At the same time, the Labour Government guaranteed certain minimum employment standards that will 'make work pay'. This latter pledge led to the introduction of the National Minimum Wage and further regulation of employment conditions, in particular through the acceptance of the Social Chapter of the Maastricht

233. On the overall policy framework, *see* the various budgets and pre-budget reports produced by the Treasury, 'Pre-Budget Report Securing Britain's Long-Term Economic Future', Cmd 3804 (November 1997); 'Budget 98 New Ambitions for Britain', HC 1997–1998, 620 (March 1998); 'Pre-Budget Report Steering a Stable Course for Lasting Prosperity', Cmd 4076 (November 1998); 'Budget 99', HC 1998–1999, 298 (March 1999). On the DfEE's objectives, *see* 'The Public Service Agreement', Cmd 4181 (December 1998) and the latest Comprehensive Spending Review, 'Modernising Public Services for Britain', Cmd 4011 (July 1998); on more specific areas of employment policy, *see* the Department for Education and Employment, 'National Minimum Wage', Cmd 3992 (May 1998) and Department for Education and Employment, 'Fairness at Work', Cmd 3968 (June 1998). On the centrality of the promotion of employment to social security reform, *see* the DSS' White Paper, 'New Ambitions for Our Country: A New Contract for Welfare', Cmd 3805 (March 1998). All works are published by TSO, London.

234. *See* below Part VII, Ch. 3 and various reports of the House of Commons Education and Employment Committee, in particular: 'Eighth Report: The New Deal Pathfinders' HC 1997–1998, 1059 (1998); 'Second Report: The New Deal' HC 1997–1998, 263 (1997) both published by TSO, London.

235. Through, for example, the cultural changes to the Employment Service, focusing it on assisting people to find work, with a renewed emphasis on careers guidance, training and assistance to improve 'employability'; moving towards compelling all benefit recipients to attend a job-focused interview as a condition of receiving benefit and subjecting the partners of long-term JSA claimants to the labour market conditions; through changes to the assessment of incapacity for work (*see* Part V); and through attention to poverty and unemployment traps, in particular via reform of the NI system (*see* Part II), the reform of in-work benefits (*see* Part X *and* Part IX on Disabled Person's Tax Credit); and through attention to in-work childcare costs.

Treaty. While there was no return to the earlier emphasis on job protection, the New Labour Government saw that there should be a 'flexible and adaptable labour market'.

353. The Coalition Government from 2010–2015 adopted this general approach. While they have abandoned some of the detailed measures contained in Labour's 'New Deal', they have replaced this with what is called the 'Work Programme'. A key feature of this programme is that it is delivered by private sector companies who, at least in part, are paid by results – that is, their remuneration is based on getting unemployed people into real jobs and keeping them there.[236] The Coalition has also set out quite bold plans to overhaul the benefit system to ensure that people are always better off in work than out of work. These general plans were further by the Conservative Government elected in 2015, culminating in welfare reforms in early 2016, as briefly considered in this volume in the opening preface and dealt with more fully in relation to the sections on UC and PIP.

354. These developments emphasize the fact that, for the last sixty years or more, many features of the social security system can still be seen to reinforce employment policy in a number of ways.

355. First, the very existence of a scheme of unemployment benefits has enabled Governments to allow economic restructuring to take place and provides the underpinning needed to sustain a 'flexible' labour market. When people lose their jobs as a result of such restructuring or flexibility, the social security system ensures that they have a bare minimum of financial resources on which to live – albeit in no great comfort.

356. Second, increasing incentives have been incorporated into the social security system to try to encourage, even to force, those without jobs back into the labour market. Thus, do benefit claimants have to demonstrate not only that they are available for work but also from 1989 that they are 'actively seeking employment', from 1996 that they have signed a written 'jobseeker's agreement'[237] outlining the steps they will take to seek employment, and from October 1999 (following changes introduced by the provisions of the WRPA) if they wished to claim on behalf of their partner, they had to sign a statement that their partner also satisfied these conditions.[238] From 1998 onwards, selected groups of the unemployed have been compelled to participate in programmes of work or training if they are to avoid temporary suspensions of all benefit payments, heightening the pressure that the social security system has long since placed on the unemployed, particularly the

236. For more information, *see* www.dwp.gov.uk/supplying-dwp/what-we-buy/welfare-to-work-services/work-programme/.
237. *See* below para. 391.
238. It is intended that this requirement will in the first instance only be imposed on those without children who are over 18 and under 25 years of age.

young school-leavers and the long-term unemployed, to seek retraining to enable them to enter or re-enter the rapidly changing labour market.[239]

357. Third, the social security system has also provided some financial underpinning for the changed employment market, in particular through significant extensions to the principle of tax credits for those in low-paid employment.[240] Other benefits, such as HB and CTB, are also paid to those in work on low pay (as well as to those not in employment at all).

358. There are, of course, those who argue that any social security provision for unemployment reduces the incentive of the unemployed to find work. It is argued that if they are better off, financially, out of work than in employment, then as rational economic beings, they will prefer a life of unemployment rather than employment. Such views ignore the apparent social reality that most people out of work would, in fact, prefer to be in employment. Nonetheless, these opinions have contributed to a reduction in what economists refer to as the 'replacement rate' of Unemployment Benefit – the degree to which Unemployment Benefit replaces income derived from work. Policymakers have sought to reduce expenditure on Unemployment Benefit by greater reliance on means-tested benefits 'targeted' to those most in need, and a reduced emphasis on contributory benefits, paid as of right. The negative effect of this, however, is that the 'poverty trap' has become ever more intense.

359. The election of the Labour Government in 1997 did not result in change on these fronts. It did not restore the value of contributory benefits for the unemployed. It was wedded to the notion that the social security system should ensure that those who are deemed capable of work should be better off in work than on benefit. Nonetheless, it placed the reduction of poverty and unemployment traps at the heart of its review of the tax and benefits system. And it sought to counter the worst effects of means-testing of benefits by:

- enhancing in-work benefits, in particular attending to those with high in-work childcare costs;
- easing the tapers through which benefits are to be withdrawn as earnings increase;
- seeking to enhance the returns from the lowest-paid work via the introduction of a National Minimum Wage; and
- seeking to ease the tax burden on the low paid through reform of NI.

360. Notwithstanding the historical and symbolic importance of contributory benefits for the unemployed, the amount of spending on these benefits has long been

239. The effectiveness of training programmes in achieving this objective is not considered in any detail here, though there are many who think that technical training, in particular, is still not taken as seriously in Britain as it is in other countries.

240. *See* below Parts X and IX.

in steady decline. Expenditure on contributory JSA is now dwarfed by that on means-tested non-contributory benefits for the unemployed.

361. There are two main reasons for the decreasing relative expenditure on contributory benefits for the unemployed. First is the fact that many unemployed are out of work for considerable periods of time – certainly more than the six[241] months to which there is entitlement to the benefit.

362. Second, the figures illustrate dramatically how far the social security system has moved away from the Beveridgean ideal that contributory social security benefit levels should be set at the officially defined 'poverty level'. Further expenditure on non-contributory income-based JSA and housing and CTB results from the fact that contributory JSA is paid at a lower level than that of the means-tested scheme.

241. Prior to the introduction of Jobseeker's Allowance in 1996, entitlement to contributory benefits lasted for twelve months.

Chapter 1. Universal Credit

363. UC is a new benefit, introduced in 2013, for people of working age who are in or out of work. UC will replace six existing benefits and is currently being rolled out across the UK. The new system is based on a single monthly payment, transferred directly into a bank account. At present UC only affects newly unemployed people in certain areas of the country.

364. UC is a single monthly payment for people in or out of work, which merges together some of the benefits and tax credits that you might be getting now.

UC will replace:

- Income-based JSA.
- Income-related ESA.
- IS.
- CTC.
- WTC.
- HB.

365. UC was announced by Work and Pensions Secretary Iain Duncan Smith at the Conservative Party annual conference in 2010 where it was stated the reform was designed to bring 'fairness and simplicity' to the British social security system. It is one of several wide-ranging welfare reforms introduced by the 2010–2015 Coalition Government in the WRA 2012.

366. UC was rolled out gradually to job centres with roll-out initially focusing on claimants in the most 'simple' circumstances namely single adults without housing costs.

367. As of January 2018, all UC areas are all full-service areas. This meant that the end to the live service or digital/full-service areas, or the 'lobster pot' principle, as it became known, where UC claimants remained in that regime and could not go back to 'live areas' where the six individual legacy benefits remained. Now, across the UK, the UC service is fully implemented.

§1. Eligibility for UC

368. To be eligible for UC, the claimant must meet the 'gateway' (basic criteria)[242] conditions as follows:

- expect to earn less than GBP 338 (after tax) in the next month;[243]
- be between 18 years old and 60 years old;
- be a British citizen;

242. Section 4 WRA 2012; Reg 8 UC Regs 2013.
243. GBP 541 if you are a couple.

- have a NI number; and
- have less than GBP 6,000 in savings or other investments (GBP 16,000 limit if you live in certain areas of Sutton or Croydon).

§2. UC Application

369. UC is an online benefit, but claimants are permitted to apply over the phone or in person if you need to.

370. Before applying for UC, claimants will need to gather some information together:

- Postcode;
- NI number;
- bank, building society, credit union or Post Office card account details;
- type of accommodation, for example private rent, council tenant or housing association tenant and rental agreement;
- landlord's contact details;
- details of any savings and any other 'capital' investments;
- details of any income that is not from work, for example from a pension or insurance plan;
- details of earnings, for example recent payslips;
- childcare costs;
- details of any other benefits.

§3. UC Interview

371. Each UC claimant must attend an interview at JCP, and this is called a 'work search interview' or 'claimant commitment interview'.

372. The interview will be with a member of staff who will become the claimant's designated 'work coach' for the duration of the claim.

373. The purpose of the UC interview is to:

- check claim details;
- explain UC to each claimant;
- devise a plan to improve work prospects.

374. Within a few days of submitting a UC application, the DWP will arrange the interview.

§4. UC 'Claimant Commitment'

375. The WRA 2012 heralded a sea change in ensuring that the claimant understood and undertook their responsibilities. To that end, the then Coalition Government proposed and eventually enacted in UC an agreement to meet certain 'work-related requirements' while getting UC. These are tasks such as applying for jobs, attending skills assessments, updating CVs or preparing a business plan. These tasks will form part of an agreement called the 'claimant commitment'.[244]

376. Under UC, requirements will be set according to individual capability and circumstance. There will be four broad conditionality groups:

(1) full conditionality – jobseekers;
(2) work preparation – people with a disability or those with a health condition which means they have limited capability for work at the current time;
(3) keeping in touch with the labour market – lone parent or lead carer in a couple with a child over age 1 but below age 5; and
(4) no conditionality – people with a disability or health condition which prevents them from working, carers, lone parents or lead carers with a child under the age of 1.

377. Therefore, certain personal circumstances will lessen the burden of the 'commitment'. For example, if the claimant:

- looks after children;
- has a disability or health condition;
- has poor literacy skills;
- has a learning disability;
- looks after someone with a disability;
- is or has been a victim of domestic violence within the last six months;
- is undertaking jury service;
- is homeless;
- is undergoing treatment for a drug or alcohol problem.

378. Where a couple are claimants, the UC rules permit them to nominate a main carer. If they are a single/lone parent, they will automatically be the main carer.

§5. UC Sanctions

379. Like most other benefits, UC has sanctions where claimants fail to meet the requirements of their 'commitment'.

244. Section 13 WRA 2012; Regs 95 & 96 UC Regs 2013.

380. In the event that the sanctioned claimant is struggling with lack of money due to the sanction, the claimant can apply for a hardship payment to get emergency money for food and bills. Alternatively, they can appeal to a tribunal in order to challenge the sanction:

> *Lowest Level:* If you only have to meet the 'work-focused interview requirement' and you fail to attend or take part in a work-focused interview. They last until you take part in one.
> *Low level*: If you fail to attend or take part in a work-focused interview and a lowest level sanction does not apply; if you fail to attend or take part in a training course; or if you fail to take a specific action to get paid work, or to increase your earnings from work. They last until you do whatever you were sanctioned for failing to do, plus *7 days* for your first low-level sanction in any 364-day period, 14 days for your second or 28 days for your third.
> *Medium Level*: If you have to meet the 'work search requirement' and you fail to take all reasonable actions to find paid work or increase your earnings from work; or, if you have to meet the 'work availability requirement' and you are not available to start work or attend interviews. You will be sanctioned for *28 days* for your first medium level sanction in any 364-day period or 91 days for your second.
> *Higher Level*: If you have to meet the 'work preparation requirement' and you fail to take part in Mandatory Work Activity; if you have to meet the 'work search requirement' and you fail to apply for a particular job when told to do so; if you have to meet the 'work availability requirement' and you refuse a job offer; or if you leave work or reduce your hours of work, whether voluntarily or due to 'misconduct' (while claiming UC or just before you claim). You will be sanctioned for *91 days* for your first higher level sanction in any 364-day period, 182 days for your second or 1,095 days for your third. There are special rules for how long your sanction will last if it is for leaving work before you claimed UC.

Standard Allowance

Your Circumstances	*Monthly Standard Allowance*
Single and under 25	GBP 251.77
Single and 25 or over	GBP 317.82
If a couple and you are both under 25	GBP 395.20 (for you both)
If a couple and either of you are 25 or over	GBP 498.89 (for you both)

Extra Amounts

Children

How Much You Will Get	*Extra Monthly Amount*
For your first child	GBP 277.08 (born before 6 April 2017) GBP 231.67 (born on or after 6 April 2017)
For your second child	GBP 231.67 per child
If you have a disabled or severely disabled child	GBP 126.11 or GBP 383.86
If you need help with childcare costs	up to 85% of your costs (up to GBP 646.35 for one child and GBP 1,108.04 for two or more children)

You only get an extra amount for more than two children if:

- you were already claiming for more than two children before 6 April 2017;
- you are renewing a claim for more than two children that stopped within the past six months.

Disability or Health Condition

How Much You Will Get	*Extra Monthly Amount*
If you have limited capability for work and work-related activity	GBP 328.32
If you have limited capability for work and you started your health-related UC or ESA claim before 3 April 2017	GBP 126.11

If You Care for a Severely Disabled Person

How Much You Will Get	*Extra Monthly Amount*
If you provide care for at least thirty-five hours a week for a severely disabled person who receives a disability-related benefit	GBP 156.45

Housing Costs[245]

You could get money to help pay your housing costs. How much you get depends on your age and circumstances.

The payment can cover rent and some service charges.

245. Section 11 WRA 2012; Regs 25 & 26 UC Regs 2013 & Schs 1–5 UC Regs 2013.

§6. CHALLENGES TO UC

381. UC has proved to be controversial and remains so. On 14 June 2018, the High Court ruled in a case brought by the Equality and Human Rights Commission that UC had discriminatory effects (*R (TP & AR) v. SSWP* (2018) EWHC 1474 (Admin). Accordingly, UC is being scrutinized by the Government, since the National Audit Office has also recently questioned this new regime's financial sustainability.

382. The most controversial element of UC is the new sanctions regime.

Sanctions

If a claimant fails to meet each of the responsibilities that they agreed in their commitment without good reason, they will have a cut in your benefit, known as a 'sanction'. This means that their UC payments will be reduced for a set period, and the period of reduction will increase the more times that the claimant fails to meet similar requirements, up to a maximum of three years (Ss. 26 and 27 WRA 2012 and Regs 101–105 UC Regs 2013).

There are four sanction levels: higher, medium, low and lowest.

Higher Level

The claimant will be sanctioned for 91 days for their first higher level sanction in any 364-day period, 182 days for their second or 1,095 days for their third if they:

- have to meet the 'work preparation requirement', and they fail to take part in Mandatory Work Activity;
- have to meet the 'work search requirement', and they fail to apply for a particular job when told to do so;
- have to meet the 'work availability requirement', and they refuse a job offer;
- leave work or reduce their hours of work, whether voluntarily or due to 'misconduct' (while claiming UC or just before their claim).

There are special rules for how long the sanction will last if it is for leaving work before they claimed UC.

Medium Level

The claimant will be sanctioned for 28 days for their first medium level sanction in any 364-day period or 91 days for their second if they have to meet either the:

- work search requirement – and they fail to take all reasonable actions to find paid work or increase their earnings from work;
- work availability requirement – and they are not available to start work or attend interviews.

Low Level

They last until they do whatever they were sanctioned for failing to do, plus 7 days for their first low-level sanction in any 364-day period, 14 days for their second or 28 days for their third if they fail to:

- attend or take part in a work-focused interview and a lowest sanction level does not apply;
- attend or take part in a training course;
- take a specific action to get paid work, or to increase their earnings from work.

Hardship Payments

The sanctioned claimant may be able to get a hardship payment if they get a sanction. They will repay it through their UC payments which will be lower until they pay it back.

The sanctioned claimant can get a hardship payment if they can show that they cannot pay for:

- rent;
- heating;
- food or hygiene needs for your or your household.

Claimants must be 18 years old or over, and your payment of UC must have been stopped or reduced because of a sanction. They cannot claim a hardship payment until this has happened. If a claimant has been sanctioned for not doing something like attending a meeting and there is no end date to that sanction, they cannot get hardship until you have done what they were asked to do.

Claimants must show that you have done everything reasonable to look for work in the seven days before claiming a hardship payment.

Chapter 2. Job Seeker's Allowance

383. From October 1996 until 2018, JSA was introduced for the unemployed. It replaced the former Unemployment Benefit and the provision of IS to the unemployed. It was replaced by UC from January 2018. However, as with ESA, JSA thus consists of two elements:

(1) *contribution-based* JSA paid to those who satisfy the requisite NICs conditions;
(2) *income-based* JSA paid to those who satisfy a means-test assessment.

There is actually a third type of JSA – *joint-claim* JSA – for couples, both of whom are unemployed; it is very similar to income-based JSA (so will not be further considered here).

384. Although JSA was a new benefit, it incorporated many of the features of the benefits it replaced, though with some additional features. In particular, the benefits are now supported by arrangements for administration of the benefit designed to ensure that unemployed claimants understand their responsibilities to go out and seek new employment. Such arrangements fall under the generic title: 'Welfare to Work'. Though started under the previous Conservative administration, they were extended by the 1997 Labour Government and remained in place under the then Coalition Government. These arrangements include requirements, which do not apply exclusively to claimants of JSA, that claimants attend 'work-focused' interviews with officials as a precondition to establishing entitlement to benefit. Claimants must also enter a jobseeker's agreement – a written statement that sets out what the claimant is going to do in order to look for work. It also requires the claimant to keep a record of the steps they have taken to find employment. (Similar arrangements are in place for recipients of ESA.) The service is delivered by JobCentre Plus, an agency within the DWP (*see* Part XI).

§1. Conditions of Entitlement to JSA

385. There are nine conditions of entitlement which a claimant must satisfy before becoming entitled to JSA. In addition, where claiming income-based JSA and the claimant is one of a couple then, the claimant's partner must also satisfy the conditions of eligibility including the receipt of advice to get them into work as well.[246]

386. First, the claimant must be 'available for employment'. This condition is not new and was brought into JSA from the old law on Unemployment Benefit and IS. Availability for employment is evidenced by the claimant attending at a local office of the DWP or JobCentre Plus to 'sign on'. Claimants are usually required to

246. WRPA 1999, s. 59.

sign on once a fortnight. Signing on involves making a declaration that the claimant is 'available for work'. This means that there is a reasonable prospect of obtaining work of the kind which the claimant states that he/she is available to do and that the claimant is willing and able to accept, generally at once,[247] any offer of work.

387. Second, the claimant must enter into a 'Jobseeker's agreement'. This was introduced by the Jobseekers Act 1995. Each claimant is interviewed by an official within the JobCentre Plus, known as an employment officer (EO). The claimant and EO enter a written agreement, which contains a statement of undertakings by the claimant as to the steps he/she will pursue in order to try and find employment.[248]

388. The third requirement is that the claimant is 'actively seeking employment'.[249] This is brought in from the old law on Unemployment Benefit. In 1989, in response to political pressure suggesting that too many of the unemployed were not taking adequate steps to get themselves back into employment (notwithstanding the apparent lack of employment opportunities), this test was added as one of the conditions of entitlement to the former Unemployment Benefit.

389. 'Actively seeking work' involves the claimants demonstrating that they have 'taken steps' in that week to find employment. The regulations provide a non-exhaustive list of examples: for example, making job applications, either written or oral; seeking information from advertisements; registering with an employment agency. The steps must be reasonable taking into account the circumstances of the claimant's situation.[250] Thus the regulations provide that in the early days of unemployment, the requirement to actively seek employment can be limited to the last occupation of the unemployed claimant, but the longer the claimant remains unemployed, the wider the field of employment he/she must consider.[251]

---

247. The harshness of the requirement for immediate availability (which has acted to preclude those unable to find work from taking on other commitments) is mitigated to a small extent by limited relaxations. Thus, those doing voluntary work or who have caring responsibilities need only be available on one week's notice; those providing a service can have twenty-four hours' notice; and there is some protection for those who are studying part-time. More recently protection was given to the long-term unemployed over 25 who are doing a full-time employment-related course approved by an EO and are in receipt of an allowance. (*See* Jobseeker's Allowance (General) Regulations SI 1996/207 (as amended) regulations 11, 15, 17A and 17D). Those participating in work-based training schemes can claim a training allowance instead, which for those aged 25 and over includes their prior entitlement to JSA.
248. Details about the Jobseeker's Agreement are prescribed in regulations made under the authority of the JSA 1995, s. 9; it is possible to vary the Jobseeker's Agreement in accordance with s. 10 of the JSA 1995. Reviews of and appeals against the terms of any such agreement are possible under s. 11 of the JSA.
249. *See* JSA 1995, s. 7. A marvellous study of somewhat similar provisions in force in the 1920s is A. Deacon, *In search of the Scrounger: The Administration of Unemployment Insurance in Britain, 1920–1931* (Occasional Papers on Social Administration, No. 60) (London: Bell, 1976).
250. Jobseeker's Allowance (General) Regulations, SI 1996 No. 207.
251. In addition, there are requirements to ensure that the claimant is willing to consider a wider range of levels of remuneration for that employment; in short, the regulations do not allow the claimant to continue to refuse to take any job that is less well paid than the job he was in when he became unemployed.

390. A person is *deemed* to be taking such steps in defined circumstances, including, for example, the two (but no more than two) weeks he/she is on holiday, the week in which he/she went back to work, any week during which he/she is on a training course for which a training allowance is paid and any week (up to three weeks) during which the claimant is on a course for which a training allowance is not payable.[252]

391. Failure to satisfy the EO that such active steps have been taken can, in the last resort, lead to the termination of entitlement to benefit, though before that stage is reached, there is a series of further interviews held with the claimants to persuade them of the desirability of continuing to take such active steps.

392. The fourth condition is that the claimant must not be *engaged in remunerative work for sixteen hours or more per week*; this, again, was brought in from the old law. Regulations provide for some exceptions to this principle. For example, certain categories of voluntary work undertaken by the claimant do not mean that he is 'engaged in remunerative work'. Furthermore, if claiming 'income-based' JSA, the claimant's partner must not be in paid work for more than twenty-four hours a week.

393. Fifth, it is important that the claimant is able to demonstrate that he is 'capable of work'. This, too, is a principle familiar from the old law. The effect of this rule is that any claimant currently entitled either to SSP or to ESA is, by definition, excluded from entitlement to JSA. An exception is made for two periods of up to two weeks in any twelve months, except for those who were recently entitled to benefits on the grounds of illness (ESA or SSP).[253]

394. The sixth requirement is that the claimant is not receiving 'relevant education'. This, in fact, excludes only those who are under 19 and (broadly) in full-time secondary as opposed to higher education.[254] Other students are excluded from entitlement on the basis that they fail the requirement to be available for work: those who are full-time students (i.e., broadly all students aged 19 or over and those under that age in tertiary education) are deemed automatically to fail this requirement;[255] there are limited circumstances in which students undertaking part-time courses only may, nevertheless, remain entitled to JSA.[256] There is also an exemption to these rules for those pursuing certain training options (as to which, *see* below Part VII, Chapter 3).

252. *Ibid.*
253. JSA (General) Regulations 1996 (SI 1996/207), regulation 51.
254. JSA Regulations, regulation 55.
255. *Ibid.*, regulation 15(a): there is an exception for student couples with a child in the summer vacation only.
256. *Ibid.*, regulation 11.

395. The next conditions are that the claimant must be under pensionable age and must also be in GB.[257] These, again, are concepts familiar under the old law. Claimants are also precluded from claiming if they are classified as persons from abroad, either because of their immigration status or because they are found not to be habitually resident in the UK.[258]

396. Finally the claimant must satisfy relevant financial conditions which relate to JSA.

§2. The Financial Conditions

397. As noted above, there are three types of JSA: a 'contribution-based' allowance, an 'income-based' allowance and a 'joint-claim' allowance. In order to claim the contribution-based element, which is payable as of right to all those who satisfy the contribution requirements, the claimant must, by definition, satisfy the contribution conditions which attach to this element.[259] The financial conditions relating to the 'income-based' element are, in effect, similar to the means-test which applies in the context of claims for IS.[260] Claimants will only be able to claim this element if their income and capital falls below the officially prescribed financial levels. 'Joint-claim' JSA is very similar to 'income-based' JSA and applies where both members of a couple satisfy the rules for getting 'income-based' JSA.

§3. The Amount of Benefit and Period of Entitlement

398. Assuming that the claimant satisfies all the conditions of entitlement summarized above, he/she will be entitled to receive the appropriate amount of JSA.[261]

---

257. There are certain exemptions to this requirement, for example for those on certain holidays, those attending interviews abroad, those travelling abroad caring for young people seeking medical treatment. In addition, those who are EU workers keep their entitlement to contributory JSA for up to three months while travelling elsewhere in the EU. Income-based JSA has, however, been listed as a special non-contributory benefit and as such is not exportable.
258. JSA Regulations, regulation 21 and Sch. 7. The rules are the same as those for IS – *see* below Part X.
259. These are set out in s. 2 of the JSA 1995.
260. The basic statutory provisions relating to the income-based conditions are set out in the JSA 1995, s. 3. Detailed Regulations are made under this provision.
261. The precise amount is determined in the Regulations made under the authority of the JSA 1995, s. 4. The effect of these provisions is, in practice, similar to the pre-existing relationship between Unemployment Benefit and IS. If the amount payable by way of the contribution-based element is as much as or more than the element payable by way of the income-based element, then the amount will consist of the contribution-based element alone; if, by contrast, the total amount under the Regulations is greater than the amount payable as the 'contribution-based' element, then the claimant will receive a 'top-up' by way of the 'income-based' element. It is also the case that entitlement to the contribution-based element ends after six months so that, from there on, entitlement will only be to the income-based component of JSA.

Entitlement does not begin until the fourth day of any period of unemployment.[262] Entitlement to the contribution-based element of the Allowance (currently GBP 73.10 a week for those aged over 25; GBP 57.90 for those aged under 25) lasts for six months only.[263] Entitlement to the income-related element lasts for as long as the claimant is unemployed. The exact amount depends on the circumstances of the claimant and is calculated by reference to a personal allowance, premiums for special needs and housing costs. In relation to both elements, entitlement may be lost by disqualification.

§4. Disqualifications

399. As under the old law,[264] there are a number of significant disqualifications from entitlement to JSA. These have been supplemented in recent years, particularly since 2012 by the use of 'sanctioning'. This as an approach has been fully adopted by UC (*see* paragraph 379).

I. Sanctions

400. Reflecting the desire of successive Governments that those in receipt of JSA should take active steps to obtain new employment, there has developed a rather complex set of measures which penalize claimants who fail to take such steps or in other ways fail to follow instructions given to them by officials within Job-Centre Plus. These measures are described generically in the legislation as 'sanctions'. Where a sanction is imposed, JSA may not be paid at all or may be paid at a reduced rate. There are three types of sanction:

(1) employment-related sanctions;
(2) jobseeker's direction sanctions; and
(3) training scheme and employment programme sanctions.

A. *Employment-Related Sanctions*

401. A claimant may be sanctioned if:

---

262. As benefit is usually paid fortnightly in arrears, there can therefore be some considerable time before a newly unemployed person receives any payment and this can cause hardship, even though it may be possible to apply for a crisis loan from the Social Fund in the interim. The 'waiting days' requirement does not apply in certain circumstances, including where the claim is linked to a previous claim, *see* Sch. 1, para. 4, JSA 1995.

263. *See* JSA 1995, s. 5. This is, of course, one of the main respects in which entitlement to Jobseeker's Allowance differs from the former mix of Unemployment Benefit and IS; entitlement to Unemployment Benefit lasted for twelve months.

264. Indeed, these disqualifications have a long history; they can be traced back to the earliest forms of Unemployment Insurance introduced in 1911.

(a) he/she has lost employment as an employed earner as a result of his/her misconduct; or
(b) has voluntarily left such employment without 'just cause';[265] or
(c) has, without good cause, after a situation in any employment been notified to him/her by an EO as vacant or about to become vacant, refused or failed to apply for it or to accept it when offered to him;[266] or
(d) has, without good cause, neglected to avail himself/herself of a reasonable opportunity of employment. It is, however, provided that a person shall have good cause for refusing any offer of employment not notified to him/her by an EO unless he/she is offered a job by an employer for whom he/she has worked in the last twelve months and on terms as good as those on which he/she was employed before.[267]

402. Misconduct cases often, in practice, become part of a wider argument between an employer and an employee as to whether the employee has been 'unfairly dismissed'. Disputes on unfair dismissal are dealt with by the Employment Tribunal.[268]

403. Many cases on voluntary leaving and alleged misconduct are appealed, where the outcome inevitably turns on questions of fact (as to whether there was in fact voluntary leaving or misconduct) and judgment (as to what the period of disqualification should be).

404. There is a 'defence' to an allegation of voluntarily leaving an employment or training opportunity that the employee has 'just cause' for so leaving. Examples of just cause might be victimization by other employees or a foreman or an unacceptable change in working conditions. In some cases, difficult personal or domestic circumstances have been held to amount to just cause. However, simply not

265. It is specifically provided that where a person is made redundant by his/her employer after having agreed to be made redundant, he/she is to be treated as not having left his/her employment voluntarily: JSA 1995, s. 19(7).
266. The reasonableness of the claimant's expectations in relation to the work he/she might be expected to do will vary with the length of time a person is unemployed. Thus a person who has lost a job of a particular specialist character may legitimately refuse to do anything else in the short term, but if the claimant cannot actually get work in that employment, then he/she must be willing to expand their horizons if they are to continue to be regarded as available for employment.
267. JSA Regulations 1996, regulation 72(8) and (9).
268. Employment Rights Act 1996, s. 111(1). There are extremely complex rules to ensure that where an Employment Tribunal makes an award of compensation for unfair dismissal, any payment of JSA paid for a period during which an Employment Tribunal award is made shall be recouped by the DSS from the employer; if the employee is held to be partially to blame for the dismissal, the employee has to contribute a proportion of the repayment. For a note on the recoupment regulations, *see* B.A. Hepple, M. Partington & R.C. Simpson, 'The Employment Protection Act and Unemployment Benefit: Protection for Whom?' *Industrial Law Journal* 54 (1977).

liking the job will not constitute just cause. It is statutorily provided that those volunteering for redundancy are not to be deemed to have left a job voluntarily.[269]

1. Trial Periods

405. Notwithstanding the provisions just considered, and in order to encourage JSA claimants to try a job, where a claimant starts a new job after having been unemployed for at least thirteen weeks, he may leave without sanction after a 'trial period of employment', namely at any point in his/her fifth to twelfth week in the job (not counting any week in which he/she has worked for less than sixteen hours).[270]

B. Jobseeker's Directions Sanctions

406. A jobseeker's direction is a written notice from an EO requiring a claimant to take a specific action to assist him/her find a job. It may take a number of forms, for example, attending a 'back-to-work session', a requirement to apply for a particular advertised job vacancy, attendance at a training course, or a requirement to improve appearance or behaviour to improve their attractiveness to a potential employer. Such directions can be given at any time and more than once. The overriding requirement is that any directions must be reasonable.

C. Training Scheme and Employment Programme-Related Sanctions

407. Rules have also been made which make it compulsory for a JSA claimant to attend a training scheme or employment programme. The details of the relevant programmes have been altered, with effect from summer 2011, by the closing of what were called 'new deal' programmes, and the introduction of the new Work Programme (*see* below paragraph 425).

408. Also, note that the mandatory attendance at training courses was recently litigated, and the UK's Supreme Court guided that the mandatory schemes were legally flawed.[271]

---

269. JSA 1995 s. 19(7) and JSA Regulations, regulations 52(3) and 72 and 73. Certain compensation payments, payable by an employer to a former employee, will have the effect of preventing entitlement to JSA, as will holiday pay paid up to four weeks after leaving a job. Compensation payments include most payments made in respect of the termination of employment but not payments made in respect of a period before which unemployment began, refunds of pension contributions, redundancy payments, unfair dismissal payments, reimbursement of expenses, pension payments, maternity pay or sick pay or lump sums under the Iron and Steel Re-adaptation Benefits Scheme. There can be quite difficult problems determining whether a particular payment does or does not disentitle a claimant to JSA.
270. *See* JSA 1995, s. 20(3) and JSA Regulations, regulation 74.
271. *R (Reilly) v. DWP* [2013] UKSC 68.

D. Sanction Periods

409. JSA sanctions regime was revised from October 2012 to December 2017. Three categories of sanction were introduced: 'higher', 'intermediate' and 'lower' – depending on the nature of the offence. Also, different levels of sanction for first, second and third offences. These new rules broadly align the rules for JSA sanctions with the rules for UC.

Those who claim JSA may be 'sanctioned' (resulting in no JSA or a reduced amount of JSA being paid) if they:

High-Level Sanction – 13 Weeks, 26 Weeks or 156 Weeks[272]

Due to for example – dishonesty or persistent poor timekeeping.

Low-Level Sanction – 4 Weeks or 13 Weeks[273]

Fail without 'good reason' to attend a place on a training scheme or employment programme.
Refuse or fail to carry out a 'jobseeker's direction' – refuse or fail without 'good cause' to follow a 'reasonable' JobCentre direction to apply for a specific job, to use the DWP 'job-posting'/'job-Matching' service or a direction to alter their appearance or behaviour in order to improve their job prospects.
i.e., Stop being available for work.
Stop actively seeking work – *see* 'actively seeking work' above.

Duration of Sanction – High-Level Sanction[274]

13 weeks – normal period of any 'high-level sanction'.
26 weeks – where there has previously been a 'high-level sanction' imposed more than 2 weeks but Less than 52 weeks since the current sanction action.
156 Weeks – where there has been a 'high-level sanction' twice previously for either 26 weeks or 156 weeks.

Duration of Sanction – Low-Level Sanction[275]

Below 13 weeks.

---

272. Section 19(2) Jobseeker's Act 1995. Regulation 70B Jobseeker's Allowance Regulations 1996. R(U)10/71 and R(U)2/76 and R(U)32/52.
273. Section 19A(2) Jobseeker's Act 1995.
274. Regulation 69(1) and (2) Jobseeker's Allowance Regulations 1996.
275. Regulation 69A(1) and (2) Jobseeker's Allowance Regulations 1996.

Level of Sanction[276]

During the period of any sanction, a single person would normally lose 100% of their JSA entitlement. In the case of couples, the amount of reduction depends on whether the JSA claim is made by one member of the couple or both members as part of a 'joint claim'. In the case of the former, the loss of JSA during the sanction period would be 100%. In a 'joint-claim' situation, the amount of the reduction would be the difference between the amount of JSA paid to a single person (i.e., typically GBP 73.10 per week) and the amount paid to a couple (i.e., typically GBP 114.85 per week), unless both members of the couple have been sanctioned in which case the loss would be 100%.

II. Trade Disputes

410. In general, a person is not entitled to a JSA for the week in which that person is unemployed where there is a stoppage of work which has caused that person not to be employed and that stoppage is due to a trade dispute at his place of work. It is possible to avoid this disqualification by showing that the claimant is 'not directly interested in the dispute'; however, the scope of 'direct interest' is very wide so that, in practice, it is hard to evade the disqualification.[277] Where a person is disqualified by reason of a trade dispute from receiving JSA, this also has the effect of reducing the sums payable in respect of other members of the claimant's family.[278]

411. The trade disputes disqualification has, historically, been by far the most controversial of the disqualifications.[279] Those on the trade union side argue that the NI Fund should be 'neutral' in industrial disputes and that benefits should not be withdrawn from strikers thus contributing to pressures forcing them back to work. Those on the employers' side argue just as forcefully that the NI Scheme should not be available in effect to subsidize those who may be regarded as 'voluntarily unemployed'. If a strike leads to financial hardship, it is their view that the trade unions themselves should provide any financial support to workers who have been called out on strike. These days, however, with the changing climate of industrial relations in GB, with far fewer strikes than some years ago, these controversies have become much less heated.

III. Persons under 18

412. There is a general disentitlement to JSA for those persons over the age of 16 but under the age of 18. This reflects the general discrimination in the social

276. Section 19 Jobseeker's Act 1995. Regulation 70 Jobseeker's Allowance Regulations 1996.
277. *See* JSA 1995, s. 14.
278. *See* JSA 1995, s. 15.
279. There is considerable literature on the issue; for an analysis of the background to the rules, *see* M. Partington, 'Unemployment, Industrial Conflict and Social Security', *Industrial Law Journal* 243 (1980).

security system against those in the 16 to 17 age bracket.[280] Generally, those in this age group are expected to apply for training and to subsist on any training allowance that may be payable. However, 16/17-year-olds can, if eligible in the usual way, still claim IS and those who are eligible to do so can choose to claim JSA instead (*see* Part X below). There are also various other groups of young people who are allowed to claim JSA (at a reduced rate), provided that they also satisfy all the usual conditions of entitlement:[281]

(1) Certain school-leavers can claim for a short period known as the 'child benefit extension period' (roughly from the start of the first school term after the young person leaves school until approximately the start of the second school term thereafter): these are broadly those who have some special reason why they need to be self-supporting. Either they are married (subject to certain additional conditions), or for specified reasons are not able to live with their parents, for example, because they are orphaned or estranged from their parents.
(2) Those leaving custody who satisfy the same reasons can claim for eight weeks after leaving custody even if those weeks fall outside the child benefit extension period.
(3) Those leaving care can claim under the usual rules for school-leavers and a further eight weeks.
(4) Finally, there is another group who can claim JSA regardless of their age: these include employees who have been laid off or put on short-time working for up to thirteen weeks, those who are one of a couple responsible for a child and those about to enlist in the Armed Forces.

413. The Secretary of State[282] has discretion to make awards of JSA to other young people who can show that they would otherwise suffer severe hardship.[283] This discretion can mitigate the hardship of disentitlement in some circumstances. However, it is necessary for the claimant to demonstrate very clearly that he/she will experience hardship if no money is received. In practice, the officials usually insist on contacting a young person's parents (or social worker/voluntary worker) before being satisfied with the need for a payment.[284] 'Severe hardship directions' must usually be renewed every eight weeks, and as a result, those (very vulnerable) young people who do qualify have no security in the continuity of their entitlement.

414. Where a claimant seeking a severe hardship payment has refused an offer of training, it will be very difficult to demonstrate that the general disentitlement to

---

280. *See* N. Harris, *Social Security for Young People* (Aldershot: Avebury, 1989). *See also* discussion of the issue in the context of IS, below, Part X.
281. These are added to in the case of 16/17-year-olds in that a young person is required to be available for and actively seeking training opportunities as well as employment.
282. There is no right of appeal to an appeal tribunal against this decision.
283. JSA 1995, s. 16.
284. This last requirement can pose problems for a young person without recourse to other sources of income, immediately following the breakdown of their relationship with their family.

benefit should be waived, and there is power to revoke any severe hardship direction on the grounds that the young person has, without good cause, failed to take up any offer of training.[285]

285. JSA 1995 s. 16(3).

Chapter 3. Back-to-Work Schemes

415. An innovation of the JSA 1995 was the introduction of a scheme, designed to encourage the return of the long-term unemployed to work. The 'back-to-work bonus' was a lump sum of up to GBP 1,000 payable to a person who had been claiming income-based JSA or IS after ninety-one days on benefit and who ceased to claim benefit following his/her reintegration into the labour market. In October 2004, it was replaced by Job Grant, a significantly less generous grant of GBP 100 (GBP 250 for those with children). Job Grant is available for individuals starting full-time paid work of sixteen hours per week who were previously in receipt of IS, income-based JSA, ESA or SDA. It is tax-free.

416. Other measures to assist the unemployed with the transition to work include an arrangement whereby HB and CTB[286] can continue to be paid for four weeks at the out-of-work level following return to work. Also, individuals starting work and coming off IS or JSA can receive mortgage interest run-on, which amounts to four weeks' housing costs. Finally, there is some protection for some of the long-term unemployed who stand to lose entitlement to enhanced rates of benefit earned through spending qualifying periods on benefit. There are rules allowing periods of unemployment separated by short periods of employment to be linked for certain purposes. This provides the unemployed with some cushion against the risk that their entitlement will be reduced should they try out a job that does not work out for them.[287] But these rules also have downsides for the claimant, who has to find longer-term employment before requalifying for a second period of contributory JSA or from accessing the more generous approach to job-seeking or the assessment of incapacity for work. A claimant also runs the risk of a work-related sanction if they leave any new job. The latter is retained under the UC regime.

286. *See* below Part X.

287. They are not, for example, required to serve again the three waiting days imposed on new claimants for JSA, nor to wait out the period before receiving some help with mortgage payments or the higher long-term rate of IB, and they can keep preserved entitlements to more generous earlier levels of benefit (e.g., they can continue to qualify for lone-parent benefit).

Chapter 4. Provision of Work: Training Schemes and Employment Opportunities

417. As noted above, from the earliest days of unemployment insurance, payment of benefit has been regarded as only part of the policy relating to dealing with the unemployed; assistance with return to work was always seen as an essential complement to the benefits.

418. Given the enormous increases in levels of unemployment which occurred in the UK during the 1970s–1990s, and also the dramatic changes that have taken place in the nature of the labour market and the types of skills required by employers, there has been increasing emphasis on the provision of training, including work experience, as a corollary to social security policy in relation to the unemployed. The last Labour Government saw training as essential to create the enhanced skills base which it believed was needed to promote economic growth and as the key to meeting its commitment to increasing the rate of employment which in turn it saw as the route to tackling poverty.[288] They introduced a large number of initiatives to try to deal with these issues.

419. The former Coalition Government retained the principle of Government sponsorship of schemes to assist the unemployed back into the labour market, but it has decided that many of the detailed initiatives taken by the previous Labour Government which operated under the generic title of 'the New Deal' were too costly and ineffective. It has also ended a programme of Employment Zones, designed to create increased incentives for employers to hire unemployed people. The Coalition Government has created in their stead the Work Programme.

420. The Work Programme,[289] which started to operate in June 2011, is, in essence, a Government-financed employment agency programme. In other words, bodies from the private, public and voluntary sectors of the economy will bid for, and if successful, be awarded contracts to place people in receipt of JSA and ESA in work. Contract holders will be incentivized to place people in real long-term employment because they will receive more money in cases where their clients stay in employment than in cases where their clients leave after only a short time. Some categories of JSA and ESA claimants will be required to engage with the Work Programme (and face the possibility of sanctions if they fail to do so); the Work Programme will also be open to others on a voluntary basis.

---

288. *See*: Her Majesty's Treasury, 'Modern Public Services for Britain: Investing in Reform', Cmd 4011 (July 1998); DfEE, 'The Learning Age: A Renaissance for a New Britain', Cmd 3790 (February 1998); DfEE, 'Learning to Succeed: A New Framework for Post-16 Learning', Cmd 4392 (June 1999); Social Exclusion Unit, 'Bridging the Gap: New Opportunities for 16–18 Year Olds Not in Education, Employment or Training', Cmd 4405 (July 1999). All reports published by London: TSO.

289. For more information, *see* www.direct.gov.uk/en/Employment/Jobseekers/programmesandservices/DG_197781.

421. In addition to the Work Programme, there are other schemes available to those who have been unemployed for certain periods of time. These schemes are frequently changed. Current schemes include:

(1) *Work Trial,*[290] in which individuals continue to receive their benefits while filling an actual job vacancy for fifteen days. Individuals in the programme also receive travel and food expenses. It is available for those over 25 who have been unemployed for six months or more.
(2) *Employment on Trial,* which allows individuals who have been unemployed for over thirteen weeks to start jobs without affecting their eligibility for benefits, as long as they remain in work for more than four weeks but less than twelve.

422. Mention may be made of Professional and Career Development Loans.[291] They were introduced on a national basis in 1988. The scheme is, primarily, provided by high street banks that have agreed to participate in the scheme. The financial commitment of the Government is limited to covering the cost of the initial interest-free period during which neither the capital nor any interest on the loan has to be paid back to the bank; this is principally during the period of the course itself and for up to one month after the course is over.

423. These loans can be used to pay the fees for Professional and Career Development Courses.[292] In addition, the loan can be used to buy essential items such as books, protective clothing, computer software and, in some cases, a computer.

424. In order to qualify under the scheme, the claimant must show that he/she intends to use the training in order to seek work in the UK or elsewhere in the EU. The scheme does not apply to normal university undergraduate courses since fees for these courses are already paid for by the Government under the Mandatory Student Award Scheme.

425. Finally, it may also be noted that the Social Fund of the European Community provides much money for vocational training in all countries of the EU, including the UK. Much of the funding goes towards training for work and other schemes. The European Social Fund, in addition, supports a range of other non-Government funded programmes provided either by the voluntary sector, by further education colleges, or by local authorities.[293]

---

290. *See*: www.direct.gov.uk/en/Employment/Jobseekers/programmesandservices/DG_173561.
291. *See* further: https://www.gov.uk/career-development-loans/overview.
292. Up to 80% of the cost of the fees can be met by the loan; the individual has to pay the balance of 20% of such fees out of his/her own pocket, unless they have not been employed for three months prior to the application, in which case 100% of course fees can be met.
293. For further details, *see* www.direct.gov.uk/en/EducationAndLearning/AdultLearning/FinancialHelpForAdultLearners/CareerDevelopmentLoans/DG_10033237.

Part VIII. Pensions

Introduction

426. Although the National Insurance Act 1911 – which introduced the first measures relating to unemployment insurance and health insurance – is widely regarded as the statute which laid the foundations for the modern welfare state, it was, in fact, preceded, by three years, by the Old Age Pensions Act 1908. Although the coverage of this early provision was extremely limited – providing a very modest benefit to certain people who reached the age of 70 – it reminds us that there is, perhaps, no more central ambition for any social security system than to provide some measure of financial security for people in their old age.

427. In common with many other countries, the British solution has been to create a framework of provision both by the State and by the private provision, the latter being created primarily through occupational pension schemes provided as part of the terms of employment.

428. The impact of the demographic changes considered in the General Introduction to this work – more people retiring from employment early, increased life expectancy and a declining birth rate resulting in fewer people in employment available to fund current expenditure on retirement pensions – has meant that over the last three decades there has been a continual adjustment of the relationship between State and private provision and increasing worry about the affordability of current arrangements.

429. The cost of the retirement pension scheme is very substantial. The Government estimated that state support for pensioners, including tax relief on pension contributions and NI rebates to those contracted out of SERPS amounted to 10% of Gross Domestic Product in 1997.[294] In the 1990s, it was estimated that GBP 42.6 billion was spent on the elderly, which is over 45% of the total of GBP 93.4 billion spent on social security in the same period. Retirement pensions dominate expenditure on contributory benefits, GBP 62.4 billion of a total of just over GBP 78 billion in 2008.[295] The most recent development was the introduction of PC, a benefit which gives a guaranteed minimum income to people aged over 60.

294. 'A New Contract for Welfare: Partnership in Pensions', Cmd 4179 (London: TSO, 1998), 21.
295. *See* www.statistics.gov.uk/downloads/theme_compendia/AA2010/aa2010final.pdf. The annual abstract of statistics provides updated figures.

430. This Part looks at the present provision of *retirement pensions* provided within the formal social security system, considers the *Additional State Pension* (which replaced SERPS) and then, in outline only, considers the main features of *Occupational and Private Pension Schemes* and the regulatory context within which they are provided. Finally, it outlines the rules governing PC.

Chapter 1. The State Retirement Pension

431. There are three main categories of State (retirement) pension in the British system. Two of these categories (A and B) are *contribution based*, and the third (Category D) is *non-contributory*.

§1. Age Limit

432. In order to qualify for any of these, the claimant has to have reached what is known as the 'pensionable age'. For many years, this was 60 for women and 65 for men. Although this rule is clearly discriminatory as between men and women, it is explicitly excluded from the equal treatment directive of the EU.[296]

433. As a result of legislative changes, the pensionable ages of women and men being harmonized, initially at the age of 65. This was to be achieved by November 2018. There will then be an overall increase in pensionable age to 66, which will be effective from April 2020.[297] As a result of further changes in the law the pension age for both men and women will rise in stages to 68; the target date is currently 2046 but may be brought forward.[298]

§2. Category A Retirement Pensions

434. Category A retirement pensions are the most generous level of retirement pension. They are pensions based on the claimant's own contribution record.

435. Category A pensions are currently up to GBP 164.35 per week. In the past, it was possible to receive an additional allowance for adult and child dependants, but in most cases, adult dependants (spouses and civil partners) now receive the Category B pension. Where there is a child dependent, the pensioner can also claim CTC.

Valuing Your NICs and Credits Made Before 6 April 2016

NI record before 6 April 2016 is used to calculate the 'starting amount'. This is part of your new State Pension.

The starting amount will be the higher of either:

- the amount the claimant would get under the old State Pension rules (which includes Basic State Pension and Additional State Pension); or
- the amount the claimant would get if the new State Pension had been in place at the start of their working life.

---

296. Article 7(1) Directive 79/7/EEC.
297. Pensions Act 1995, s. 126 and Sch. 4, and Pensions Acts 2008 and 2014.
298. Pensions Act 2007.

Though, note the starting amount will include a deduction if the claimant was contracted out of the Additional State Pension.

If the Claimant's Starting Amount Is Less Than the Full New State Pension

The claimant can obtain more State Pension by adding more qualifying years to their NI record after 5 April 2016.

Each qualifying year on your NI record after 5 April 2016 will add about GBP 4.70 a week to their new State Pension. The exact amount the claimants gets is calculated by dividing GBP 164.35 by 35 and then multiplying by the number of qualifying years after 5 April 2016.

If the Claimant's Starting Amount Is More Than the Full New State Pension

The part of their starting amount which is above the full new State Pension is called the 'protected payment'. This is paid on top of the full new State Pension.

Any qualifying years you have after 5 April 2016 will not add more to their State Pension.

If the Claimant Did Not Make Any NI Contributions or Get NI Credits Before 6 April 2016

Their State Pension will be calculated entirely under the new State Pension rules.

> The claimant will usually need at least ten qualifying years on your NI record to get any State Pension.
> They need thirty-five qualifying years to get the full new State Pension.

The claimant will receive a proportion of the new State Pension if they have between ten and thirty-five qualifying years.

Annual Increases

The new State Pension increases each year by whichever is the highest:

- earnings – the average percentage growth in wages (in GB);
- prices – the percentage growth in prices in the UK as measured by the Consumer Prices Index (CPI);
- 2.5%.

If you have a protected payment, it increases each year in line with the CPI.

§3. Category B Retirement Pensions for Spouses and Civil Partners and Widows, Widowers and Surviving Civil Partners

436. Category B Retirement Pensions are pensions payable to the spouses, civil partners, widows and widowers of those claiming Category A pensions. Those entitled do not have a contribution record of their own but rely on that of the person receiving the Category A pension. There are, in effect, two sorts of Category B Retirement Pension:

(1) those paid to the spouse or civil partner while the Category A pensioner is still alive; and
(2) those paid to the former spouse/civil partner of a Category A pensioner who has now died (Men, or women with civil partners, can only claim where the former wife or civil partner was born after 5 April 1950. This is because prior to the passing of the Civil Partnership Act 2004, Category B Retirement Pension was only available to widows).

437. In order for a spouse, former spouse or civil partner to claim, both partners must be over pensionable age. Category B Retirement Pension is also payable irrespective of any contribution record if the spouse or civil partner died as the result of an industrial accident or disease.[299]

438. As with Category A pensions, the benefit comprises a basic weekly sum, supplemented, where relevant, by additions for dependent children, the Christmas bonus, and the age addition for those aged over 80.

439. He/she will also receive any benefit under SERPS/Additional State Pension Scheme (*see* paragraph 451) based on the spouse/surviving civil partner's earnings while he/she was in work (however, the maximum a widow can claim is 50% of the additional pension).

440. If the claimant's spouse or civil partner did not have a full contribution record, then the amount payable is reduced, pro rata.

441. The weekly monetary value of the Category B pension for those falling into category (i) above is currently up to GBP 71.50 a week; for widows and widowers and surviving civil partners in category (ii), the sum is considerably higher, currently up to GBP 119.30. This means that a widow or widower approaching pensionable age, and who is contemplating remarriage, might be considerably better off delaying such a happy event until they have passed that age.

442. Once in payment, Category B pension is payable indefinitely, until the death of the claimant; entitlement is *not* affected by remarriage to or cohabitation with another person.

443. As a result of changes introduced by the Pensions Act 2007, the detailed rules relating to Category B Pensions were amended, with effect from 6 April 2010.

444. The Act removed the former restriction on a person's entitlement to a Category B pension that their spouse or civil partner must have made a claim for their Category A pension. As a result, where one member of a married couple or civil partnership has deferred his/her Category A pension and the other member has reached pension age, the other member now has the choice of claiming a Category

299. *See* generally, Part VI.

B pension (and where applicable any Category A pension based on their own contributions) or deferring their Category B pension (and any Category A pension to which they are also entitled) in order to accrue either increments or a lump sum.

§4. Category D Retirement Pensions

445. Category D retirement pension is, by contrast with Category A and Category B Pensions, a *non-contributory* benefit. It is a pension for those who reach the age of 80 and are entitled either to no other form of retirement pension or where the amount that is payable (perhaps because of reduced entitlement arising from an incomplete contribution record) is less than that payable by way of Category D retirement pension.

446. Unlike other categories of retirement pension, however, it is essential that the pensioner be 'ordinarily resident' in GB and have been ordinarily resident for ten years in the last twenty years.

Chapter 2. Additional State Pension

447. One of the long-term consequences of the failure of successive Governments to implement the Beveridge principle that levels of social security benefit should be set at the officially defined poverty line was that, during the 1950s and 1960s, it became clear that one of the largest groups facing poverty in Britain was the elderly.

448. Despite having worked for forty years, they faced an old age with an inadequate retirement pension, topped up, at least in theory, by a means-tested supplement (then called Supplementary Benefit – the precursor of the present IS). The practical problem with this arrangement was that many elderly people were either too proud or otherwise deterred from claiming means-tested benefits. Thus the additional resource that was available to them in theory was, in many cases, not available for them in practice.

449. As a consequence from the late 1960s onwards, successive Governments – both Labour and Conservative – sought to create a scheme which would guarantee a more financially secure old age for people but at the same time be one that was affordable in terms of public expenditure. They have sought to find a politically acceptable balance between provision by the State and provision by individuals providing their own funding for pension provision. They have also tried to find a balance between imposing requirements on individuals to make provision for retirement and providing economic and fiscal incentives to encourage individuals to make such provision. The outcome has been a series of complex initiatives which is hard to summarize succinctly.

450. The initial conclusion reached was the creation of the SERPS.[300]

451. By the time SERPS was to become fully operational (like many changes to the pensions system, though the relevant Act was passed in 1975 it was going to take many years to bring fully into effect), Governments had decided it could not be afforded. New initiatives to encourage private provision were introduced including 'appropriate personal pensions' and 'stakeholder pensions'. Under current rules, individual employees have the right to choose their own pension scheme, and as long as the scheme has been certified by HMRC, employers and the Government must make contributions.

452. In April 2002, SERPS was replaced with a more generous scheme – additional State Second Pension – which it was hoped would nevertheless be more affordable by the State because people had made greater pension provision for themselves. Among other changes, the Additional State Pension was a 'better buy' for the low paid, as it was based on statutorily determined minimum levels of earnings,

300. Social Security Pensions Act 1975; for analysis *see*, for example, J. Mesher, 'Social Security Pensions Act 1975', *Modern Law Review* 39 (1976): 321.

rather than actual wages. The intention was that the higher paid were expected to top up Additional State Pension with their own private provision.

453. In the longer term, this expectation may be extended to those falling within the middle-income group as well. Thus, State support can be targeted more closely on those who are seen as not in a position to make realistic private pension contributions. At present, the system is means-tested, but in the future, it may be replaced by a flat-rate system.

454. These changes are supplemented by changes to the private pension market considered in Chapter 3 below designed to make private pensions more accessible to those on middle incomes. The expected result is that the overall proportion of private to public provision will change from the current 40:60 to 60:40.

455. It is intended that the Additional State Pension should raise those pensioners in receipt of means-tested benefits, off incomes below IS levels.

456. It should be noted that the level of the universal basic pension was for many years not raised in real terms. However, after fierce political lobbying by groups representing pensioners, the Coalition Government has decided that, while increases in pension levels should not be linked to earnings, they should be linked to the Consumer Price Index, rather than the Retail Price Index. The Government also created a new PC, discussed below in Part VIII Chapter 4.

Chapter 3. Occupational and Personal Pensions Schemes

457. As noted above, in order to encourage employees to opt out of SERPS/the Additional State Pension, successive Governments have sought to encourage alternative private provision. These come, essentially, in two forms: occupational pension schemes, created by employers for the benefit of their employees, and personal pensions schemes, which individuals may decide to purchase for themselves.

458. A variety of tax advantages – relating both to the contributions paid into schemes and the benefits taken from the schemes – have been created in relation to both provide financial incentives for employees to opt for one or other of these alternatives.

459. There are detailed rules designed to ensure that occupational pensions are at least as generous in terms of the benefits provided as SERPS, now the Additional State Pension.[301] Also as a result of a major scandal in the operation of pension schemes, a complex new regulatory regime has been introduced, designed to ensure that the trustees of pension funds and the asset managers operate their schemes in such a way as to ensure that the assets available are in fact sufficient to meet the liabilities arising under the scheme.[302]

460. Part I of the WRPA introduced a new category of money-purchase occupational and personal pensions to be known as 'stakeholder pensions'. These have to meet certain 'minimum standards' which are designed to make them more accessible to those with lower incomes and more uncertain career patterns. Minimum contributions have to be set at low levels. It must be possible for people to transfer in or out of the schemes without charge. They also have to be flexible over breaks in contributions. They have to meet restrictions on the amount of any overall charges imposed by pension providers on those who are purchasing stakeholder pensions. They have to provide specified information to investors at least annually. Employers are required to nominate a stakeholder scheme to be available to their employees. They have to give those running the scheme access to their employees in the workplace for the purpose of giving them information about the scheme, and employers will be required to pay contributions to the scheme as a direct deduction from wages if an employee so requests. The Government is able to provide a tax regime for stakeholder pensions that differ from that applicable to other pension schemes. These reforms were accompanied by a programme of public education on available pension schemes designed to reflect the then Government's belief that those who are able to make private provision should do so.

---

301. These are now found in the Pension Schemes Act 1993 and regulations made thereunder.
302. *See* Pension Law Reform Committee (Chair: Prof. Roy Goode Q.C.) 'Pension Law Reform: The Report of the Pension Law Review Committee', Cmd 2343 (London: HMSO, 1993) and the consequent Pensions Act 1995. Further changes to the regulatory framework for occupational and personal pensions were introduced in the WRPA, 1999, Part II.

461. Despite this, the evidence by the mid-2000s was that not enough people were taking advantage of 'stakeholder pensions'. The then Labour Government, therefore, provided, in the Pensions Act 2007, that all employers should be required to enrol their employees into a workplace pension. Thus a benefit that was common for better-paid employees should effectively be extended. The Coalition Government's Pensions Act 2014 has made some detailed amendments to the operation of the scheme, but the basic principle has been retained. For employers who do not have their own pensions scheme, it will be possible to enrol employees into a new scheme run by the National Employment Savings Trust.[303] The intended result is that the State should provide a reduced percentage of total pension provision, particularly for the better off.

462. The details of all the provisions relating to private pension schemes are beyond the scope of this work. It is, however, clear that in this area of pension provision, the shifting relationship in the Welfare State between benefits provided directly by the State and benefits being provided by the individual within a framework prescribed by the State[304] can most clearly be seen.

303. The scheme sets the benchmark for occupational pensions schemes. For more detail, *see* www.nestpensions.org.uk/schemeweb/NestWeb/public/home/contents/homepage.html.

304. Referred to in the General Introduction, above. On this theme, *see* Frank Field, 'Inside the Whale: Redrawing the line between State and Government', *Political Quarterly* 69 (1998): 252–257.

Chapter 4. Pension Credits

463. PC is a benefit for the over 60s[305] giving them a minimum income guarantee, while also rewarding individuals who have saved for retirement. It is administered by the Pension Service, an executive agency of the DWP. PC was introduced in 2002.

464. The benefit consists of a *guarantee credit* and a *savings credit.* Both are available only to UK residents who are free of immigration control. For the guarantee credit, applicants must currently be over 60 (though this is in the process of being increased). They must have either no income at all or income below the minimum income guarantee (*see* paragraph 465) plus any additional allowable amounts.[306] Not all income is included in this calculation; for example, benefits relating to disability or children are subject to disregards. Capital over GBP 6,000 is deemed to give an income of GBP 1 for every GBP 500 the claimant owns.

465. The current weekly standard minimum guarantees are GBP 155.60 for a single person and GBP 237.55 for a couple. This guarantee credit is designed to ensure that all over the age of entitlement in the UK receive at least this amount every week. Where a claimant also has caring responsibilities, a disability or housing costs, the level of the guaranteed income is increased, as it is if the claimant is in receipt of income-based JSA or IS when they reach entitlement age and without any addition, there would be a drop in their income.[307]

466. Savings credit is available only to applicants over 65 who have income which exceeds the 'savings credit threshold'.[308] The savings credit threshold is currently set at GBP 133.82 a week for an individual and GBP 212.97 for couples. Above this threshold, the benefit is paid on a sliding scale with claimants receiving a benefit worth 60% of their income[309] above the threshold, up to a maximum of GBP 13.07 for an individual and GBP 14.75 for a couple. Once income exceeds the minimum guarantee (including any additional amounts), the amount of excess income will count against the credit.[310] Therefore, claimants with too high an income will not be able to claim any PC.

---

305. In line with other changes to pensionable age, namely the alignment of the pensionable age for men and women and the overall increase in pensionable age – initially to 66 – this will increase up to 2018.
306. State Pension Credit Act 2002, s. 2.
307. *See* State Pension Credit Regulations 2002, SI 1792, regulation 6(6)(b) and Sch. 1, para. 6.
308. *See* State Pension Credit Act 2002, s. 3.
309. Income is the same as income for the purposes of guarantee credit but excludes WTC, IB, contribution-based JSA, SDA, Maternity Allowance and maintenance payments from a former spouse of the claimant or their current spouse. *See* regulation 9 of the State Pension Credit Regulations 2002.
310. About 40% of the claimant's total income above the minimum income guarantee is set against the amount of savings credit until the credit is wiped out.

467. In general terms, PC seems to have had a positive impact on the income of UK pensioners. At present, around 2.73 million households receive the benefit, with an estimated 1.99 million pensioner households receiving more money than they had before its introduction. Furthermore, most of this additional money goes to the poorest pensioner households. Research has shown that it has made a noticeable difference in the quality of life of pensioners.[311] However, the system has been much criticized for its complexity and because it is means-tested.

311. *See* 'Pension Credit', the Third Report of 2004–2005 by the Work and Pensions Committee, published on 9 Mar. 2005, paras 17 and 18. For data on current expenditure, *see* the Annual Abstract of Statistics at www.statistics.gov.uk/downloads/theme_compendia/AA2010/aa2010final.pdf.

Part IX. Disabled Persons

Introduction

468. A wide range of social security benefits and other services are provided for those with mental or physical disabilities. In the early 1990s, policy, and the resulting law, underwent radical reform in Britain with the development of a more integrated programme of assistance for the disabled. This may be seen as another example of Government policy attempting to target benefits to those special categories most in need.

469. In this case, the primary focus for this range of social security benefits is the provision of compensation for the consequences of disability, and the extra living expenses that arise as a result of this, rather than simple lack of resource, which may be said to be the primary focus of the means-tested benefits to be discussed in the next Part.

470. Up until the introduction of WTC in 2002, there was a special tax credit for the disabled, known as Disabled Persons Tax Credit. (Before that, it was called Disability Working Allowance). WTC subsumed this separate benefit. Now disabled people can claim additional disability and severe disability elements as part of their WTC claim (*see* Part X). The special rules relating to payments to the disabled are currently under review.

471. The benefits discussed in this Part include:

(1) Attendance Allowance for the over 65s (AA 65+);
(2) PIP;
(3) SDA (now abolished);
(4) other benefits and measures to assist the disabled.

In addition, it should be noted that for those disabled as a result of industrial injury or disease, special industrial disablement benefits are also payable, as discussed in Part VI. Furthermore, disabled persons in receipt of IS also receive additional weekly amounts of benefit; this is discussed in Part X.

Chapter 1. Disability Living Allowance

472. DLA was introduced in April 1992 and replaced by PIP (*see* later) from October 2013. Similarly, DLA when enacted replaced two earlier benefits: *Mobility Allowance* and *Attendance Allowance*. Notwithstanding this point, the current statutory provisions do in fact provide that Attendance Allowance is still payable to those who claim it for the first time over the age of 65; this is known as 'AA 65+'.

473. DLA is a non-contributory benefit, payable, as of right, to all those who satisfy the qualifying conditions. The benefit is *not* means-tested.

474. DLA was introduced after a major Government survey of the disabled population, their special needs and the cost of meeting those needs.[312] While not meeting all the demands of pressure groups representing the disabled, the new benefit nevertheless represented a considerable improvement in provision from what existed before its introduction. Certainly, it has proved to be a 'successful' benefit, in the sense that more people have come forward to claim the benefit than it was anticipated would do so at the time it was introduced.

475. Following the increased public expenditure that has gone hand in hand with its success, the benefit came in for criticism on the grounds that it is not targeted on those with the greatest need; is not the best way to meet need and because of the high levels of inaccuracy in decisions and the administrative difficulties caused by the complexity of its eligibility criteria.[313]

476. The basic law is found in the SSCBA 1992, Part III, and regulations made thereunder.

§1. The Benefit Structure

477. DLA comprises two separate components:[314]

(1) a 'mobility component' targeted at those who have to meet extra costs when they wish to get out of the house; and

312. The Social Survey Division of the Government's Office of Population Censuses and Surveys published six reports on the extent of Disability in the UK in 1988 and 1989. The background to the legislation is set out in the Government's White Paper, 'The Way Ahead: Benefits for Disabled People', Cmd 917 (London: HMSO, 1990). More recent surveys have examined again the financial costs of disability: *First Findings from the disability follow-up to the Family Resources Survey.* Research Summary No. 5, 1998.

313. *See* Social Security Committee, '4th Report Disability Living Allowance', HC Paper 1997–1998 No. 641 (London: TSO) which contained a critical report from the Disability Living Allowance Advisory Board. The Government responded: *see* Cmd 4007 (London: TSO, 1998).

314. SSCBA 1992, s. 71.

(2) a 'care component' targeted on those who need assistance with their disabilities in their homes.[315]

478. Each of these components is paid at different rates, depending on the degree of disability of the claimant.

§2. The Mobility Component

479. In order to qualify for the mobility component,[316] a claimant must satisfy the appropriate age conditions. To claim the lower rate of DLA mobility, he/she must currently be over the age of 5[317] but still be under the age of 66 when the claim is first made. However, severely disabled 3- and 4-year-olds can claim the higher rate.[318] The claimant must show that he/she was suffering from the condition which satisfies the statutory test before he/she reached the age of 65; a claimant has a period of 1 year's grace, until their 66th birthday, actually to make the claim. If a claim is not made by then, however, then no entitlement to this benefit can arise. Once entitlement is established, the benefit remains payable until either the person no longer satisfies one of the other conditions for the benefit, or dies, whichever is the earlier.[319] The claimant must show that he/she is able to benefit from 'facilities for enhanced locomotion'.[320]

480. In the case of young claimants aged under 16, they must additionally show that they require *substantially* more guidance or supervision than persons of their age in normal physical or mental health would or that persons of their age in normal physical or mental health would not require *any* such guidance or supervision.[321]

481. Claimants must also satisfy *residence conditions* which provide that they are 'ordinarily resident' in GB;[322] are present in GB; and have been present in GB

315. The Government's view is that DLA is intended to meet the general costs of disability. High mobility and care needs have been found to be a good index to those with high consequential costs, but it is not these costs alone which DLA is intended to cover.
316. *Ibid.*, s. 73.
317. Although mobility component cannot be paid to anyone under 5, the three-month qualifying period can start from before the 5th birthday so that claims for the benefit may be made from the age of 4 years 9 months, and thus payment of benefit can start on the 5th birthday.
318. WRPA 1999, s. 67.
319. There was a rule that the former mobility allowance was not payable to those over the age of 80, but this was repealed in April 1992.
320. Not a difficult test to satisfy in practice; only the very severely bedridden would be caught by the test.
321. SSCBA 1992, s. 73(4).
322. This term is not capable of precise definition: there must be some degree of continuity about the person's residence, however. Thus, periods of residence abroad will not interrupt ordinary residence in GB, as long as they are temporary in nature. The burden of proof is on the claimant to demonstrate that they are ordinarily resident in GB, in any case where there is any doubt.

for a total of twenty-six weeks out of the last twelve months.[323] Entitlement to DLA is lost if a claimant moves from the UK even within the EU.[324]

I. Qualifying Period

482. Since the object of the benefit is to assist with the cost of long-term problems associated with disabling conditions, the claimant must demonstrate that he/she has satisfied these conditions for a period of three months prior to the date of claim and that they are likely to continue to satisfy those conditions for the next six months.[325]

II. Higher Rate Mobility Component

483. The higher rate of the mobility component (currently GBP 57.45 per week) is paid to:

(1) those who are suffering from a physical disability so that they are unable to walk; or
(2) those who are virtually unable to walk; or
(3) those who are both deaf and blind;[326] or
(4) those born without feet or who are a double amputee; or
(5) those who are severely mentally handicapped[327] and have severe behavioural problems[328] and who also qualify for the highest rate of the care component (*see* paragraph 500).

---

323. The terminally ill are exempted from this provision. An absence from Britain for more than twenty-six weeks, if for the purpose of medical treatment, will not destroy entitlement to the benefit, though the Secretary of State must issue a certificate that the absence was reasonable.
324. DLA was listed as a non-exportable special non-contributory benefit under R 1408/71, Art. 10(a)(1). *See Snares v. Adjudication Officer* ECJ C20/96 (1997) All ER (EC) 886.
325. These rules do not apply to the 'terminally ill' who are deemed to satisfy the qualifying period and have a fast track to the benefit: SSCBA 1992, s. 73(12).
326. SSCBA 1992, s. 73(3). This test is satisfied if the degree of disablement resulting from the loss of vision is 100% (which is not the same as total blindness); and the degree of disablement resulting from the loss of hearing is 80% on a scale where 100% represents total deafness; and the combined effect of the blindness and deafness means that the claimant is unable to walk to any destination out of doors without the help of another: Social Security (Disability Living Allowance) Regulations 1991, regulation 12(2) and (3).
327. This means that the person must suffer from a state of arrested development or incomplete physical development of the brain, which results in severe impairment of intelligence and social functioning: Social Security (Disability Living Allowance) Regulations 1991, regulation 12(5). This excludes those (like most Alzheimer's sufferers) who suffer damage to an already fully developed brain (*R(DLA) 2/1996*); and those who have severe mobility problems but an unimpaired intelligence (e.g., those with autism or schizophrenia but an IQ over 55). (*C(DLA) 1678/1997, C(DLA) 6219/1997, C(DLA) 3253/1995*).
328. This means they must exhibit extreme disruptive behaviour, combined with a requirement that someone else regularly intervene and physically restrain them to prevent them causing injury to another or damage to property, and their behaviour is so unpredictable that another person has to

From April 2011, the higher rate mobility component was also payable to those who are 'severely visually impaired'.[329]

484. The 'virtually unable to walk' test is one of the most difficult to apply in British social security law. It has been subject to further elaboration both in regulations and in decisions from the Social Security Commissioners, now the Upper Tribunal. The test is only satisfied if one of the following three conditions is satisfied:

(1) the claimant is unable to walk; or
(2) the claimant's ability to walk out of doors is so limited, as regards the distance over which, or the speed at which, or the length of time for which, or the manner in which he/she can make progress on foot without severe discomfort (i.e., walking *with* severe discomfort is to be ignored), that the claimant is virtually unable to walk; or
(3) the exertion required to walk would constitute a danger to the claimant's life or would be likely to lead to a serious deterioration in his/her health.[330]

In assessing ability, account must be taken of any artificial aids that are used, for example, a stick or crutches. If the claimant can walk with such aids, he/she will not qualify. However, the claimant who can 'get about' (e.g., with one leg only and the use of crutches) is not technically able to 'walk' and thus will qualify for the benefit. Since April 1991, those with no feet where both legs have been amputated either through or above the ankle or have had one such amputation and no other leg or are without both legs to the same extent as if they had been amputated automatically qualify for the higher rate of the mobility component.[331]

485. Those qualifying for the higher rate may, if they are otherwise able to drive a car, be able to pay the benefit to a special charity, *Motability*, which will help claimants to lease or purchase a car. However, to take advantage of this, the higher rate mobility component of DLA must have been awarded for a period of at least a year from the date of the claim.

III. Lower Rate Mobility Component

486. The lower rate (currently GBP 21.80 a week) is payable to those who are able to walk, but who are so severely disabled, either physically or mentally, that

be awake and watching over them whenever they themselves are awake: Social Security (Disability Living Allowance) Regulations 1991, regulation 12(6).

329. This means that they must have been certified as blind or severely visually impaired and to have combined visual acuity of less than 3/60 on the 'Snellen scale'.

330. Social Security (Disability Living Allowance) Regulations 1991, regulation 12(1).

331. *Ibid.*, regulation 12(1)(b).

(ignoring familiar routes) they are unable to walk out of doors without guidance or supervision from another person for most of the time.[332]

§3. The Care Component

487. In order to qualify for the care component, a claimant must satisfy the same residence conditions as for the mobility component.

488. The benefit cannot be paid to those living in hospital for more than twenty-eight days (eighty-four days for children)[333] nor to those living in residential care accommodation, provided out of public or local authority funds.[334] Where such a person would remain entitled to coming out of hospital, it is necessary for them to put in a claim for the benefit in the normal way.

489. The basic conditions for care component are:

(1) that a claimant must satisfy one or more of the supervision or attention conditions (*see* paragraph 500); or
(2) if over 16 that the claimant can satisfy the 'cooking test'; and
(3) that the claimant, unless terminally ill,[335] has done so for three months before the claim was made and is likely to continue to satisfy the conditions for the next six months.

490. As with the mobility element, the benefit is, therefore, not intended for those experiencing short-term care problems (except the terminally ill).

---

332. SSCBA 1992, s. 73(1)(d). This test is intended to cover a wider group of people than those falling in the group with severe behavioural problems just discussed above. This rule will commonly apply to autistic children. Other qualifying conditions might be dementia or severe agoraphobia (where a person cannot go out unless accompanied by another). Although the test is not based on a physical inability to walk, the guidance or supervision required must be needed to enable the claimant to take advantage of the faculty of walking and not required in case of some other health difficulty which might affect the claimant in any circumstances (such as likely panic or migraine attacks). (*C(DLA) 591/1997*).
333. This exception does permit the possibility of the carer having periods of respite from his/her caring responsibilities by placing the person cared for in hospital for a short period of time, without the claimant losing entitlement to benefit. Those long term in hospital are denied benefit on the basis that as hospital treatment provided by the NHS is free, all care needs are met through the NHS and therefore there would in effect be a double payment if DLA remained in payment. *See also* above Part III.
334. This restriction does not apply in certain cases, for example, to the terminally ill, to those who have always paid the cost of their accommodation or who are living in accommodation as a permanently fostered child.
335. SSCBA 1992, s. 66(2) defines the phrase 'terminally ill' as suffering from a progressive illness such that the claimant can reasonably be expected to die within six months. This is not a test 'on the balance of probabilities', rather that the death would not be unexpected within that time. The claim must be made on that basis. If this is done, there is a special 'fast-track' administrative procedure to ensure that it is dealt with administratively within ten days. If terminally ill, the claimant is automatically taken to satisfy the care conditions for the higher rate care component.

I. Age Limits

491. Unlike the mobility component, there is no lower age limit for claiming the care component, though, as with all other claimants, even babies will have to meet the qualifying conditions for three months (unless they are terminally ill) before the benefit can be paid. Furthermore, where a claim is made in relation to a child, it has to be shown that the level of care needed is either substantially in excess of that provided for a normal child or of a nature not normally required for a normal child of the same age.

492. However, there *is* an upper age limit for claiming which, as with the mobility component, is usually 65. Those who do not satisfy the conditions of entitlement until after the age of 65 must claim Attendance Allowance (AA 65+). There is no upper age limit for the *receipt* of the care component; therefore, once entitlement is established, it will continue until the claimant dies or his/her condition improves so that the qualifying conditions are no longer satisfied.[336]

II. Rates of Benefit

493. The care component of DLA is payable at three different rates[337] depending on which of the qualifying conditions is satisfied by the claimant:

(1) a *lowest rate* (currently GBP 21.80 a week) for those who satisfy the 'cooking test' or the lower rate 'limited attention' test;
(2) a *middle rate* (currently GBP 55.10 a week) for those who satisfy either the day or night attention test or the day or night supervision test;[338] or
(3) a *highest rate* (currently GBP 82.30) for those who satisfy *both* the day attention or supervision test *and* the night attention or supervision test *or* those who are terminally ill.

The details of these qualifying conditions are discussed in the following paragraphs.

III. The Cooking Test

494. This test, first introduced in April 1992, requires claimants to demonstrate that they are so severely disabled physically or mentally that they cannot prepare a

336. A claimant who establishes entitlement to the middle rate care component, before the age of 65, but who subsequently improves so that, were they still under 65 they would become entitled to the lower rate care, will, if the improvement takes place after their 65th birthday, lose benefit altogether, as there is no equivalent to the lower rate under AA 65+.
337. The precise rates are determined by the Government annually and are effective from April to April in each calendar year.
338. Special regulations also provide that those undergoing kidney dialysis two or more times a week and who need supervision or help while it is going on are entitled to the middle rate.

cooked main meal for themselves if they had the ingredients.[339] This test is a qualifying test for the lower rate of the care component. Those under 16 cannot qualify by this route. It does not matter that the claimant has never learned how to cook; the essential issue is whether they would be capable of undertaking the task, assuming they had the ingredients and the know-how.

IV. The Attention Tests

495. In order to satisfy these tests, the claimant must show that he/she is so physically or mentally disabled that he/she requires[340] assistance from another person in connection with her/his 'bodily functions'.[341] There are three separate tests which can be satisfied in a variety of ways which are listed below.

---

339. The test is an abstract one, in the sense that no official will come into the claimant's kitchen and inspect the actual process. The evidence on which decisions are based is derived from the claim form which asks claimants about whether they are able to peel vegetables, chop up ingredients, etc. Claimants must also have the mental capacity to organize the cooking process. The mere fact that a claimant has a microwave oven into which he/she can put frozen meals does not mean they have failed this test (and so disqualify them from the benefit), since to do that would not, by itself, show that they can *prepare* a meal. The claimant is not to be disqualified on the basis that he/she would be able to prepare a meal if he/she had a kitchen adapted in certain ways; however, adaptations which are actually available to the claimant are not to be ignored. (*C(DLA) 17329/1996*).

340. The fact that assistance is provided does not prove that it is required: R(A) 1/73. However, nor does the fact that it is not provided prove that it is not required. Claimants who live on their own, and who struggle to remain independent, may on occasion suffer from a failure to apply this rule correctly since there can be a tendency for decision-makers to assume that those who cope on their own do not require assistance. The assistance does not have to be required as a matter of survival. It must be 'reasonably required to enable the severely disabled person as far as reasonably possible to live a normal life', including a normal social life insofar as is reasonable in all the circumstances (*Cockburn v. Chief Adjudication Officer* and *Secretary of State v. Halliday* (1997) 1 WLR 799 (HL)). To qualify as 'attention', assistance must probably be delivered in the presence of the disabled person (*per* the majority, Lord Slynn dissenting).

341. Bodily functions include: breathing, seeing, eating, drinking, walking, sitting, sleeping, getting in and out of bed, dressing and undressing, eliminating waste products. They also include the operation of the senses (*Cockburn* and *Halliday*) and metabolism (in the case of a diabetic) (*C(DLA) 126/1996*). To be attention in connection with a bodily function, the attention must be active, close, caring and personal, with a high degree of personal intimacy. Usually it will involve doing something which a fit person does for himself/herself, enabling the bodily function to operate or providing a substitute for it. Such attention does not include cooking (unless, possibly, very precise weighing and measuring is required for a very specialized diet), shopping or the other things done by one member of the household for another: *R v. National Insurance Commissioner ex parte Secretary of State for Social Services* (1981) 1 WLR 1017 (CA); R(A)2/80 (Appendix), although the decision in *Cockburn* and *Halliday* has made it plain that there is no simple distinction between domestic activities and attention in connection with a bodily function. This decision suggests it is important to consider the purpose of the attention and the nature of the link with a bodily function. Thus doing the laundry can constitute attention if, for example, it is part of treatment of a skin condition, and, on the majority view, if carried out for an incontinent person physically unable to do his/her own washing where it is carried out in the presence of that person.

496. First is the *limited attention* condition: Here the claimant must show he/she requires a limited amount of attention but for a 'significant portion of the day',[342] either in a single period or a number of periods.

497. Second is the *day attention* condition: Here the claimant must show he/she needs attention *frequently* throughout the day. A pattern of need has to be established.

498. Third is the *night attention* condition: Here the claimant must show that he/she requires either 'prolonged'[343] or 'repeated'[344] attention during the night. Such attention does not have to be given every night so long as it is part of a regular pattern of attention.

499. It will be appreciated that each of these tests is laid down in the statutory rules in language that is somewhat 'open-textured' in character. The conditions are not prescriptively described by relation to precise numbers of minutes or hours. Rather they allow for flexible application to meet the particular circumstances of the individual and the justice of the case. The risk with such tests, of course, is that claimants in very similar situations may be treated differently by different officials or in different parts of the country.[345] Further, the language has been subject to the criticism that it is difficult for administrators and claimants alike to understand. There has also been criticism that the imprecise language has led to the benefit being implemented in ways not intended by Parliament.[346]

V. The Supervision Tests

500. There are two tests which fall under this heading.

501. First is the *day supervision* test: This is satisfied where the claimant requires continual[347] supervision from another throughout the day in order to avoid substantial danger to himself/herself or others. The substantial danger must be one which is reasonable to guard against, looking to the future as well as to the past.

342. The phrase is not defined in the Act. During Parliamentary debate, a Minister stated that 'an hour or thereabouts' would do. Help for an even shorter period might suffice if the attention related to something significant for the claimant.
343. Interpreted by officials as at least twenty minutes.
344. This has been interpreted by the Social Security Commissioners as meaning twice or more.
345. For a research report on the operation of DLA, *see* R. Sainsbury, M. Hirst & D. Lawton, 'Evaluation of Disability Living Allowance and Attendance Allowance', Department of Social Security Research Report No. 41 (London: HMSO, 1995).
346. *See also* the report of the Disability Living Allowance Advisory Board, reproduced in Social Security Committee, 'Fourth Report: Disability Living Allowance', HC Paper 1997–1998 No. 641 (London: TSO).
347. This is not the same as continuous but must be more than occasional or spasmodic: R(A) 1/73.

502. The second is the *night supervision* test: This is satisfied where the claimant requires another to be awake for a prolonged period or at frequent intervals[348] to watch over[349] the claimant in order to avoid substantial danger to himself/herself or to others.

503. Similar comments may be made about the nature of the legal language used to describe the supervision tests as were made in the context of the attention tests, which therefore give scope for argument and judgment in their application.

§4. Administration and Adjudication of DLA

504. There are special features relating to the administration and adjudication of DLA which are discussed in Part XI.

348. This probably means more than twice.
349. This can include taking precautions or anticipatory action that never in fact results in any direct intervention with the claimant.

Chapter 2. Attendance Allowance for Those over the Age of 65 (AA 65+)

505. Attendance Allowance – first introduced in 1970 – is the benefit *still* paid to those who first become so physically or mentally disabled after the age of 65 that they have attendance requirements which entitle them to receipt of this benefit. It should be noted, however, that AA 65+ does not provide for any mobility component. Given that many elderly people suffer from reduced mobility that is a serious omission. Of course that fact also explains the omission. As a substantial proportion of, if not all, elderly people experience limitations on mobility, to compensate them for this would, in the Government's view, be just too expensive for the State to bear.

506. Nevertheless, for those over the age of 65, AA 65+ remains an important benefit. There are many similarities between AA 65+ and the care component of DLA. But there are also important differences. The main ones are:

(1) the benefit is payable only at two rates, a higher and a lower rate (equivalent to the higher and middle rate under DLA). The lower rate available under DLA is not part of AA 65+;
(2) as a consequence, the 'cooking test' condition and the 'limited attention' condition are not relevant to AA 65+;
(3) claimants must show that they have satisfied the conditions for benefit for six months prior to the date of their claim rather than the three-month period under DLA, unless they are terminally ill.

507. The higher rate of AA 65+ (currently GBP 82.30 per week) is payable to those satisfying *both* the day attention or supervision test *and* the night attention or supervision test *or* those who are terminally ill; the lower rate (currently GBP 55.10 per week) is payable to those who satisfy *either* the day *or* night attention test or the day or night supervision test.

Chapter 3. Personal Independence Payment

508. Over 3.2 million people were in receipt of DLA.[350] The WRA 2012 made provision for DLA to be replaced by Personal Independent Payment (PIP). However, the changeover to PIP only applies if the claimant is aged between 16 and 64 on 8 April 2013 or the claimant became 16 years of age, after that date. Therefore, claimants aged 65 or over (on 8 April 2013) who are already getting DLA will be unaffected (thus, DLA still applies to them, as discussed above).

509. From April 2013, a PIP Pilot scheme was run in the North West and North East of England. However, since June 2013, PIP has been rolled out, nationally. In fact, from 6 October 2013, those DLA claimants whose claims were due to expire were reassessed under PIP, save for those aged over 65 years of age.

510. From 7 October 2013, any DLA claimant can claim PIP and will, subject to notification of any change in circumstances and/or be due for reassessment, will be dealt with under PIP.

511. The WRA 2012 establishes the framework for PIP:

- a person's ability to carry out daily living activities being limited or severely limited by the person's physical or mental condition;[351]
- a person's ability to carry out mobility activities being limited or severely limited by the person's physical or mental condition.[352]

This change in terminology from the pre-existing statutory references in sections 72–73 SSCBA 1992 where 'limited ability' under PIP replaces 'disablement and severe disablement' formerly found in DLA & AA.

512. However, PIP remains comprised of two components. Accordingly, the payment is made up of two components. Each component can be paid at either the standard or the enhanced rate. Whether the claimant obtains one component or both, and whether the standard or the enhanced rate applies, depends on how the claimant's condition affects their ability.

PIP Rates

Component	*Weekly Rate*
Daily living – standard rate	**GBP 57.30**
Daily living – enhanced rate	**GBP 85.60**
Mobility – standard rate	**GBP 22.65**

350. DLA Reform, Equality Impact Assessment, May 2012, DWP.
351. Section 78 WRA 2012.
352. Section 79 WRA 2012.

Component	*Weekly Rate*
Mobility – enhanced rate	**GBP 59.75**

§1. Eligibility for PIP

513. Eligibility for PIP is based upon the practical effects of a condition on a person's life, rather than the condition itself. It is not currently available to children; it can be claimed by adults under the State Pension age, and people already on the benefit will continue to receive it after they retire. PIP and the benefit it replaces are predominantly received by older people because increasing age is the main risk factor for developing disabling diseases.

§2. PIP Assessment Process

514. Each claimant having completed their claim form (PIP2) are required to attend a face-to-face assessment with a Health care Practitioner (HCP)[353] or a paper-based review or by advice produced for DWP. At such assessments, the claimant's functionality/'ability' is appraised in relation to a points-based system on daily living and mobility activities, as below:

Daily Living Activities

(1) Preparing food:[354]
  (a) Can prepare and cook a simple meal unaided – 0 point.
  (b) Needs to use an aid or appliance to be able to either prepare or cook a simple meal – 2 points.
  (c) Cannot cook a simple meal using a conventional cooker but is able to do so using a microwave – 2 points.
  (d) Needs prompting to be able to either prepare or cook a simple meal – 2 points.
  (e) Needs supervision or assistance to either prepare or cook a simple meal – 4 points.
  (f) Cannot prepare and cook food – 8 points.
(2) Taking nutrition:[355]
  (a) Can take nutrition unaided – 0 point.
  (b) Needs:
    – to use an aid or appliance to be able to take nutrition; or
    – supervision to be able to take nutrition; or
    – assistance to be able to cut up food – 2 points.

353. Section 80(3)(b) WRA 2012.
354. *SD v. SSWP* [2017] UKUT 310; *EG v. SSWP* [2015] UKUT 275 and *GB v. SSWP* [2015] 546; *LC v. SSWP* [2016] UKUT 150; and, *LB v. SSWP* [2017] UKUT 436 and *JT v. SSWP* [2018] UKUT 101.
355. *MM v. SSWP* [2017] UKUT 17; *DF v. SSWP* [2017] UKUT 160.

(c) Needs a therapeutic source to be able to take nutrition – 2 points.
(d) Needs prompting to be able to take nutrition – 4 points.
(e) Needs assistance to be able to manage a therapeutic source to take nutrition – 6 points.
(f) Cannot convey food and drink to their mouth and needs another person to do so – 10 points.

(3) Managing therapy or monitoring a health condition.[356]
(a) Either:
- does not receive medication or therapy or need to monitor a health condition; or
- can manage medication or therapy or monitor a health condition unaided – 0 point.

(b) Needs either:
- to use an aid or appliance to be able to manage medication; or
- supervision, prompting or assistance to be able to manage medication or monitor;
- health condition – 1 point.
- Needs supervision, prompting or assistance to be able to manage therapy that takes no more than 3.5 hours a week – 2 points.
- Needs supervision, prompting or assistance to be able to manage therapy that takes more than 3.5 but no more than 7 hours a week – 4 points.
- Needs supervision, prompting or assistance to be able to manage therapy that takes more than 7 but no more than 14 hours a week – 6 points.
- Needs supervision, prompting or assistance to be able to manage therapy that takes more than 14 hours a week –8 points.

(4) Washing and bathing:[357]
(a) Can wash and bathe unaided. 0 point.
(b) Needs to use an aid or appliance to be able to wash or bathe. 2 points.
(c) Needs supervision or prompting to be able to wash or bathe. 2 points.
(d) Needs assistance to be able to wash either their hair or body below the waist. 2 points.
(e) Needs assistance to be able to get in or out of a bath or shower. 3 points.
(f) Needs assistance to be able to wash their body between the shoulders and waist. 4 points.
(g) Cannot wash and bathe at all and needs another person to wash their entire body. 8 points.

(5) Managing toilet needs or incontinence:[358]
(a) Can manage toilet needs or incontinence unaided. 0 point.
(b) Needs to use an aid or appliance to be able to manage toilet needs or incontinence. 2 points.

356. *DC v. SSWP* [2016] UKUT 11; and, *AS v. SSWP* [2017] UKUT 104.
357. *SP v. SSWP* [2016] UKUT 190.
358. *KW v. SSWP* [2017] UKUT 54.

(c) Needs supervision or prompting to be able to manage toilet needs. 2 points.
(d) Needs assistance to be able to manage toilet needs. 4 points.
(e) Needs assistance to be able to manage incontinence of either bladder or bowel. 6 points.
(f) Needs assistance to be able to manage incontinence of both bladder and bowel. 8 points.

(6) Dressing and undressing:[359]
(a) Can dress and undress unaided. 0 point.
(b) Needs to use an aid or appliance to be able to dress or undress. 2 points.
(c) Needs either:
– prompting to be able to dress, undress or determine appropriate circumstances for remaining clothed; or
– prompting or assistance to be able to select appropriate clothing. 2 points.
(d) Needs assistance to be able to dress or undress their lower body. 2 points.
(e) Needs assistance to be able to dress or undress their upper body. 4 points.
(f) Cannot dress or undress at all. 8 points.

(7) Communicating verbally:[360]
(a) Can express and understand verbal information unaided. 0 point.
(b) Needs to use an aid or appliance to be able to speak or hear. 2 points.
(c) Needs communication support to be able to express or understand complex verbal information. 4 points.
(d) Needs communication support to be able to express or understand basic verbal information. 8 points.
(e) Cannot express or understand verbal information at all even with communication support. 12 points.

(8) Reading and understanding signs, symbols and words:[361]
(a) Can read and understand basic and complex written information either unaided or using spectacles or contact lenses. 0 point.
(b). Needs to use an aid or appliance, other than spectacles or contact lenses, to be able to read or understand either basic or complex written information. 2 points.
(c) Needs prompting to be able to read or understand complex written information. 2 points.
(d) Needs prompting to be able to read or understand basic written information. 4 points.
(e) Cannot read or understand signs, symbols or words at all. 8 points.

(9) Engaging with other people face-to-face:[362]
(a) Can engage with other people unaided. 0 point.
(b) Needs prompting to be able to engage with other people. 2 points.
(c) Needs social support to be able to engage with other people. 4 points.

359. *DP v. SSWP* [2017] UKUT 156.
360. *EG v. SSWP* [2017] UKUT 101.
361. *KP v. SSWP* [2017] UKUT 30.
362. *SSWP v. AS* [2017] UKUT 454; *RC v. SSWP* [2017] UKUT 352; and, *DV v. SSWP* [2017] UKUT 244.

(d) Cannot engage with other people due to such engagement causing either:
   - overwhelming psychological distress to the claimant; or
   - the claimant to exhibit behaviour which would result in a substantial risk of harm to the claimant or another person. 8 points.

(10) Making budgeting decisions:[363]
   (a) Can manage complex budgeting decisions unaided. 0 point.
   (b) Needs prompting or assistance to be able to make complex budgeting decisions. 2 points.
   (c) Needs prompting or assistance to be able to make simple budgeting decisions. 4 points.
   (d) Cannot make any budgeting decisions at all. 6 points.

Mobility Activities

(1) Planning and following journeys:[364]
   (a) Can plan and follow the route of a journey unaided (0 point).
   (b) Needs prompting to be able to undertake any journey to avoid overwhelming psychological distress to the claimant (4 points).
   (c) Cannot plan the route of a journey (8 points).
   (d) Cannot follow the route of an unfamiliar journey without another person, assistance dog or orientation aid (10 points).
   (e) Cannot undertake any journey because it would cause overwhelming psychological distress to the claimant (10 points).
   (f) Cannot follow the route of a familiar journey without another person, an assistance dog or an orientation aid (12 points).

(2) Moving around:[365]
   (a) Can stand and then move more than 200 metres, either aided or unaided (0 point).
   (b) Can stand and then move more than 50 metres but no more than 200 metres, either aided or unaided (4 points).
   (c) Can stand and then move unaided more than 20 metres but no more than 50 metres (8 points).
   (d) Can stand and then move using an aid or appliance more than 20 metres but no more than 50 metres (10 points).
   (e) Can stand and then move more than 1 metre but no more than 20 metres, either aided or unaided (12 points).
   (f) Cannot, either aided or unaided:
      - stand; or
      - move more than 1 metre (12 points).

363. *RB v. SSWP* [2016] UKUT 393.
364. *SSWP v. IV* [2016] UKUT 420.
365. *KR v. SSWP* [2015] UKUT 547; *DT v. SSWP* [2016] UKUT 240; and, *KL v. SSWP* [2016] UKUT 545.

The PIP Regulations & PIP (Amendment) Regulations 2013 detail the assessment required.

§3. PIP SCORING

515. To get an award of either component:

- 8 points are required for the standard rate.
- 12 points are required for the enhanced rate.

I. Variability

516. Regulation 7[366] provides a 50% rule. In effect, this rule ensures that the descriptor/activity is satisfied over 50%. Where the descriptor is not satisfied under this rule, then essentially the claimant fails to score any points under that descriptor. In contrast to the situation where the claimant exceeds the 50% rule, in such a scenario then the claimant evidences the enhanced rate.

II. Duration of PIP Awards

517. PIP Awards can be short-term (up to two years) or longer-term awards (e.g., five or ten years).

III. Future of PIP

518. There has been widespread condemnation of PIP across the disability sector. In particular that the assessment with which the DWP assesses eligibility for PIP is not fit for purpose. For instance, SCOPE (the disability charity) declared that PIP's '… assessment – the principles underlying it; the activities it focuses on, and the descriptors – goes against the Government's stated commitment to adopting a social model for DLA reform'.[367] To that end, the primary arguments made against PIP in its current form are:

(1) that the assessment and the principles underlying it are highly medical, and there is not enough consideration of the social model of disability;
(2) that the assessment will be of limited use in achieving the objectives of reform;
(3) that the aims of achieving an assessment that is both totally 'objective' and accurate, and that achieves its original objectives for reform, contradict one another; and

366. PIP Regulations 2013, SI 2013/377.
367. The Future of PIP – social model, Scope, 2013.

(4) that the draft assessment criteria against which prospective recipients are to be assessed is restricted to the point of being counter to the original purpose of both PIP and its predecessor, DLA. That is, as a benefit designed to contribute towards meeting the additional costs of disability.

519. Notwithstanding the controversy, the DWP in December 2015 launched a consultation aimed at slashing the number of people eligible for the daily living component of PIP by up to 35%. The cuts will be aimed at claimants who qualify for PIP because of their use of aids and appliances and may include replacing awards with discretionary voucher payments. The DWP's press release and consultation document asserts that 35% of all daily living allowance awards are based solely on the claimant's need to use aids and appliances. Further, the DWP argued that the use of readily available or low-cost items as aids or appliances is not a reliable guide as to whether a person has to meet additional costs because of their disability. As a result, the DWP's brief consultation ended on 29 January 2016, and we await the fuller details on whether and how changes will be made to the current PIP system.

However, the Government's PIP Regulations were challenged in December 2017. The UK's High Court Judge, Mr Justice Mostyn, allowed the claim in the case of *RF v. Secretary of State for Work and Pensions, where* a disabled PIP claimant with mental health support needs to be challenged the changes the Government made to PIP Regulations in March 2017.

These changes were urgently introduced to reverse the impact of the Upper Tribunal Judgment in the case of *MH v. Secretary of State for Work and Pensions (2016) UKUT 531.* These changes prevented thousands of disabled people from claiming for not being able to plan and follow a journey due to psychological distress. The Public Law Project which represented RF argued that the changes are discriminatory and unlawful.

Chapter 4. Severe Disablement Allowance

520. One of the limitations of the Beveridge model of social insurance was his assumption that those who fell sick or otherwise became incapable of work would do so having built up an adequate contribution record while in work. In the years since the end of Second World War, policymakers came to realize that there was a substantial group of people who were so mentally or physically disabled that they would never enter the workforce and who would therefore not be able to build up an entitlement to the contributory benefits.

521. The response to this issue was the SDA,[368] a non-contributory, non-means-tested benefit – currently GBP 74.65 a week, plus an 'age addition' of GBP 11.15 – payable to those who are *incapable* of work.

522. SDA replaced an earlier benefit, the Non-Contributory Invalidity Pension in 1984.[369]

523. SDA was a widely claimed benefit. In 1997–1998, it was estimated that some 369,000 persons claimed the benefit at an annual cost of just over GBP 1 billion.

524. Nevertheless, the Labour Government, 1997–2010, came to the view that SDA, which was set at a financial level below that paid to those in receipt of IS, provided inadequate support to those disabled early in life.[370] They therefore abolished SDA for all new claimants from April 2001.[371]

525. Since then, those who become incapable of work before the age of 20 (or in some circumstances 25) became eligible for IB.[372]

526. For those who become incapable of work in later life and who do not have an adequate NI contribution record entitling them to IB, there is no special benefit to replace SDA. They have to rely wholly on IS on the ground of disability.

527. As the contribution conditions for entitlement to IB were also made stricter, this resulted in substantial savings in public expenditure.

368. SSCBA 1992, ss 68 and 69. In addition to the benefit for the person in question, additions are also payable for those dependent upon the claimant.
369. This benefit, introduced by the Labour Government in 1975, was particularly controversial since women claimants had to satisfy a 'normal household duties' test that was not applied to men. This meant that only women who were unable to carry out such duties were eligible for the benefit. The test was eventually acknowledged to be unlawfully discriminatory by the Government, and this led to its replacement by SDA in 1984, in anticipation of the coming into force of EC Council Directive 79/7 on the progressive implementation of the principle of equal treatment for men and women in matters of social security.
370. *See* 'A New Contract for Welfare: Support for Disabled People', Cmd 4103 (London: TSO, 1998).
371. WRPA 1999, s. 65.
372. WRPA 1999, s. 64; *see* above Part V.

528. With the introduction of ESA, those who in the past might have qualified for IB or IS on the grounds of disability now claim ESA. There are some people who for historical reasons are still in receipt of SDA. The Government intends to reassess all these people between 2011 and 2014, and those who qualify for ESA will be moved onto the new benefit.

Chapter 5. Other Benefits and Measures to Assist the Disabled

§1. Carer's Allowance

529. Carer's Allowance (CA)[373] is a non-means-tested and non-contributory but taxable benefit that is paid to persons over the age of 16 and under the age of 65 who are regularly and substantially engaged in caring for another who is a severely disabled person. The recipient of CA is also given credits towards his/her contribution record.[374] A claim can be made within three months of becoming entitled.

530. The conditions of entitlement are:

(1) that the carer is over 16, is neither gainfully employed[375] nor in full-time education;[376]
(2) that the carer is looking after the other person for at least thirty-five hours in the week;[377]
(3) that the carer satisfies the normal residence conditions;
(4) that the person cared for is in receipt of either the middle or higher rate of the care component of DLA; or Attendance Allowance; or constant attendance allowance in respect of industrial or war disablement.

531. The amount payable is GBP 64.60 a week.

§2. Vaccine Damage Payments

532. The Vaccine Damages Payments scheme originally provided a lump sum of GBP 30,000 for a person who is (or who was immediately prior to his/her death) severely disabled as a result of vaccination against specific diseases.[378] The test of severe disability is the same as for SDA (*see* below, paragraph 538). The vaccination must have been carried out, in the UK, when the person was under 18, or at the time of an outbreak of one of the relevant diseases. The sum will not be payable unless the person is now at least 2 years old. The claim must be made within six

373. SSCBA 1992, s. 70. Before April 2003, this benefit was called Invalid Care Allowance.
374. *See* further Part II.
375. This is defined in the Social Security (Invalid Care Allowance) Regulation 1976 regulation 8 which provides that a person is not regarded as being in gainful employment in any day in a week if he/she has earned less than GBP 50 in the preceding week. This rule does not apply when the carer is on 'holiday'; *ibid.* Note that the claimant does not have to have given up a job in order to qualify. There used to be a rule that wives looking after their husbands could not qualify, but this has been repealed.
376. *Ibid.*, regulation 5.
377. *Ibid.*, regulation 4. Once the carer has been in receipt of benefit for some time, it is possible to take a break from caring without losing entitlement to the benefit. The rules are complex, but their effect is that a break of up to four weeks in a six months' period is allowed.
378. Diphtheria, tetanus, whooping cough, polio, measles, rubella, tuberculosis, smallpox, haemophilus influenzae type B (HIB), meningococcal group C (meningitis C) or pneumococcal infection.

years of the vaccination, or within six years of the claimant's second birthday. The claimant must normally live in the UK or the Isle of Man.

533. After years of campaigning by the parents of a number of seriously disabled children, the scheme was recently expanded. The tax-free lump sum is now GBP 120,000. The time limits have also been extended. Now claims must be made before the disabled person's 21st birthday or within six years if later.

§3. Residential Care

534. Although the primary policy of Government is to provide care in the community, that is, in the person's own home, there are cases where disabled persons have to receive residential care. If they can afford it, they can pay privately. If not, care services are, subject to complex needs assessment, provided by local authorities or private or voluntary organizations which can also provide residential care. Standards in homes run by bodies other than local authorities are maintained through a residential home's registration scheme.

535. Very seriously disabled people, who need full nursing care, are placed in nursing homes, which are run by local health authorities, or by private providers registered with local health authorities. Some homes are also run by NHS health authorities. Nursing services in local authority or privately run homes may be provided by the NHS or by others. There are no clear lines to define in what circumstances care is the responsibility of the NHS and when it is the responsibility of the local authority.[379]

536. Those living in NHS homes are treated as hospital inpatients and are not charged fees.[380] Those living in private or local authority homes are charged fees. However, those with limited resources may have those fees met, in some cases through IS, more usually paid for by benefit provided by the local authority – the exact amount being determined by the application of a means-test.[381] It is very similar to the means-test which applies to IS/UC. However, because of the fundamental principle that the State should not pay twice for the same thing, those in residential accommodation do not receive the full amount of social security benefit which they would if they lived outside the home, but only a 'personal expenses allowance' to enable them to purchase extra items which are not provided directly by the home in

379. The issue was considered at length by the Court of Appeal in *R v. North and East Devon Health Authority ex parte Coughlan, The Times* [2001] QB 213 and has been much litigated on since.
380. The impact of this on entitlement to other benefits is considered above in Part III.
381. The details of both the fees to be charged and the basis for their remission are to be found in National Assistance (Assessment of Resources) Regulations 1992 (as amended); *see also* the *Charging for Residential Accommodation Guide*, LAC(92)19, as amended published by the Department of Health.

question.[382] This is an area of social policy that is undergoing very close scrutiny at the present time as the population ages and more elderly people need residential care.

§4. EQUIPMENT

537. Disabled persons may also require special items of equipment to help them with day-to-day living. Such equipment is provided primarily by local authorities through social services departments. In some cases, equipment may be provided by health authorities.

§5. WAR PENSIONS

538. A very special set of provisions relates to the payment of War Pensions to those who have been injured or disabled while serving in the Armed Forces during periods of war or other hostilities. This is an area of social security law and administration that has not perhaps had the detailed attention it deserves.[383]

539. Until 1978, the scheme did not operate under any statutory provisions at all, but rather under the inherent powers of the Crown known as the 'Royal Prerogative'. In 1978, the scheme was put on a statutory footing in a special Order in Council.[384] All support services for veterans and current serving armed forces personnel are now managed by the Service Personnel and Veterans Agency (SPVA, created in April 2007), an executive agency of the Ministry of Defence (MOD).

540. Where a serviceman was injured prior to April 2005, they are entitled to a War Pension. The primary test for entitlement to a War Pension is that the disablement or death in question must be attributable to war service. One notable feature of the scheme is that the onus of proof is on the MOD to show that the disablement or death is *not* so attributable, rather than on the serviceman to show that it was. Thus the normal burden of proof on the claimant to prove the factors necessary to establish entitlement to a social security benefit – which applies throughout the rest of the social security system – is in this case reversed; this no doubt reflects the very special position that service personnel have in the politics of a nation.

541. The pension is made up of a basic award, plus, where relevant, increases for the dependants of the service person, and allowances, for example, for loss of

382. *See* Part X, and the National Assistance (Sums for Personal Requirements) Regulations 1998, SI 1998, No. 498.
383. An outline of the law is to be found in A.I. Ogus, E. Barendt & N. Wikeley, *Law of Social Security*, 5th edn 2002, Ch. 8. (London: Butterworths).
384. SI 1978 No. 1525.

earning capacity or to cope with the extra expenses associated with serious disablement. In the case of death, payment is by way of a pension paid to the widow or widower, as relevant.

542. Where the injury to a serviceman occurs on or after 6 April 2005, they will now be covered by the Armed Forces Compensation Scheme.[385] The new scheme gives a lump sum and/or regular payments to cover the loss of earnings to any current or former service personnel who are injured while in service, irrespective of fault. Payments are made by reference to a tariff of severity of injury ranging from the most severe in tariff 1 to the least in tariff 15, and payments to members of the serviceman's family are also available on death. The current maximum payment is GBP 285,000. However, the new system has been heavily criticized by injured servicemen and their families as providing too little financial support. It is currently under review by the MOD.

There are two main types of War Pensions Scheme Awards:

(1) pension, an ongoing payment paid weekly or monthly;
(2) gratuity, a lump sum payment.

The amount of money depends on how disabled the claimant is, and it does not matter how much they earn.

The requisite conditions are:

- a wound;
- an injury;
- a disease;
- something that happened as a result of an accident.

The amount of money paid is dependent on the extent of the disablement, that is any physical or mental injury or damage, or loss of physical or mental capacity.

The assessment of the disablement is calculated as a percentage. If the disablement is assessed at less than 20%, a lump sum called a gratuity will be paid. Otherwise, a War Pension is payable over 20%.

385. *See* The Armed Forces and Reserve Forces (Compensation Scheme) Order 2005, SI 439 (as amended).

Part X. Social Benefits and Tax Credits

Introduction

543. Although, as noted throughout this Encyclopaedia, the British social security system has a variety of policy objectives, there is no doubt that one of its principal objectives is relief of poverty. (The measures which fall into this classification are discussed below in this Part.) This statement, however, raises the politically very controversial question of how poverty should be defined.

544. Some[386] argue that a 'relative' measure should be used. In this definition, the poor are to be regarded as those who are relatively worse off, as compared with the population as a whole and who as a consequence are not able fully to participate in all the opportunities that life provides. By contrast, others argue that such an approach means that, in the absence of a truly egalitarian society, there will always be a defined percentage of the population in poverty, and that this may mask real social progress. They, therefore, argue that what should be used is an 'absolute' measure of poverty. Only those falling below a defined level of income should be regarded as being in poverty.

545. On this basis, it is argued that people – even the poorest – are better off than their predecessors in the 1930s or 1950s. Such an approach tends, however, to ignore the extent to which peoples' expectations change. Thus what might have been the basis for an adequate subsistence existence in the 1930s cannot be regarded in the same way in the very much more affluent present day. Between these two possibly rather extreme positions, there is scope for an almost infinite variety of alternative definitions.

546. As will by now be clear, one of the major respects in which the British social security system failed to meet up to the Beveridge blueprint was the failure to set contributory benefits at the so-called poverty line. Instead, increasing reliance has been placed on the use of means-tested benefits, including now tax credits, to

386. The issue is discussed most fully in P. Townsend, *Poverty in the United Kingdom: A Survey of Household Resources and Standards of Living* (Harmondsworth: Penguin, 1979). *See also* B. Abel-Smith & P. Townsend, *The Poor and the Poorest: A New Analysis of the Ministry of Labour's Family Expenditure Surveys of 1953–1954 and 1960* (London: Bell, 1965) and V. George, *Social Security and Society* (London: Routledge and Kegan Paul, 1973).

ensure that the poorest members of society have a minimum on which to live. Beveridge thought that means-tested National Assistance, as it was initially called, should simply be the 'safety net' of the Welfare State, catching a small minority of those who had otherwise fallen through the contributory framework. The present reality is far removed from that vision. The current position is that, far from representing a residual part of the social security system, the combination of means-tested assistance payments and tax credits represent a very substantial part of the total social security budget.

§1. Scope of This Part

547. Four means-tested benefits are discussed in this Part which are designed to provide support by way of social assistance for persons and families on low incomes. They are:

(1) IS;
(2) Working Tax Credit;
(3) HB;
(4) CTB.

548. In addition, there is a consideration of the *Social Fund*, which provides loans and grants in defined situations to the very poorest in society. Two further means-tested benefits – CTC and PC – have been considered above.[387]

549. Total expenditure on these benefits is enormous, around one-third of total social security expenditure. The numbers in receipt of these benefits at any one time are also very large. By comparison, expenditure on the Social Fund is extremely modest.

550. Of course, many people are in receipt of more than one of these benefits. But if it is assumed that a substantial number of these recipients are also members of families and that therefore they are having to provide for not only themselves but also their dependants, it is likely that around a quarter of the total population of Britain is, either wholly or in part, dependent on these basic-level social security benefits.[388]

551. The Government argues that, by increasing the prosperity of the better off, this has a 'trickle-down' effect which works to the benefit of the less well off. But there are only limited signs that this has occurred, and many would argue that it has

387. *See* respectively above Parts IV and VIII.
388. Will Hutton, *The State We're In,* revised edition (London: Vintage, 1996) describes Britain as a 40:30:30 society, with 40% in a privileged group at the top with good incomes and relative job security; 30% marginalized, with limited income and insecure employment opportunities; and 30% disadvantaged, unable to play a full part in the life of the community.

not occurred at all.[389] The Labour Governments, 1997–2010, sought to use the welfare system, and in particular tax credits, as the means to reduce child poverty. Indeed, in the final months of the New Labour Administration, the Child Poverty Act, 2010 was passed into law which set statutory targets for reducing child poverty. Although the Coalition Government that followed, 2010–2015, did not repeal this Act, they did little, if anything to promote it and consequently, compliance with targets was ignored.[390] Further, the current UK Conservative Government has sought to pursue tax credits as a poverty reliever.

552. There has always been considerable debate in the UK about the extent to which the means-test levels do in fact enable claimants to acquire the bare necessities of living. Many argue that Governments are always too mean when they set their means-test levels. Against that, the Government replies that they have to strike a balance between those arguments and more general arguments about 'what the country can afford', given other demands on the public purse.

553. All these benefits and credits are paid for out of general taxation. They are not part of the contributory social insurance benefit scheme.[391] They are also means-tested benefits. That is to say, they are only payable to those claimants whose *resources* (as defined in the relevant legislation) are less than their *requirements*, that is to say, the required level of income that they are deemed, again as defined by the legislation, to need in order to survive. In the case of tax credits, they are payable where the statutorily defined 'guaranteed minimum' falls below what the person receiving the credit is able to earn in employment.

§2. OBJECTIVES OF SOCIAL ASSISTANCE BENEFITS AND TAX CREDITS

554. Each of the benefits considered in this Part has different objectives. The primary object of IS was to ensure that those outside the workforce have at least a bare minimum of financial resource on which to live. Until the introduction of the JSA,[392] IS provided the main source of social security payments for the unemployed; this has been taken over by the income-related element of the JSA.[393] Similarly, IS used to supplement the resources available to those in receipt of long-term sickness benefits; these have now been replaced by the income-related component of ESA.[394] For many years, IS was a primary source of income for families, in particular lone-parent families, in which the claimant – usually the mother – would not

389. The best overview of information about poverty and its causes is to be found in J. Flaherty, J. Veit-Wilson & P. Dornan, *Poverty: The Facts,* 5th edn (London: CPAG, 2004). The CPAG is the most active anti-poverty pressure group and publishes a wide range of literature on poverty in Britain.
390. Current information about the Coalition Government's Child Poverty policy is at www.dwp.gov.uk/policy/child-poverty/.
391. *See* above General Introduction.
392. See above Part VII.
393. *See* above Part VII.
394. *See* above Part V.

be required to register for employment. It was the cost of this support that led successive Governments to try to ensure that the parents of children – in particular fathers – contributed more to the cost of their children through the Child Support system.[395] IS was also used as a 'top-up' for old-age pensioners and the long-term sick, whose other sources of income were below the officially defined poverty line; to an extent, this function has been replaced by the PC. IS may be claimed by those in (limited) part-time work (up to sixteen hours per week)[396] if their earnings are below the means-test limit. In this context, it will provide a limited wage subsidy. However, despite all the changes of detail, the primary function of IS remains to ensure that those without a bare minimum of financial resources coming from other directions – whether wages or benefits – have a bare minimum of cash on which to live.

555. In contrast, the primary objective of WTC is wage subsidy. It is designed to encourage those who might otherwise be unemployed to go into poorly paid employment. Indeed, entitlement to the tax credit arises only where the claimant is in remunerative employment, of thirty hours or more per week (or if they fall into one of the other categories).

556. The primary objective of HB is to provide a mechanism for subsidizing the housing costs of the poor. It used to complement the indirect subsidies that were available to better-off owners–occupiers which used to be made through the tax system via tax relief on mortgage interest payments.[397] HB replaced the structure of housing subsidy that used to be in place until the early 1980s whereby Government would provide direct financial assistance with the actual costs of providing the dwellings; the bulk of this funding was provided by way of subsidy to the local authorities who were the primary providers of public sector housing for the less well off. HB is payable both to the unemployed and to those in employment but on low wages.

557. CTB is a subsidy payable both to the unemployed and those in low-wage employment, designed to assist with the payment of those taxes which are levied directly by local authorities (councils). It is not possible to provide here a full account of the details of the major changes in the structure and regulation of local authority finance that have taken effect over the last twenty-five years in Britain. However, an outcome of this is that councils have needed to raise their tax levels considerably during this period; the provision of CTB was designed to soften the impact of those changes on the least well off and thereby make the changes more politically acceptable.

---

395. *See* above Part IV.
396. Until April 1992, the limit was twenty-four hours per week. The effect of the new rule will be to deny entitlement to Income Support to a substantial number of part-time workers; they may be entitled to FC, but only if they have a child.
397. The relief was abolished in 2000.

I. Passporting

558. A consequence of establishing entitlement to one or more of the main means-tested benefits considered in principle above is that automatic entitlement to other benefits may also be established. The process of automatic entitlement is known, informally, as 'passporting', that is to say, entitlement to the primary benefit provides a passport of entitlement to other benefits. Passporting arises as follows:

(1) *IS, Income-Based JSA and Income-related ESA* passports to Social Fund payments, both discretionary and non-discretionary; health benefits; free school meals for children; and housing renovation grants.
(2) Some recipients of *WTC* get a passport to the payment of maternity and funeral expenses payments from the Social Fund and also to the health benefits.
(3) *PC* passports to the Social Fund and maternity grant.
(4) *HB and CTB* passport to payments of Social Fund funeral expenses payments.

559. There is no apparent rationale for the differences in passporting rules, save that those on IS are regarded as being most in need and thus requiring the most additional support.

II. Take-Up of Means-Tested Benefits and Tax Credits

560. As was noted in the General Introduction, one of the practical problems associated with the administration of means-tested benefits in Britain is that, for a variety of reasons – ignorance, pride or (possibly) laziness – they are not fully taken up by those entitled to them. The Government attempts to estimate the level of take-up of the main means-tested benefits.[398] While it is clear that take-up rates are significantly higher now than they were in the 1970s, there is still a significant gap between the numbers expected to claim and the numbers who actually claim.

III. The Poverty Trap (the So-Called Lobster Pot)

561. The welfare trap (or poverty trap, as it is more widely known) theory asserts that taxation and welfare systems can jointly contribute to keeping people on social insurance because the withdrawal of means-tested benefits that comes with entering low-paid work causes there to be no significant increase in total income. Therefore, an individual sees that the opportunity cost of returning to work is too great for too little a financial return, and this can create a perverse incentive to not work. Plainly, one of the consequences of increased use of means-tested benefits and tax credits is the increased impact of the 'poverty trap'. This concept refers to the inevitable consequence of means-testing and the provision of tax credits which is that if a person seeks to increase her income, for example, by working for longer

398. *See* www.hmrc.gov.uk/stats/personal-tax-credits/cwtc-take-up.htm for the latest estimates.

hours and therefore earning more money in the form of wages, this simply has the effect of reducing the amount of money received by way of benefit or credit. There have been some attempts to alleviate the effects of the poverty trap, for example, by allowing some increases in wages to be disregarded. But it is the almost inevitable consequence of the policy of increased targeting of means-tested benefits and use of tax credits on the poor that, notwithstanding Government rhetoric which seeks to encourage people back into work, the disincentive effect of the poverty trap is in many cases greater than any incentives to return to work, or, if in work, to work longer hours.

562. Despite all these difficulties, policies designed to ensure that people are better off in work than out of work were central to the New Labour Government's programme of welfare reform. Measures to address these problems included renewed emphasis on in-work benefits and tax credits and their more gradual withdrawal as wages increase, as well as the introduction of the National Minimum Wage and the easing of the tax and NI burden on the lower paid, which have been considered in context above.

563. Ensuring that a person is financially better off in work than out of work is also the fundamental principle that is at the heart of the former Coalition Government's plans, as contained in the WRA 2012, which introduced UC. This is designed to ensure that it will always be financially beneficial to be in work rather than out of work.

564. The benefit cap introduced in seeks to place a limit on the total amount of certain benefits you can get if you are in working age. Yet the benefit cap will only affect HB or UC claimants.

The level of the benefit cap is:[399]

For claimants who reside outside Greater London, the cap is:

- GBP 384.62 per week (GBP 20,000 a year) – couple;
- GBP 384.62 per week (GBP 20,000 a year) – single with child/children;
- GBP 257.69 per week (GBP 13,400 a year) – single with no children.

For claimants who reside in Greater London, the cap is:

- GBP 442.31 per week (GBP 23,000 a year) – couple;
- GBP 442.31 per week (GBP 23,000 a year) – single with child/children;
- GBP 296.35 per week (GBP 15,410 a year) – single with no children.

399. *See* https://www.gov.uk/benefit-cap/benefit-cap-amounts.

Chapter 1. Income Support

565. This benefit, together with income-based JSA and income-related ESA, is the principal 'safety net' of the British Welfare State. IS replaced National Assistance and thereafter Supplementary Benefit. Together they are the benefits which are designed to ensure that people have the ability to survive physically, albeit at a pretty basic level.

§1. CONDITIONS OF ENTITLEMENT

566. The fundamental conditions for claiming IS (UC now replaces, since January 2018, this benefit) are:

(1) the claimant's income (as defined in Regulations)[400] must be less than the claimant's 'applicable amount' – a statutorily defined sum which is intended to represent the weekly sum of money which is expected to cover the claimant's day-to-day living expenses;
(2) the claimant's savings and capital must be worth no more than GBP 16,000;[401]
(3) neither the claimant nor the partner of the claimant (if any) can be in full-time remunerative employment, which is defined in regulations as work of sixteen hours or more per week;
(4) the claimant cannot usually be in full-time education, either at 'non-advanced' (broadly sub-degree) level or 'advanced' (broadly degree) level though part-time students may qualify.[402] There are certain exceptions to these general rules;[403]

400. It will exclude certain income which the claimant does actually receive but which is not counted for IS purposes as income: for example, payments to the holders of the Victoria and George Crosses – awarded for bravery in time of war; and Disability Living Allowance. Income can, however, include 'notional income' – money which the claimant does not actually have but which he/she is deemed under the regulations to receive.

401. Certain capital, in particular the value of the claimant's home is ignored. Claimants whose saving are less than GBP 6,000 will receive the full amount of IS to which they are entitled; those with savings between GBP 6,000 and GBP 16,000 have their weekly entitlement reduced by GBP 1 for every GBP 250 (or part thereof) in excess of GBP 6,000.

402. The distinction between full time and part time is not entirely clear. The essential factor is the nature of the course, not the pattern of attendance of the student on the course. The nature of the course will usually be determined by the college or other institution providing the course.

403. There are very limited exceptions for those who are either over or under 19 and who are in advanced education: for example, if the claimant qualifies for IS as a lone parent or single foster parent, as a disabled, long-term sick or deaf student, or as a refugee learning English; or is a person from abroad who qualifies for urgent cases payments because their usual source of income has been interrupted; or, for the duration of the summer vacation only, is a member of a student couple responsible for a child. Different exemptions apply for those students who are under 19 in secondary education.

(5) the claimant must be over the age of 16[404] and under the qualifying age for PC (currently 60 but rising over the coming years to 65);[405]
(6) the claimant must not be entitled to contribution-based JSA or ESA, and neither the claimant nor their partner are entitled to income-based JSA or income-related ESA; and
(7) claimants must usually be present[406] and habitually resident[407] in GB and not be subject to immigration control.

567. In addition, the claimant must fall within one of the closely prescribed categories who are not expected to work:[408]

(a) parents:
  - a lone parent responsible for a child under 7 (the age is reduced to 5 for claims made after October 2011);
  - a parent on 'parental leave'[409] from work who is not receiving payment from an employer, who lives in the same household as the children and who was entitled to certain benefits before the parental leave began;[410]
  - a parent on paternity leave who is not entitled to SPP or any other payment and who was entitled to certain benefits before the paternity leave began (these benefits being the same as in previous footnote);
  - new mothers for fifteen weeks from her child's birth;
  - those fostering a child under the age of 16 through an arrangement made by a local authority;[411] or where a child has been placed with a couple by an adoption agency.

(b) carers:
  - carers in receipt of Carers' Allowance or caring for someone who is in receipt of Attendance Allowance or the higher or middle rate care component of DLA/enhanced PIP;[412]
  - those who are caring for a member of their family who is temporarily ill or a child whose parent is temporarily unwell or away from home.

---

404. SSCBA 1992, s. 124.
405. IS has been replaced for those over the age that entitles them to Pension Credit, *see* Pt VIII. Claimants with partners entitled to Pension Credit are also not entitled to claim IS.
406. As always, there are limited exceptions. Temporary absence of less than four weeks may be possible, so long as the claimant is not required to sign on; a parent taking a child abroad for medical treatment may continue to receive IS for up to eight weeks. IS is not exportable within the EEA, since it is listed as a special non-contributory benefit in Annex IIa to EC Regulation 1408/71.
407. This test was introduced in 1994 and was designed to prevent what had been described by Government Ministers as 'benefit tourism' – payment of benefits to persons from overseas, allegedly attracted to Britain by generous rules of entitlement. IS is not now payable unless the claimant can, in effect, demonstrate a commitment to living in Britain by showing that he is habitually resident here. Residents in the EEA are automatically deemed to be habitually resident in Britain. However, they must still satisfy the condition of actual presence in the country in order to qualify.
408. *See* regulation 4ZA and Sch. 1B Income Support (General) Regulations 1987, No. 1967.
409. *See* the Maternity and Parental Leave, etc. Regulations 1999 (as amended).
410. WTC, CTC at a higher rate than the family element, HB or CTB.
411. Or a member of a couple where the other member of the couple is temporarily absent from the UK.
412. Carers continue to be eligible for eight weeks after their caring responsibilities come to an end or their caring ceases to qualify.

(c) the unwell and disabled:
  - those entitled to SSP;
  - those who are incapable of work but who are treated as capable of work because they were disqualified from ESA for misconduct or failure to accept treatment.[413]

(d) those who are pregnant:
  - a pregnant woman who is incapable of work because of her pregnancy or who has eleven weeks or less before her pregnancy.

(e) certain students/trainees:
  - certain groups of 16-to 18[414]-year-old students in secondary education do qualify for IS. These are those who are parents living with their child; or students who have been incapable of work for twenty-eight weeks; or are orphans with no one acting in the place of their parents; or have of necessity to live away from their parents or anyone acting in the place of their parents because they are estranged from them, or they are in physical or moral danger or there is a serious risk to their mental or physical health; or care-leavers who have of necessity to live away from their parents for any reason; or those whose parents cannot support them because they are disabled, in custody or not allowed to enter the country;[415]
  - those 16-to 24-year-olds participating in work-based training for young people can claim although some trainees are classified as being in remunerative employment and so are ineligible. IS is only intended to top up (where appropriate) the training allowance that is otherwise payable;
  - refugees learning English in order to enable them to find work for up to nine months;
  - students from abroad with limited leave to remain in the UK without recourse to public funds but who are temporarily without funds for a period of six weeks.

(f) others:
  - those required to attend a court; those prisoners who are able to claim benefit;
  - those affected by a trade dispute who can claim;
  - persons from abroad entitled to reduced payments of IS: a person who has been maintaining himself/herself but whose remittances from abroad have been temporarily interrupted; whose sponsor has died; or who is an asylum seeker who qualifies for IS.

568. IS claimants are not currently required to attend at an office of JobCentre Plus in person as a matter of course in order to claim benefit. However, they are

---

413. *See* above Part V. Also entitled are some of those who are appealing against decisions that they are capable of work.
414. This upper age limit can cause problems for those who qualify for IS only because they have been forced to be self-supporting from an early age while still at school. If (as is not unusual) they do not complete their secondary education before their 19th birthday, they will then usually lose entitlement to both IS and HB and are likely in practice to be forced to leave school.
415. Those who fall into these groups are deemed not to be in 'relevant education'.

required to attend a 'work-focused' interview as a condition of claiming benefit.[416] Failure to attend means that no entitlement to benefit arises. At the interview, an official discusses with the claimant the possibility of employment and seeks to identify any obstacles to employment. He/she also discusses the range of benefits available to the claimant both in and out of work.

§2. Calculation of IS: The Application of the Means-Test

569. The amount of IS to which a claimant is entitled involves a three-stage process of calculation, which is now described in outline.

570. First, there must be determined the 'applicable amount' for the claimant and any family or other dependants. This is an amount prescribed by Parliament as the basic amount of money which a person in the circumstances of the claimant is deemed to need. The applicable amount is made up of three components:

(1) *personal allowances* which vary depending on whether the claimant lives alone or with a partner and whether he/she has children to bring up;
(2) *premiums* for special needs,[417] such as old age or disability or bringing up a child alone; and
(3) for those who are not renting housing (and who are therefore entitled to *HB*, *housing costs*, which are basically the interest payments on mortgages.[418]

571. Once the applicable amount has been worked out, the weekly income[419] of the claimant must be calculated. Some income is taken into account in full, such as payments of Child Benefit and many other social security benefits; some income is taken partially into account; yet other income is ignored completely.[420]

416. *See* WRPA 1999, s. 57 and *see* 'A New Contract for Welfare: The Gateway to Work', Cmd 4102 (London: TSO, 1998).
417. The full list of premiums is as follows: family premium, disabled child premium, severe disability premium, carer's premium – all of which can be paid in addition to any other premium; and lone-parent premium, disability premium, pensioner premium and higher pensioner premium, of which only one (the highest for which the claimant qualifies) is payable.
418. Complex amendments to the Income Support regulations now mean that mortgage interest payments are only made in respect of mortgages up to GBP 100,000 in value. Furthermore, for new claimants, since 2 Oct. 1995, no mortgage interest payments are payable for the first nine months of a period of entitlement to Income Support; mortgagors are in effect required to purchase insurance to cover this initial period. *See* Income Support (General) Regulations, 1987 (as amended) Sch. 1 for the full details. The amount of housing costs may also be limited in defined circumstances where the amount payable is regarded, in the context of the detailed regulations, as 'unreasonable'. Furthermore, where the rate of mortgage interest payable is 5% or more, IS payments are made on the basis that the claimant is paying interest at a prescribed rate, not the actual rate charged by the mortgagee.
419. Since entitlement to IS is on a weekly basis, all sums have to be converted into weekly sums, however received by the claimant.
420. Income Support (General) Regulations 1987 (as amended), Schs 8–10.

572. Capital *over GBP 6,000 but under GBP 16,000* is deemed to produce an income of GBP 1 per week for every GBP 250 or part thereof over GBP 6,000.

573. With these two steps completed, the third stage takes place, in that the level of IS payable to the particular claimant is the difference between the 'applicable amount' and the 'weekly income' which is available to the claimant.

574. Claimants who have a 'non-dependant'[421] living with them have their entitlement reduced by a statutory deduction, which is a sum deemed to be paid by the non-dependant to the claimant as a contribution towards the living costs for which the claimant would otherwise be liable to pay, such as the cost of heating and lighting and cooking. This deduction is made automatically, whether or not the non-dependant actually makes a contribution.

575. It used to be possible for those outside the normal rules of entitlement to claim an *urgent cases payment*, but this was abolished in 2010. Asylum seekers – who were the principal group to receive these payments – now receive special treatment under schemes designed specifically for asylum seekers (e.g., Asylum Support).

§3. Special Rules

576. Special rules apply to special groups.

I. 16- to 17-Year-Olds

577. All 16-and 17-year-olds are entitled to IS provided they qualify in their own right in the usual way.

578. A small group of 16-and 17-year-olds who are still at school can also qualify, as can those participating in training schemes.

579. Other 16-to 19-year-olds in full-time education used to be able to qualify for an Educational Maintenance Allowance and may now be entitled to bursaries.

580. There is no residual discretion for others who remain at school full time to be awarded IS even to avoid severe hardship: if a young person leaves home without falling within the prescribed categories, he/she will either have to become self-supporting or reduce the time spent in education sufficiently to allow himself/herself to meet the prohibition on full-time study and the labour market conditions that are imposed on claimants of JSA.

---

421. Basically, someone who normally resides with the claimant, but who is not a member of the claimant's family (as defined). The full definition is in Income Support (General) Regulations 1987 (as amended) regulation 3.

II. Persons Involved in Trade Disputes

581. Individuals involved in trade disputes are treated as being in full-time work for the first seven days of the dispute and so cannot claim IS for this period. Thereafter IS can be paid, but only at a reduced rate.[422]

III. Persons from Abroad

582. The rules relating to the treatment for the purpose of IS (and indeed of entitlement to social security benefits generally) of persons from abroad are extremely complex. The rules differ as between different benefits; they are riddled with exceptional cases. The details are far beyond the scope of this work. The general point to make is that any idea that immigrants to the UK can easily obtain social security benefits is an urban myth. Three factors have to be taken into account: first, the immigration status of the claimant and whether that person is 'subject to immigration control'; second, whether the claimant is 'habitually resident' in the UK; and third, whether the claimant is an asylum seeker.

A. Immigration Status

583. Broadly speaking, British citizens and those who do not require leave to enter or remain in the UK[423] together with nationals of the EEA[424] are treated in relation to the social security system more favourably than citizens of other countries. In addition, persons with 'indefinite leave' to remain in the UK are treated more favourably than those with only 'limited leave' to be in the country[425] as are those with current work permits. Those granted refugee status are also treated more generously as are the nationals of Croatia, Macedonia and Turkey. Persons who fall into these groups, and who are also actually or deemed to be 'habitually resident' in the UK (or the Common Travel Area), are entitled to claim IS in the normal way.

584. Persons with other more limited types of immigration status or in relation to whom no decision has been taken, or who are asylum seekers or who are 'overstayers' or are subject to a deportation order or are illegal immigrants are treated as 'persons from abroad' and are not entitled to IS under the normal rules.

585. The Immigration and Asylum Act 1999 removed rights to all means-tested and non-contributory benefits (and almost every other source of public assistance)

422. *See* Income Support (General) Regulations 1987, SI 1967, regulation 5(4).
423. This group includes (usually) those from the 'Common Travel Area', of the Channel Islands, the Isle of Man and the Republic of Ireland.
424. Members of the EU plus Norway, Iceland and Liechtenstein.
425. Unless the terms on which the person has such 'limited leave' do *not* prohibit the person from having recourse to public funds – a status which is a rare privilege in current conditions.

from those 'subject to immigration control', which is given a new (narrower) definition, comprising those (other than nationals of the EEA) who require leave to enter or remain in the UK and do not have it, or who have leave to enter or remain on condition that they do not have recourse to public funds or on an undertaking by someone else to maintain them. A new form of benefit, *Asylum Support*, was created to provide some minimal assistance to those claiming refugee status, pending the outcome of their application.[426]

B. Habitual Residence

586. The requirement that claimants of IS should be habitually resident in the UK, the Channel Islands, the Isle of Man or the Republic of Ireland was introduced in August 1994, as a response by the Government to what it perceived to be a problem of 'benefit tourism' – people coming from abroad to the UK in order to take advantage of the allegedly more generous benefit system then operating in the UK.[427] The test applies to all claimants of IS (though not their partners or dependants). Potential claimants must show that they are *in fact* habitually resident in the UK. In addition, since May 2004, a claimant must also have the right to reside. This is defined in such a way that even persons from the EEA who have come to seek work in the UK do not have the right to reside in the UK for the first three months that they are in the UK. In addition to this general rule, there were further restrictions on people coming from the then eight countries (A8) that joined the EU in May 2004,[428] and from the two countries (A2) that joined in 2007.[429]

587. The following groups are exempt from the test:

(1) citizens of the EEA[430] who are classed under European law as 'workers' but only if they have the right to reside;[431]
(2) those who have the right to reside in the UK under EU legislation;[432]
(3) refugees; or
(4) those granted 'exceptional leave to enter or remain in the UK' by the immigration authorities.

Around 3.6 million EU nationals currently live in the UK, including nearly 600,000 children.

---

426. *See* www.ind.homeoffice.gov.uk/asylum/support/.
427. Income Support (General) Regulations 1987, Regulation 21(3), as amended from 1 August 1994, by SI 1994 No. 1807.
428. The so-called A8 countries were: Czech Republic, Estonia, Hungary, Latvia, Lithuania, Poland, Slovakia and Slovenia; these restrictions ended in April 2011.
429. The A2 countries are: Bulgaria and Romania; the restrictions were initially to be lifted in December 2011 but may be extended to December 2013.
430. Members of the EU, plus Norway and Iceland.
431. Regulation 1612/68 or 1251/70; this includes many who are not actually working. There is considerable, not wholly consistent, case law on the meaning of these regulations.
432. Directive 68/360 or 73/148.

The British Prime Minister, Theresa May, confirmed in June 2018 that all EU nationals living in the UK will now be able to gain 'settled status' and stay here indefinitely. After an initial agreement on 'divorce issues' with the EU was reached on 8 December, Mrs May pledged that EU citizens' rights would be written into UK law. Notably, any EU citizen arriving between March 2019 and 2021 will have a right to residency. They will also be able to bring their family.

Papers released in March 2018 explained that EU nationals arriving after 30 March 2019 will be given a 'temporary status' allowing them to stay beyond the end of a transition phase in December 2020.

The Government said: 'This means that they will be able to remain lawfully in the UK working, studying or being self-sufficient for the five years needed to obtain settlement.'

588. Those who were entitled to and in receipt of IS on 31 July 1994 do not have to satisfy the test unless in the meantime they have come off benefit and have subsequently made a new claim.

589. 'Habitual residence' is not a concept which is defined with any precision in the regulations. It is, however, a concept on which there is a rich jurisprudence, both in European case law and in British case law.

590. Under European law[433] requiring equal treatment between workers and their families in the EEA[434] on social security questions, certain benefits, which are ancillary benefits protecting against various risks including unemployment, are classified as special non-contributory benefits. IS is one such benefit. It is a condition of receipt of these benefits that the claimant is habitually resident in the State by which they are paid.

591. The European Court of Justice (ECJ) has held that in the interpretation of this regulation, national courts must apply the European jurisprudence on the term 'habitual residence'. This holds that an individual is habitually resident where he/she habitually lives and where the centre of his/her interests lies. Relevant factors include the claimant's family situation, the reasons for the move, the length and continuity of residence, the stability of any employment and the workers' intentions as they appear from all the circumstances. The court also held that in the case of a migrant worker returning from another EEA country to his/her native country where his/her family lives, there can be no intrinsic requirement for the worker to have lived for any specific period in the country before he/she can be said to be habitually resident there. To find otherwise, according to the court, would be to discriminate against workers who seek to exercise their right to work elsewhere in the EU.[435]

---

433. EC Regulation 1408/71 as amended.
434. Individuals can continue to fall within the definition of 'worker' even during periods of unemployment.
435. *Swaddling v. Adjudication Officer* Case C-90/97 (1999) All ER (EC) 217.

592. There is a separate English case law defining 'habitual residence', however, which remains applicable to those who do not fall within thc scopc of the European legislation. The concept has a considerable history particularly in the field of UK family law and private international law. Interpretations developed in other contexts have been found to be of relevance to the understanding of the concept in the social security context. It has been held that the phrase is to be understood in its usual meaning and that the decision whether or not someone is habitually resident is a question of fact to be decided by reference to all the circumstances. However, that is subject to the finding that (at least in circumstances where one residence is abandoned for a totally new one) an appreciable period of time and a settled intention to make a home in the new country are necessary conditions which must be satisfied before someone can be held to be habitually resident in the UK.[436]

593. The UK's Upper Tribunal has also given guidance, largely similar to that of the European Court, on some of the key factors to be considered in deciding if someone is habitually relevant: these include the mental element; the intention to reside; and the length, continuity and general nature of the claimant's residence in the country. It is for the decision-maker to show that the claimant's residence is not habitual and not for the claimant to prove it is habitual. More recently, the UK's Supreme Court[437] has clarified that where an EEA National is not a worker, self-employed or a student, then such economic inactive migrants place a substantial burden on a host Member State contrary to the 2004 Directive.[438]

C. Asylum Seekers

594. As a result of other legislative changes, there is a general disbarment from social security benefits of those in the UK who claim that they are refugees from another country and are therefore seeking asylum in the UK. There was an exception to this general principle in that those who declared themselves as asylum seekers at the time of entry to the UK might remain entitled to some assistance while their claim is determined. But if there was any delay in declaring themselves so entitled, they were barred by statute from social security entitlement.[439]

595. Since April 2000, a new system of support for asylum seekers – outside the mainstream benefit system – has been in operation.[440] Under this scheme, asylum seekers are disbarred from entitlement to all social security benefits and to mainstream housing and social services. The Secretary of State has a power (but not, save in the case of families with children, a duty) to provide support to those who appear to be destitute or likely to become so. A person is defined as being destitute

436. *Nessa v. Chief Adjudication Officer* [1999] 1 WLR 1937.
437. *Mirga v. SSWP* [2016] UKSC 1.
438. Cf. C-67/14 *Jobcenter Berlin v. Alimanovic.*
439. Full details of this very complex and controversial area of the law of social security is set out in *Benefits for Migrants Handbook,* 6th ed (London: CPAG, 2013).
440. Immigration and Asylum Act 1999. For the background to the proposals *see* 'Fairer, Faster, Firmer – a Modern Approach to Immigration and Asylum', Cmd 4018 (London: TSO, 1998).

where he/she lacks adequate accommodation or any means of obtaining it or he/she cannot meet his/her other essential living needs. Those with any savings, however small, are excluded from the system until those savings are exhausted.

596. Those who meet the qualifying criterion are eligible for housing to be provided by the Home Secretary. They are required to live where the Home Secretary dictates, and the Home Secretary is statutorily prevented from taking into account any preferences they may have about where they should live. This is to enable asylum seekers to be distributed around the country to where accommodation is available. Accommodation provided to asylum seekers should be supplied with pots, pans and bed linen; and basic utilities should be provided free of charge. They are also eligible for assistance with their living expenses and expenses (other than legal costs) related to their asylum claim. Except in exceptional circumstances, support is not provided 'wholly or mainly' in cash. Instead, it is provided through a voucher system at a rate equivalent to 70% of IS. Additionally, there will be a 'single payment element' payable after six months of approximately GBP 50 to assist with any other needs such as that for clothing for a family.

597. This new system is designed partly to 'contain costs through incentives to asylum seekers to look first to their own means or those of their communities for support'.[441] The low level of payments is justified on the basis that asylum decisions are to be taken swiftly, and the speed of asylum decisions has undoubtedly improved following the more recent introduction in 2005 of the New Asylum Model. However, not all cases are resolved quickly, and the tighter deadlines and fast-track procedure has attracted criticism from asylum support charities who argue that it often leads to injustice.[442]

IV. Those in Residential and/or Nursing Care

598. Those who go into residential or nursing care establishments, for example because they are elderly and unable to look after themselves, or because they are recovering from an operation, are entitled to claim IS but special rules apply. The system of funding such persons altered substantially on 1 April 1993. In broad terms, primary responsibility for funding persons in residential and nursing homes was transferred from the Central Government to local authorities, working through their social work departments.

441. 'Fairer Faster Firmer – a Modern Approach to Immigration and Asylum', Cmd 4018 (London: TSO, 1998), para. 702, p. 38 para. 8.17.

442. *See*, for example, the Refugee Council briefing on the New Asylum Model, August 2007, available online at www.refugeecouncil.org.uk.

599. Those in receipt of IS on 31 March 1993 and who were then living in an independent[443] residential care or nursing home have what are known as 'preserved rights'[444] which entitle them to higher rates of IS than those claiming after that date.

600. Those who went into independent homes after 31 March 1993, who thus by definition do not have preserved rights, are nevertheless still entitled to claim IS, but if they qualify for the benefit, it is paid at a considerably less generous level than that paid to persons with preserved rights. Those who cannot afford to pay the fees of the independent home are able to apply for financial assistance from the local authority, but if payments are made by the local authority, this has the effect of greatly reducing the amount of social security benefits available directly to the claimant.

601. Those in homes run directly by local authorities do not have 'preserved rights'. They are entitled to claim IS.

V. People in Hospital

602. Due to the general principle that the Welfare State should not pay twice for people's needs, those in receipt of IS who go into hospital (where the bulk of their essential needs are met) suffer a reduction in their IS.[445] To avoid administrative inconvenience, there are no reductions in IS for the first twenty-eight days of a stay in hospital, and after this time, the disability premiums of IS will stop. The level is then further reduced for those who have to stay in hospital for more than fifty-two weeks.

VI. Prisoners

603. Those in custody are not entitled to IS.[446]

VII. People Without Settled Accommodation

604. Persons with no settled address are still entitled to the normal personal allowance provided for under the IS scheme but cannot usually receive any other payment, for example, a premium.[447]

---

443. That is, one run privately, and not by a local authority.
444. The preserved rights are lost if the claimant is absent from the home for defined periods of time: for example, fifty-two weeks in hospital.
445. *See also* above Part III.
446. Income Support (General) Regulations, Sch. 7 para. 8; there is a limited exception for those detained pending trial or awaiting the sentence of the court.
447. *Ibid.*, Sch. 7, para. 6. A recent appeal on this point employing ECHR Art. 14 and Art. 1, Protocol 1 was unsuccessful, *see R (RJM) v. Secretary of State for Work and Pensions* [2007] EWCA Civ 614, 28 Jun. 2007.

Chapter 2. Working Tax Credit

§1. Introduction

605. *WTC* remains a line of policy initiatives designed to support those on low pay by giving them tax credits to bring them up to defined levels of income.

606. The Labour Government in 2002 introduced WTC to replace FC in order to increase in-work incomes and provide enhanced support with childcare. It was anticipated then that over 1.5 million families would be in receipt of the benefit by 2002 at an annual cost of GBP 5 billion.

607. It was intended that the effect of the new WTC/CTC would be reinforced by the introduction of the National Minimum Wage, a lower starting rate of income tax and greater provision for childcare.

608. The WTC in fact replaced FC from October 1999.[448]

609. The benefit was structured in a very similar way to its predecessor. The qualifying conditions were the same as those for the predecessor benefit, and like FC it remained in payment for six months irrespective of any changes.

§2. Working Tax Credit

610. Commonly, only those with a family qualified. The Tax Credits Act 2002 completely restructured the tax credit system. CTC and PC have been discussed in, respectively, Parts IV and VIII. Here we consider WTC.

611. To qualify for WTC, claimants must be in full-time paid work, and their income must fall below a statutorily prescribed limit. They must also be both present and ordinary resident in the UK and not subject to immigration control.

612. Individuals will be in full-time paid work[449] if:

- they work at least sixteen hours or more a week and they have responsibility for a child or young person; or
- they work at least sixteen hours a week, have a disability which puts them at a disadvantage in getting a job, and qualify for the disability element of WTC;[450] or

448. Tax Credits Act 1999.
449. *See* Working Tax Credits (Entitlement and Maximum Rate) Regulations 2002, SI 2005, regulation 4.
450. *See* WTC(EMR) Regulations 2002 regulation 9(2). This includes individuals receiving the higher rate of IB; long-term IB; SDA; a higher pensioner or disability premium as part of IS, income-based JSA, HB or CTB; Disability Living Allowance; Attendance Allowance; mobility supplement/ constant attendance allowance as part of a War Pension/Industrial Injuries disablement benefit; with

- they work at least sixteen hours a week, are over 50 (or their partner is over 50) and qualify for the 50-plus element of WTC;[451] or
- they are over 25 and work at least thirty hours a week.

613. The amount of benefit payable is calculated by a three-stage process. First, the claimant's maximum WTC is calculated. This is ascertained by adding together all of the potential elements which apply to the claimant. These elements are revised annually. These include:

The Rates for the 2018 to 2019 Tax Year

Element	*Yearly Amount*
For a couple applying together or a single parent (the 'couples and lone-parent element')	Up to GBP 2,010
If you work at least 30 hours a week (the '30-hour element')	Up to GBP 810
If you work and are disabled (the 'disability element')	Up to GBP 3,090
If you are severely disabled (the 'severe disability element')	Up to GBP 1,330
If you are paying for registered or approved childcare (the 'childcare element')	Up to 70% of your childcare costs

614. Second, the claimant's income must be calculated. Claimants on IS, income-based JSA, income-related ESA or PC are automatically passported to the maximum WTC elements to which they are entitled. Other claimants need to calculate their income.

---

an invalid carriage or similar vehicle; sick pay, statutory or otherwise, short-term IB, IS due to incapacity for 140 days and be expected to be injured for a further six months and have reduced earnings by the greater or 15% or GBP 20 per week; or have undertaken training for work at least one day in the fifty-six days preceding the claim and be receiving long-term IB, higher rate short-term IB or SDA. For further details of these benefits *see* Part IX.

451. *See* WTC(EMR) Regulations 2002, regulation 18. This includes individuals who, for six months before they started work, received IS, JSA, IB, SDA, State retirement pension plus Pension Credit or a training allowance (or individuals who enabled another person to get an increase in one of these benefits). The six months can be consecutive or can be cumulative so long as there is no more than twelve weeks separating the periods (except where the claimant enabled another to get an increased benefit). It also covers individuals who, for six months immediately preceding starting work, were entitled to be credited with NI contributions or earnings. Finally, in all these cases where the six months was consecutive, individuals satisfy this condition if it has been less than six months but they received CA, bereavement allowance or widowed parent's allowance and the periods together equal six months.

Chapter 3. HB and CTB

615. Both these schemes are underpinned by a great body of detailed legislative provision, which has in turn been amplified by a number of decisions of the courts.[452] It is not intended to give more than the barest outline of these two further means-tested benefits.

616. The primary purposes of these benefits have been mentioned earlier; HB is designed to subsidize the costs of renting accommodation;[453] CTB is designed to help with the payment of the form of local taxation known as Council Tax.[454]

617. Both benefits can be claimed both by people who are out of work (as is the case with IS) and by those who are in remunerative but low-paid employment (as with WTC).

618. In structural terms, both benefits work on a basis which combines elements of both IS and WTC.

619. For example, like IS, the *applicable amount* element of the HB or CTB calculation incorporates both the personal allowance and the premiums.

620. But when it comes to calculating the amount of benefit which is payable, the structure is more like WTC. If the claimant's weekly income is the same as or less than the applicable amount, the claimant is entitled to the full amount of benefit to which he is entitled. (Claimants in receipt of IS and the guarantee credit of PC automatically get the full entitlement.) If the weekly income exceeds the applicable

452. The best legal analysis of the Housing Benefit and Council Tax scheme is L. Findlay, R. Poynter & M. Ward, *CPAG's Housing Benefit and Council Tax Benefit Legislation,* 28th edn (London: Sweet & Maxwell, Annual, 2015); *see also* Chartered Institute of Housing and Shelter Housing Aid Centre, *Guide to Housing Benefit and Council Tax Benefit* (London: Chartered Institute of Housing/Shelter, Annual).

453. The cost of HB has grown dramatically in recent years, partly the result of Government housing subsidy policy which reduced subsidies on the capital costs of building dwellings, and replaced them with this benefit which subsidizes individual families; partly because the Government has sought to increase levels of local authority housing rents, to bring them closer to private rent levels; and partly the result of the deregulation of rents in the private rented sector of the housing market. There is also evidence that the costs have been inflated further by a degree of highly organized fraud associated with the administration of HB. The issue is discussed in Social Security Committee, 'Housing Benefit Fraud', HC 1995–1996 No. 90 (London: HMSO, 1996); *see also* National Audit Office, 'Remote Control: The National Administration of Housing Benefit' (London: HMSO, 1993); National Audit Office, 'Measures to Counter Housing Benefit Fraud', HC Paper No. 164 (London: TSO, 1997–1998). The most recent estimate, as of March 2006, was that GBP 770 million, or 5.5% of HB expenditure, was overpaid through fraud and error and that it is likely that there was an increase in overpayment in the period 2002–2006.

454. Council Tax replaced two earlier forms of local Government taxation: the first was known as the 'Domestic Rate', and had existed for many years until Mrs Thatcher determined that it should be replaced by a new 'Community Charge' or 'Poll Tax'. This latter was one of the most unpopular taxes which Governments have sought to levy in recent years, and indeed led to a certain amount of civil disobedience and unrest. Commercial properties still have their local taxation levied on the basis of a 'Business Rate'.

amount, then that full amount is reduced, in the case of HB by 65 pence for every GBP 1.00 of excess, in the case of CTB, by 20 pence for every GBP 1.00 of excess.

621. The maximum payable under the HB scheme is 100% of the 'eligible rent'; this is often the full rent, in particular where the claimant is a tenant of a local housing authority or housing association. However, where the tenant rents from a private landlord, there are further mechanisms in place to prevent abuse of the system by unscrupulous landlords who charge excessive 'market' rents and then expect to get the full amount from the HB scheme. (Officials, known as rent officers – who historically had the task of regulating rents between landlords and tenants under earlier rent regulation legislation – now have the job of ensuring that private market rents are in fact reasonable.)[455] There are also special rules which limit the amount of HB that can be paid to single people living on their own. Currently, this applies to those under the age of 25; the Coalition Government has announced that it intends to raise this threshold to 35.

622. As a result of changes introduced in April 2008, those who rent from private landlords now receive up to 100% of what is called the 'Local Housing Allowance'. This is a figure, determined by the Rent Officer, which reflects private sector rents in particular localities. At present, if a person can find a rent cheaper than the allowance, she can keep the difference; if the only accommodation available is at a rent which exceeds the Local Housing Allowance, the tenant has to find the difference.

623. In the case of CTB, the maximum payable is 100% of the Council Tax assessment for the year in question.

624. More controversially, the former Coalition Government, 2010–2015, introduced its HB changes aimed at reducing the cost of HB. This so-called bedroom tax, which was aimed at ensuring that those in social housing did not reside in houses where empty rooms were not utilized, proved most unpopular and was challenged before the courts. Recently, the UK's Court of Appeal[456] deemed these flagship HB reforms, that is Regulation B13 of the HB Regulations 2006, as amended in 2013, unlawful on the grounds of discriminatory practice. However, permission to appeal to the Supreme Court was granted on 28 January 2016.[457]

455. *See* M. Partington, 'The Re-Introduction of Rent Control', *Journal of Housing Law* 1 (1997): 8–11.
456. *Rutherford v. SSWP* [2016] EWCA Civ 29.
457. UKSC 2014/0125 & 0129.

Chapter 4. The Social Fund

625. One of the challenges of any social assistance programme[458] is how to meet the unexpected or exceptional expenditures that confront individuals and families. The former National Assistance and Supplementary Benefits schemes attempted to address this major challenge by building into their structure the ability to provide special payments to meet exceptional needs. Under the Supplementary Benefit scheme, which was in operation from 1966 to 1988, there were initially two sorts of such payment which were paid on the basis of administrative discretion: exceptional needs payments, which were 'single payments' to meet one-off exceptional needs – for example, the provision of a cooker or furniture for people who had to move home and exceptional circumstances additions, which were additions to the basic benefit provision to meet regular needs, for example additional laundry costs associated with the support of someone who was ill.

626. Partly as a result of the fact that expenditure on these discretionary payments had risen rapidly, partly because there had been considerable criticism of the use of discretion as a source of authority for the making of these payments, in 1980, these administrative discretionary rules were abandoned and replaced by a highly detailed set of legislative-regulatory provisions.[459] This both had the effect of making social security law substantially more complex and also failed to achieve the Government's objective of reducing, or curbing, public expenditure.

627. A new approach was adopted when the Social Fund was created in 1988.[460] This reintroduced a discretionary approach to the meeting of financial hardship. At the same time, the Government imposed an annual financial limit on the amount of funding available to the Social Fund. The resources thus made available were made to go further by the fact that a substantial proportion of the payments made through the Social Fund were by way of loans, which had to be paid back, rather than through grants which were not recoverable.

628. The Social Fund has two parts to it: a non-discretionary part, and a discretionary part. Apart from the fact that the former element is paid for, as of right, there is an important distinction in the process of adjudication: appeals against decisions relating to the non-discretionary part go to the Social Security and Child Support Appeals Tribunal, but those against the discretionary part are determined by a special review procedure.[461]

458. For a detailed analysis of the law and practice relating to the Social Fund, and also to the policy context within which it was established, *see* the excellent account by T. Buck, *The Social Fund,* 3rd edn (London: Sweet and Maxwell, 2009).
459. For analysis of the issue, *see* M. Partington, 'Rules and Discretion in British Social Security Law', in *Essays in Memory of Sir Otto Kahn-Freund,* eds. B.A. Hepple et al. (Munich: Beck, 1980).
460. Legislative authority for the Social Fund is now found in SSCBA 1992, Part VII, ss 138–140.
461. *See* further below Part XI.

§1. The Non-discretionary Social Fund

629. The non-discretionary (regulated) Social Fund provides modest financial assistance in three sets of circumstances: birth, death and the onset of cold weather.[462]

I. Maternity Expenses

630. Under the original NI Scheme, a maternity grant used to be payable to nearly all mothers. However, the value of this reduced substantially over the years, and it has now been abolished. More 'targeted' arrangements have been put in its place.

631. Now, in relation to a birth, the Social Fund provides a payment of GBP 500 – called *Sure Start Maternity Grant* – to a person who has been awarded UC, IS, income-based JSA, income-related ESA, WTC which includes the disability or severe disability element, CTC at a rate which exceeds the family element, or PC on the day on which the claim for a payment towards maternity expenses is made (or where an award is backdated), and the claimant or a member of her family is expecting a child, is at least twenty-nine weeks pregnant, or is to adopt a baby or has given birth. The claim can be made at any time from then until six months after the baby has been born. The sum is not affected by any capital held by the claimant.

632. Payments can also be made where parents have a baby as the result of surrogacy, or where a baby is adopted, though not where the baby so adopted is more than 12 months old. Then the claim must be made within three months.

II. Funeral Expenses

633. Similarly, in relation to a death, the former NI death grant has been abolished, and more targeted payments from the Social Fund have been introduced. Under the current rules, a payment can be made to a low-income claimant who has taken responsibility for the funeral of a deceased person.

634. When this benefit was first introduced, no specific sum was set. However, as a result of changes to the regulations, the payment now comprises two elements:

462. *See* the Social Fund Maternity and Funeral Expenses (General) Regulations 1987, SI 1987 No. 481; the Social Fund Cold Weather Payments (General) Regulations 1988, SI 1988 No. 1724; and the Social Fund (Winter Fuel Payments) Regulations 1998, SI 1998 No. 19.

a payment of up to GBP 700[463] to meet the fees of a funeral director or the costs of the person arranging the funeral.[464] In addition, an extra amount may be claimed to cover other defined expenses.[465]

635. In order to make a claim (SF200 Form), the claimant must at the time of claiming be in receipt of UC, IS, income-based JSA, income-related ESA, WTC which includes the disability or severe disability element, CTC at a rate which exceeds the family element, PC, HB or CTB. The claimant or her/his partner must have taken responsibility for paying the costs of the funeral. The claimant must be the partner of the deceased or a close relative[466] or close friend of the deceased (in these latter two cases, it must be shown that it was reasonable for the claimant to take on the responsibility).[467] The funeral – whether by burial or cremation – must take place in the UK or the EEA.[468]

636. The grant is reduced by any other payment received, for example, under an insurance policy, occupational pension scheme, prepaid funeral plan, burial club or similar source; any contribution from a charity or relative; any other funeral grant paid by the Government to a war disablement pensioner; arrears of other social security benefits (e.g., Attendance Allowance/PIP); and the value of the deceased person's assets if any. Finally, the Government is able to recover any funeral expenses payments which have been made from the estate of the deceased person, once all their affairs have been wound up, though personal possessions left to relatives and the value of the house occupied by a surviving spouse do not count as assets for these purposes.

III. Cold Weather Payments

637. In addition to the above, the non-discretionary part of the Social Fund provides for the payment of extra money – GBP 25 for each week of cold weather – to cover additional heating costs arising from periods of cold weather during the winter months. The conditions for payment are that the claimant is already in receipt of

463. *See* https://www.gov.uk/funeral-payments.
464. These include the costs of collecting and transporting the deceased up to 50 miles within the UK to the premises of a funeral director or a place of rest; caring for the deceased prior to the funeral; providing a simple coffin and plain robe; hiring a hearse and one other vehicle for mourners; and paying for the other services provided by the funeral director.
465. For example, the fees for a priest and organist; fees for the provision of documentation such as a doctor's certificate; the cost of cremation; flowers up to GBP 25; some travelling expenses; and other expenses.
466. Defined in the regulations as: parent, parent-in-law, step-parent, son, daughter, son- or daughter-in-law, stepson or stepdaughter, stepson- or stepdaughter-in-law, brother or sister, brother- or sister-in-law.
467. In order to prevent what the Government would regard as inappropriate calls on the Social Fund, payments to a close friend or close relative will not be made where it can be shown that another person was in fact in closer contact with the deceased or there is another person who was in equally close contact who is not in receipt of any of the qualifying benefits.
468. Only limited groups, principally EEA workers and their families, have a right to a funeral payment for a funeral outside the UK.

IS or income-based JSA and that the calculation of IS or income-based JSA includes one of the following premiums: pensioner, disability, higher pensioner, severe disability or disabled child. In addition, claimants in receipt of PC qualify, as do those in receipt of IS or income-based JSA who also have a child under the age of 5.

638. Entitlement arises if the qualifying benefit has been awarded for at least one day during a 'period of cold weather'. A period of cold weather is defined as a period of seven consecutive days during which the average of the mean daily temperature[469] forecast or recorded for the period is at or below 0 degree Celsius. For the purposes of determining entitlement, the country is divided into seventy-two areas, in each of which there is an official weather station which records or forecasts such temperatures. If the address of the claimant, as determined by the relevant postcode falls within one of the areas so defined, then entitlement to the payment arises.

639. The award is not affected by any savings the claimant may have. Further, no actual claim has to be made; the payments are, or should be, sent automatically by the DWP. However, it is not a huge amount of money, and it is reducing annually in real terms because it has not increased in line with inflation.

IV. Winter Fuel Payments[470]

640. In 1997, flat-rate payments to all pensioner households[471] in receipt of a qualifying benefit[472] were introduced, to assist with the cost of winter fuel. These payments were initially introduced pending reform to the pensions system, for two years only, but were extended for a further three years from 1999. They are now a permanent fixture.

§2. The Discretionary Social Fund

641. By contrast, the Discretionary Social Fund does not create any entitlement to benefit but is designed to provide additional financial assistance to meet individual need, and on the basis that there are still funds available from which payments can be made. Until 1 April 2013, the Social Fund could also pay community care grants and crisis loans, but these have now been abolished. They have been replaced by different welfare assistance schemes and advance payments of benefit. The extent to which individual needs can, in fact, be met from a cash-limited fund is one of the intellectual challenges of the scheme.

469. The mean daily temperature is the average of the maximum and minimum temperature recorded for that day.
470. *See* https://www.gov.uk/winter-fuel-payment.
471. Except those who are in nursing residential care or who are hospital inpatients.
472. Retirement pension, Attendance Allowance, Disability Living Allowance, IB, Invalid Care Allowance, SDA, any industrial injuries benefits, war disablement pension, war pension or war widow's pension, widowed mother's allowance or widow's pension.

642. Budgeting loans are loans, not grants. The Government's intention is that by requiring money loaned to be paid back, this increases the total funds available and thus go some way to mitigating any hardship resulting from the cash-limiting of the fund. This does, however, cause a further problem. Loans are only made to those who are judged to have some, albeit limited, ability to pay the loan back. It is possible, therefore, that those with the most severe shortage of resources may be denied help from the fund, not because they have no needs but because of their inability to pay.

643. Decisions in relation to the discretionary part of the Social Fund are taken by specially designated officials, who are required to act on the basis of official *directions* and *guidance* provided by the Secretary of State. The directions set out the conditions which must be satisfied in relation to each category of payment. Furthermore, the directions provide that the Social Fund cannot be used to meet certain categories of expense.[473] The guidance is what it says: guidance to officers as to how they should exercise their discretion, in particular in determining priorities. In practice, officials tend to follow the guidance, particularly at the initial decision-making level; there may be some additional flexibility if an application is subject to review.

§3. Budgeting Loans

644. These are interest-free loans, intended to assist those who have been in receipt of IS, PC or income-based JSA for six months or more with meeting particular one-off expenses. Any capital available to the applicant in excess of GBP 1,000 (GBP 2,000 if the claimant or his/her partner is over 60) reduces the amount of any loan awarded. The amount of a loan can vary between GBP 100 and GBP 1,500. Again, claimants or their partners who are involved in a trade dispute are excluded.

645. The intention is that the loan should be used to meet important but intermittent expenses for which it is hard to budget when living at IS levels. Loans are available to cover only certain categories of expenditure: furniture and household equipment, clothing and footwear, rent in advance and/or removal expenses, household repairs and security, travelling expenses, expenses incurred in looking for or going back to work and also to repay debt incurred to meet expenditure falling within these categories.

646. All applicants are given a weighting reflecting the size of their family. A maximum amount of loan is set locally for each weighting. The amount that the claimant can actually receive is reduced if he/she has existing debt or it is thought that the maximum exceeds his/her ability to repay over an eighteen-month period.

473. *Social Fund Directions*, Directions 12, 23 and 29. These include, for example, expenses on a need which arises outside the UK or certain expenses which are either not regarded as essential or in relation to which there may be other sources of payment such as the expense of a distinctive school uniform for a child or payments to meet the cost of domestic assistance or respite care.

Given that many people on low incomes do in fact borrow money, often at very high rates of interest from lenders of dubious commercial reputation, the possibility of a loan at a zero interest rate may appear to be not wholly unattractive to some applicants. But the practical difficulty of finding the resource to repay, assuming that the applicant remains on subsistence income benefits, cannot be overstressed.

Part XI. Claims and Adjudication

Introduction

647. Having considered the principal areas of substantive law which regulate the entitlement to benefits within the British social security system, this final Part considers some of the practical questions about the administration and adjudication of social security claims in the UK: how are claims made? Who administers the social security system? How can decisions once made be reviewed or appealed against?

648. Central to the UK's administration of its social security system is the key government department – the Department of Work & Pensions (DWP). The DWP is headed by a cabinet Minister (i.e., the Secretary of State for Work & Pensions), supported by a ministerial team, comprising a Department of State which works with thirteen separate agencies.

Chapter 1. Claims

649. It is a fundamental principle of British social security law that entitlement to any particular benefit is, with very rare exceptions, dependent upon a claim for that benefit being made.[474] The necessity for making a formal claim still arises, even though all other conditions of entitlement to any particular benefit are satisfied. As an anti-fraud measure, claims must be supported by the provision of the claimant's individual 'NI number'[475] which is an individual identifying number allocated to each individual worker or claimant.

650. The precise rules about claiming are laid down in very great detail in the Claims and Payments Regulations 1987.[476] They provide that claims should be in writing and be made on official claim forms (although PC does not have to be unless the claimant is specifically required to put their claim in writing). For all benefits other than UC, IS, income-based JSA or income-related ESA (the principal means-tested benefits), the Secretary of State – in other words, in practice, officials working in the Government agencies responsible for administering claims – does have a discretion to treat other forms of communication, for example, a letter, as a claim. Claim forms for UC, IS, JSA and ESA must be properly completed and accompanied by all the evidence required for the claim to be valid,[477] although IS claimants have a month within which to remedy any deficiency as, at the Secretary of State's discretion only, do claimants for JSA and ESA. For increasing numbers of benefits, claimants are now able to submit claims online.

651. The basic requirement that claims must usually be in writing clearly makes administrative sense since only in this way can officials obtain, in permanent form, the evidence which they need on which a claim to benefit can be determined. However, steps have also been made to enable initial contact with the different agencies of the DWP to be made by telephone, although this must be followed up by a claim in writing. This reflects in part awareness of the high numbers of benefits claimants with literacy problems.[478]

---

474. SSAA 1992, s. 1.
475. A claimant who does not have a number may supply evidence that he/she has made an application for one.
476. SI 1987 No. 1968 as amended, although this has been repealed in relation to Child Benefit and GA which is now administered by HMRC; administration of these benefits is now governed by Child Benefit and Guardian's Allowance (Administration) Regulations, 2003, SI 492.
477. There are very limited exceptions to these rules, including some protection for those with learning, mental or communications difficulties who cannot practicably secure assistance in filling in the form. The introduction of these rules was extremely controversial. They were intended to facilitate speedy administration but can have the effect of penalizing those otherwise entitled to benefit for failure to provide information promptly: *see* Social Security Advisory Committee, 'The Social Security (Miscellaneous Amendments) (No. 2) Regulations', Cmd 3586 (London: TSO, 1997).
478. *See* Social Security Committee, 'Welfare Reform and the DSS Departmental Report: Minutes of Evidence', HC Paper No. 587-ii (London: TSO, 1997–1998) 42 et seq.; Social Security Committee, 'Active Modern Service: Minutes of Evidence', HC Paper 1997–1998 No. 587-iii (London: TSO, 1998) Q236ff.

652. Claimants for UC, JSA and (in most cases) ESA must also attend at a JobCentre Plus office before their claim is valid. It is a condition of claiming any benefit that the claimant attends a 'work-focused interview', at which there will be discussion of the claimant's training needs, opportunities for work and in-work benefits, as well as any other benefits that might be available to the claimant in their current situation. This innovation was presented as a key part of the effort to change the focus of benefits administration from a focus on providing cash support to providing support and services which enable a claimant to leave the benefits system.[479]

653. In defined cases, where a claim for one benefit is made to which a claimant is not entitled, such a claim may be treated as a claim to another benefit to which he is entitled. Unfortunately, this sensible principle does not apply generally; there are only certain specific situations in which it will operate, all of which are defined with extraordinary precision in regulations.[480]

654. Normally, a claimant does not seek a benefit until the circumstances have arisen which give entitlement to benefit. However when it is clear that, other things being equal, entitlement will arise in the near future, there are specific rules which permit the claiming of benefit in advance.[481]

655. The Claims and Payments Regulations[482] also prescribe time limits within which claims must be made. These vary as between different benefits. Broadly means-tested benefits (UC, IS, JSA and ESA) must be claimed immediately; whereas claims for most other benefits[483] can be backdated for a maximum of three months. PC, bereavement payments and the retirement pension can be backdated for twelve months. Failure to claim in time does not (usually) destroy the entitlement to the benefit in question, but it limits the time for which the benefit is payable. Benefits cannot normally be paid before the first day on which an effective claim has been made.

656. There is, of course, always the possibility that the impact of such rules will be that injustice will be caused. There is minimal power to extend the time limit for claims for UC, IS, JSA and ESA.[484] Thus, there is a power to extend payment for up to three months where there is a prescribed reason justifying the delay in making an earlier claim (e.g., in some circumstances where the delay was due to illness or disability, to wrong advice from an authoritative source, or, sometimes, to the need to deal with a personal crisis). Claims can also be backdated for up to a month where the Secretary of State is satisfied that this would be consistent with the proper administration of the SSAs and, again, one of a set of specified justifications can be

479. WRPA 1999, s. 57. *See also* 'A New Contract for Welfare: The Gateway to Work', Cmd 4102 (London: TSO, 1998).
480. Claims and Payments Regulations, regulations 9, 10 and 11.
481. *Ibid.*, regulations 13, 14, 15 and 19.
482. Regulation 19.
483. As can applications for social fund funeral and maternity payments. Claims for DLA and AA cannot be backdated at all.
484. Claims and Payments Regulations, regulation 19 as amended.

given: there were administrative difficulties, the claimant was recently separated or divorced, or recently bereaved, or where the delay relates to a claim for an in-work benefit made by an individual who was previously claiming IS, JSA or ESA.

657. These minimal powers replaced earlier provisions which allowed much more extensive scope for extending the time limits for claiming, including a power to backdate claims for any benefit by up to a year where there was 'good cause' for doing so.[485]

658. The rules outlined above apply to the main categories of social security benefits. There are separate rules, though similar in effect, that apply to specific categories of benefit, in particular HB and CTB.

485. The phrase 'good cause' was the subject of considerable interpretation by Social Security Commissioners. The former rules, including the jurisprudence developed by the Commissioners, are discussed in detail in M. Partington, *Claim in Time*, 3rd edn (London: Legal Action Group, 1994).

Chapter 2. The Administration of Social Security

659. Assuming that a proper claim for benefit has been made, the claim will then need to be determined by those responsible for administering the social security system. The system was the subject of fundamental and far-reaching change implemented throughout 1999 and into 2000.

660. The changes, introduced primarily by the SSA 1998, were intended by the Government to introduce a 'less complex, more accurate and cost-effective system' for initial decision-making and appeals.[486] There are fewer institutions in the decision-making landscape.[487] The changes however are wide-ranging and were much criticized. In particular, it was argued that they would lead to a diminution in the levels of institutional independence among decision-makers and in other respects would erode long-established standards of procedural justice.[488]

661. On an administrative level, there were moves to develop better cooperation and to facilitate the sharing of information between the different organizations which remain involved in social security decision-making. In the longer term, the Government proposed reform to its computer systems which would enable information collected in response to an application for one benefit to be linked with the programmes that deal with, and the information collected in connection with, other benefits.[489]

662. Running counter to the move to minimize the number of institutions involved in social security administration was the policy of transferring responsibility for various aspects of the system, in particular responsibility for NI contributions generally and for the administration of in-work benefits, to the Inland Revenue, now HMRC. This was born in part out of moves to harmonize income tax and NI and to make tax credits a key part of social security provision.

486. DSS 'Improving Decision Making and Appeals in Social Security', Cmd 3328 (London: HMSO, 1996). The notion of uniformity in decision-making structures has long since been a contested virtue itself particularly in second or higher tier decision-making structures: it is argued that individuals use appeals processes rarely and are likely to be unfamiliar with any system; while diversity allows systems to cater to the different forms of questions that fall to be decided. (*See*, for example: 'Report of the Committee on Administrative Tribunals and Enquiries', Chairman: Lord Franks, Cmnd 218 (London: HMSO, 1957), 30).

487. The DSS rejected the notion that it might train its decision-makers to be competent to decide on all aspects of any one individual's claim: the system is too complex for that to be a realistic option. There will therefore continue to be diverse categories of decision-makers operating within the new, ostensibly simplified, system.

488. *See* R. Sainsbury, *Consultation on Improving Decision Making and Appeals in Social Security: Analysis of Responses* (London: DSS, 1997); R. Sainsbury, 'The Reform of Social Security Administration'. In *Administrative Justice in the 21st Century,* ed. M. Harris & M. Partington. Oxford: Hart Publishing, 1999; and M. Adler & R. Sainsbury, *Adjudication Matters: Reforming Decision Making and Appeals in Social Security* (Edinburgh: Department of Social Policy, University of Edinburgh, 1998).

489. Social Security Committee, 'Welfare Reform and the DSS Departmental Report: Minutes of Evidence' HC Paper 1997–1998 No. 587-ii; and WRPA 1999, ss 71 and 72 allowing further sharing of functions and information.

663. The following sections offer an outline account of the main players in the decision-making process.

§1. The DWP and HM Revenue and Customs

664. Primary responsibility for determination of policy on all aspects of the system remains firmly within Central Government. However, the rebalancing of responsibilities as between the DWP (as the former DSS became) to HM Revenue and Customs (as the former Inland Revenue has become) means that many of the key decisions are now made by HMRC, in particular on tax credits, statutory pay and child benefit.[490] DWP retains policy control of most other benefits. Behind both, of course, lies the Treasury, who has ultimate control on decisions both on the raising and spending of public money.

§2. Executive Agencies

665. Delivery of social security policy to the public is undertaken within a number of executive agencies.[491]

I. JobCentre Plus

666. JobCentre Plus was created from the old Employment Service and parts of the former Benefits Agency (BA) with the objective of having a single agency responsible for the promotion of work. It is responsible for all benefits administered by DWP which relate to employment and work.

667. The BA of the former DSS had been established in 1991 as part of a policy of devolving areas of Government administration to semi-independent governmental agencies. The Employment Service was an executive agency of the Department for Education and Employment as it was then called. The new agency was created in 2002.

668. In 2015, JobCentre Plus employed over 70,000 staff, deployed in an extensive network of local offices (currently 272) all across the country. Many of the social security benefits are directly administered, at the local level, in these offices of the agency, to which members of the public can go in order to claim benefit.

490. Over the years, these organizations have had a number of different names: the Ministry of Pensions and National Insurance; the Department of Health and Social Security; and the Department of Social Security. Unemployment Benefit (now JSA) has been administered by the Department of Employment, formerly the Ministry of Labour, on behalf of the DWP. HMRC was created in 2005 from a merger between HM Customs and Inland Revenue, a non-ministerial Department, which is overseen by the Treasury.

491. For links to more information, *see* www.dwp.gov.uk/contact-us/.

669. However, administration of certain aspects of some benefits, for example many severe hardship directions for 16/17-year-old claimants of JSA, are administered at the national level in a single centralized office. Yet other benefits are administered on a regional rather than either a local or national basis. While one of the purposes of concentrating administrative resources at a national or regional level was to encourage efficient use of those resources, a consequence is that, inevitably, contact with the public in these offices is indirectly by post or telephone rather than through direct, face-to-face contact. This may have a negative impact on the public perception of those offices.

II. The Child Maintenance and Enforcement Commission

670. Decisions relating to Child Support are taken by officials working within a second executive agency of the DWP, the CMEC, previously known as the CSA. As noted in Part IV, Chapter 3, this Agency has become part of a new organization, the Child Maintenance and Enforcement Commission.

III. Pension Service

671. The Pension Service is another executive agency of the DWP. It deals with retirement pensions and PC and also has a network of local offices.[492] Formally, the Pension Service and the Disability and Carers Service are part of the same organization.

IV. The Status of Officials Within DWP Executive Agencies

672. With the coming into effect of the SSA 1998, all decisions on claims for (mainstream) benefits are formally decisions of the Secretary of State.[493] In practice, they are taken by civil servants acting in his/her name.

673. Previously only a small category of decisions were said to be taken by officials acting in the capacity of Secretary of State.[494] The bulk of decisions were taken by officials who had conferred upon them the title 'adjudication officers' (or in the context of Child Support administration, 'Child Support Officers').

674. These labels signified three important factors: first, that the officials in question were supposed, when acting as adjudication officers, to act with a degree

492. *See* www.dwp.gov.uk/about-dwp/customer-delivery/the-pension-service/.

493. SSA 1998, s. 8, although in relation to Child Benefit and GA, these functions were transferred to the Commissioners of Inland Revenue (now HMRC) by s. 50 of the Tax Credits Act 2002, as was the exercise of decision-making power in relation to tax credits.

494. For a full analysis, *see* M. Partington, 'Secretary of State's Powers of Adjudication in Social Security Law' (School for Advanced Urban Studies, University of Bristol, Working Paper No. 96, April 1991).

of independence from the Department;[495] second, it was only decisions of adjudication officers that could be appealed to the appropriate appeal tribunals (now the First-Tier Tribunal) and thence, on points of law, to the Social Security Commissioners (now Upper Tribunal) (*see* further, Part XI, Chapter 3 below); third, it was only in relation to the decisions taken by adjudication officers that the Central Adjudication Service monitored performance,[496] set standards of adjudication and provided guidance as to the decision-making process.

675. In place of independent monitoring system of decision-making, the Secretary of State is now required to provide an annual report to Parliament on the standards achieved by his own decision-makers,[497] and the President of the unified appeals tribunals service is required to provide an annual report on the standards of decision-making in those first-tier decisions which are appealed to the tribunals.[498] There is also an independent Decision Making Standards Committee, reporting to the heads of JobCentre Plus and the Pension Service which monitors the quality of decision-making across the DWP and recommends methods of improvement.

676. It remains the case that not all decisions are open to appeal. Questions which were formerly decided by adjudication officers continue to be appealable to the Tribunal Service. Some of the former Secretary of State's decisions are now open to independent review. Most questions relating to NI contributions become appealable within the tax appeals system. However, many decisions are not appealable: these include what might be seen as administrative rather than substantive entitlement questions, but also many important issues, such as decisions on the severe hardship directions that are required before most 16- or 17-year-olds can claim any benefit.[499]

V. Social Fund Applications

677. Decisions on applications to the Social Fund are taken by staff in the local JobCentre Plus offices who have been specially designated as 'appropriate officers'.[500] There is no appeal, as such, from the discretionary decisions of a Social Fund Officer.[501] But there is a very detailed review procedure, whereby decisions

495. For further analysis of the status and discussion of the practical implications of the attempt to create this sense of independence, *see* now J. Baldwin, N. Wikeley & R. Young, *Judging Social Security* (Oxford: Clarendon Press, 1992).
496. This service was disbanded under the new arrangements.
497. SSA 1998, s. 81.
498. Tribunals, Courts and Enforcement Act 2007, s. 43.
499. The exceptions are listed in SSA 1998 Sch. II and in regulations made thereunder.
500. They were called 'Social Fund Officers' prior to the implementation of the SSA 1998.
501. Any appeal against a decision relating to one of the mandatory components of the Social Fund – maternity or funeral expenses or cold weather payments – *see* above Part X – goes to the normal social security appeal bodies.

can be looked at further on two occasions, first in the local office, and then by further application to Social Fund Inspectors[502] who work from a single centralized office.

§3. MEDICAL ADVICE, EXAMINATION AND ADJUDICATION

678. As has been noted in the context of considering specific benefits, particularly relating to the sick and the disabled, but also industrial injuries, there are many contexts in which entitlement to benefit is dependent upon medical evidence. While much of this evidence is provided by the claimant himself/herself, with the additional support of his/her own doctor, it is also important that the social security administration has access to its own medical inputs.

679. There are essentially two forms of medical input that are available to the social security system: *medical advice* and *medical adjudication.*

680. Medical advice is provided by doctors employed within the *Medical Service*[503] (these are undertaken by contractors, formerly ATOS now Capita and/or Maximus). Technically, they do not actually take decisions relating to the entitlement of claimants to benefit, but rather provide medical evidence on the basis of which decisions are taken by DWP officials in relation to any incapacity or disability benefit. For example, in the context of ESA, when the point is reached where the claimant, having completed a questionnaire, is examined by a doctor although the doctor's report is very influential in the context of the decision to be taken on the claim, the status of the report is, technically, that it is advisory to the official, and not actually, of itself, determinative of the issue whether a claimant is entitled to ESA.

681. Medical adjudication used to arise in other contexts where an actual medical issue has to be determined.

682. Similarly, decisions about disablement arising in the context of industrial injuries *disablement benefit*[504] were taken by doctors.

502. Known collectively as the Independent Review Service.

503. This service is now contracted out to a private medical consortium.

504. The disablement questions were: has the relevant industrial accident or disease resulted in a loss of faculty? What is the extent of disablement arising from such loss of faculty? And what is the period to be taken into account for such assessment?

683. However, this system of medical adjudication has also been abolished.[505] Questions on industrial injuries benefit are now referred to the standard decision-making process, with provision for medical advice.[506]

§4. Local Authorities

684. HB and CTB, which are properly regarded as social security benefits since the policy in relation to both is determined by the Secretary of State for Social Security, are administered by local authorities.

685. Again there are special provisions relating to appeals, considered below in the context of review and appeals.

§5. HM Revenue and Customs

686. As mentioned above, HMRC is now responsible for decisions relating to tax credits, child benefit, in-work benefits; to disputes over SSP and SMP; and to NI contributions.

§6. Employers

687. SSP and SMP are, in effect, administered by employers on behalf of the HMRC, though any disputes as to entitlement are settled by officials operating within the Department.

§7. Asylum Support

688. Support for asylum seekers is administered by the UK Border Agency, an executive agency of the Home Office.[507]

§8. Counter Fraud

689. A constant concern of Government has been the potential for the social security system to be the subject of abuse by persons making fraudulent claims. This is a controversial issue. Commentators point to the draconian steps often taken by

505. SSA 1998, Sch. 1.
506. Section 32 provides that the general procedural regulations can be modified for questions relating to industrial injuries benefit that were previously referred to Adjudicating Medical Authorities. However, the new procedural regulations merely provide that they may be referred to a doctor for advice.
507. *See* www.ukba.homeoffice.gov.uk/asylum/support/.

the social security authorities to deal with claim fraud, compared with what is perceived as the 'softer' approach taken by the taxation authorities to deal with tax fraud.[508] The present Government has sought to address this issue as part of its programme of reform and modernization of the welfare system.

690. The Social Security Fraud Act 2001 contains four key elements. First is improving methods for the obtaining and sharing of information. This involved: introducing additional powers to obtain information from specified private and public sector organizations to tackle benefit fraud and error; providing the authority for DSS (now DWP) to supply information to countries outside of the UK in line with agreed arrangements, where those countries have adequate safeguards against improper use of that information; and changing the requirement on authorities administering HB or CTB to supply information to DWP, the Northern Ireland Department or other authorities from one based in regulations to one based on directions. Second, there was the introduction of powers to reduce or withdraw specified benefits where an offender was convicted twice of benefit offences within a period of three years. Third was the introduction of financial administrative penalties as an alternative to prosecution.

508. *See*, for example, D. Cook, *Poverty, Crime and Punishment* (London: CPAG, 1997). Frank Field M.P. has argued that the very reliance of the social security system on means-testing has the perverse effect of encouraging social security benefit fraud.

Chapter 3. Reviews and Appeals

691. Once a claim is made, it is adjudicated upon by officials working within one of the executive agencies of the DWP. If the claimant is dissatisfied with the decision, there exists a range of opportunities to obtain a review of the decision or to make an appeal. It is important to distinguish between review and appeal. In fact, mandatory review was introduced from April 2013, as part of the WRA 2012.

§1. Reviews

692. *Review* is essentially an internal process whereby a decision is looked at again by officials to see if it is correct. Two forms of review are available for decisions of the Secretary of State: revisions or supersessions.[509] Both processes can be initiated either by the Secretary of State or by the claimant.

693. Revisions take effect from the date of the original decision; supersessions take effect only from the date on which the application for a new decision, or in some cases the new decision itself, is made.[510]

694. Applications for a revision must usually be made within one month of the date on which notice of the original decision was posted to the applicant. Decisions can be revised on any grounds other than a change of circumstances.[511] The time limit can be extended in special circumstances where it is reasonable to do so, provided that a claimant makes an application within fifteen months of the original decision. By contrast, supersessions can be applied for generally at any time on the basis of a change of circumstances.[512]

695. Review processes generally are classified as either *formal* or *informal*. Formal review takes place when the regulations relating to the benefit in question prescribe a process of review before any further steps can be taken to challenge the decision. Formal reviews are prescribed, for example, in relation to discretionary

509. SSA 1998, s. 9 and s. 10; and Social Security and Child Support (Decisions and Appeals) Regulations 1999 SI 1999/991, regulations 3 to 7. Decisions on the discretionary Social Fund continue to be exempt from the mainstream review and appeal process.

510. There are exceptions to this rule designed to assist a claimant who notifies a change of circumstances within a period of one month from the change.

511. There is, for example, no time limit for the revision of questions on which no appeal is allowed, on decisions concerning sanctions imposed on a claimant for JSA, or of decisions which are based on an official error or which are made in ignorance of or mistake as to a material fact and are more generous than they should have been.

512. A decision (other than one on which there is no appeal) can also be superseded where it was founded on an error of law or a significant error of fact, where the application is made outside the time limit for seeking a revision. A decision to pay JSA can be superseded where a sanction is imposed. Any decision to award benefit can be superseded where a claimant or member of his family becomes entitled to another benefit or an increase in another benefit. A decision of a tribunal or Commissioner can also be superseded (without time limit) if shown to have been reached in ignorance of or on the basis of a mistake as to a significant fact.

Social Fund decisions. Informal reviews take place where officials decide it would be sensible to review a decision. Neither of the new processes of revision and supersession constitute formal reviews.[513] Informal reviews – which by definition are not prescribed – continue to be initiated by the Secretary of State whenever an appeal against a decision is lodged. In the past, this practice resulted in the lapsing of considerable numbers of appeals, as decisions were revised before an appeal is heard. The extent to which appeals lapse for this reason can be taken as one index of the quality of the first-tier decision-making system.

696. In relation to non-discretionary Social Fund decisions, there is a further process of review, known as 'second-tier review', rather than appeal in the sense to be considered below. Second-tier review of Social Fund decisions is undertaken by a special centralized Social Fund review – the Independent Review Service – unit under the control of the Social Fund Commissioner.[514]

I. Mandatory Reconsideration

697. Since April 2013, mandatory reconsideration of PIP & ESA claims has taken place. The main reasons for introducing mandatory reconsideration were to:

- resolve disputes as early as possible;
- reduce unnecessary demand on Her Majesty's Courts and Tribunals Service (HMCTS) by resolving more disputes internally;
- consider revising a decision where appropriate;
- provide a full explanation of the decision; and
- encourage claimants to identify and provide any additional evidence that may affect the decision so that they receive a correct decision at the earliest opportunity.

698. Furthermore, mandatory reconsideration allows the DWP to look again at their decisions in a fair and thorough way. The mandatory reconsideration process involves an outbound call from decision-makers, to talk through disputed decisions with claimants and inviting them to provide any additional evidence at the earliest opportunity. Then, where appropriate, the DWP can change its decision at the earliest possible point rather than having to go through a long and costly appeals process.

513. They do, however, replace formal review processes that existed previously in relation to DLA decisions and Child Support decisions.

514. The Independent Review Service publishes an annual report as well as a more regular newsletter about their work.

§2. Appeals: Social Entitlement Chamber

699. The structure of administrative justice in the UK has undergone fundamental change over recent years. This has come about primarily through the creation of a new Tribunal Service, which brought together under one administrative structure a number of formerly quite separate tribunals.[515] Since October 2008, it was judicially integrated under a new Senior President of tribunals.[516]

700. The Tribunal Service is divided into two tiers: the first tier which largely deals with appeals against decisions taken by officials; and the Upper Tier which largely deals with appeals from the first-tier. Both the first-tier and the Upper Tier are further divided into 'chambers'. The bulk of social security cases go to the Social Entitlement Chamber of the First-Tier Tribunal and to the Administrative Appeals Chamber of the Upper Tribunal.[517]

701. At the first-tier, the Social Entitlement Chamber deals with Asylum Support and Criminal Injuries Compensation appeals, as well as Social Security and Child Support Appeals. The Social Security and Child Support part deals with disputes about: UC; IS; JSA; IB; Employment Support Allowance, DLA; Attendance Allowance; Personal Independent Payment; and Retirement Pensions. It also deals with disputes about: Child Support; Tax Credits; SSP; SMP; Vaccine Damage and decisions on HB and CTB.[518]

702. The tribunals consist of panels of between one and three judges, of whom at least one must be legally qualified. In many instances these days, they sit as one-person tribunals in 01 regime and as panels in 02–06 regimes.[519] Appeals may be disposed of on the papers or after an oral hearing. The appellant is required to state whether or not he/she wants an oral hearing. Failure to state a preference can result in the appeal being struck out, and this must be given within a fourteen-day period. Oral hearings must be held where the appellant so requests, and a tribunal chairman can also insist on an oral hearing if satisfied of the need for one.[520]

---

515. More detail about the tribunal structure is available at www.justice.gov.uk/about/hmcts/tribunals.htm#1.
516. These changes follow a major review of tribunals in 2001 led by Sir Andrew Leggatt, a former Lord Justice of Appeal. The changes were implemented in the Tribunals, Courts and Enforcement Act 2007.
517. For more information on the old appeals system, *see* J. Baldwin et al., *Judging Social Security* (Oxford: Oxford University Press 1992).
518. For exclusions from the jurisdiction of the SSCSA, *see* SSA 1998, s. 12 and Sch. 2 and Social Security and Child Support (Decisions and Appeals) Regulations, SI 1999 No. 991, regulation 27 and Sch. 2. Also *see* SSA 1998, Sch. 3 and SI 1999 No. 991, regulation 26 for decisions which have specifically been brought into the jurisdiction of the tribunal.
519. *See* SSA 1998, s. 7 and Social Security and Child Support (Decisions and Appeals) Regulations, SI 1999 No. 991, regulation 36. These arrangements constitute a substantial and controversial departure from the previous requirement that tribunals should consist of three persons.
520. Social Security and Child Support (Decisions and Appeals) Regulations SI 1999 No. 991, regulation 39.

703. A tribunal may refer an appellant for a medical examination on specific questions[521] and may seek the assistance of an expert if necessary.[522]

§3. APPEALS: UPPER TRIBUNAL (ADMINISTRATIVE APPEALS CHAMBER)

704. The Upper Tribunal (Administrative Appeals Chamber) has taken over the functions of the Social Security, Child Support and Pensions Appeals Commissioners. The judges in the Upper Tribunal are lawyers who have been specially appointed to hear appeals from the First-Tier Tribunal. They consider points of law only. They normally determine cases sitting on their own. Particularly unusual or important cases are dealt with by a tribunal of judges. The bulk of their cases are determined on the papers; in a small number of cases, they hold a hearing.

§4. TAX (HMRC) APPEALS

705. Appeals from decisions taken by HMRC, with the exception of appeals about tax credits which go to the Social Entitlement Chamber, go to the Tax Chamber of the First-Tier Tribunal. Appeals from the Tax Chamber go to the Tax and Chancery Division of the Upper Tribunal.[523]

---

521. SSA 1998, s. 20 and SI 1999 No. 991, regulation 41.
522. SSA 1998, s. 7(4).
523. *See* further www.justice.gov.uk/guidance/courts-and-tribunals/tribunals/tax/index.htm.

Appendix 1. UK Benefits & Pensions Rates 2018-19

Benefit and Pension rates 2018/2019		
	RATES	**RATES**
(Weekly rates unless otherwise shown)	**2017-18**	**2018-19**
ATTENDANCE ALLOWANCE		
higher rate	83.10	85.60
lower rate	55.65	57.30
BEREAVEMENT BENEFIT		
Bereavement payment (lump sum)	2000.00	2000.00
Widowed parent's allowance	113.70	117.10
Bereavement Allowance		
standard rate	113.70	117.10
age-related		
age 54	105.74	108.90
53	97.78	100.71
52	89.82	92.51
51	81.86	84.31
50	73.91	76.12
49	65.95	67.92
48	57.99	59.72
47	50.03	51.52
46	42.07	43.33
45	34.11	35.13
BEREAVEMENT SUPPORT PAYMENT (for deaths occurring on or after 6 April 2017)		
Standard rate (lump sum)	2500.00	2500.00

Appendix 1: UK Benefits & Pensions Rates 2018-19

Standard rate monthly payments	100.00	100.00
Higher rate (lump sum)	3500.00	3500.00
Higher rate monthly payments	350.00	350.00
BENEFIT CAP - Rates introduced November 2016		
Reduction in annual level of Benefit Cap (Greater London)		
Couples (with or without children) or single claimants with a child of qualifying age	23000.00	23000.00
Single adult households without children	15410.00	15410.00

Reduction in annual level of Benefit Cap (Rest of Great Britain)		
Couples (with or without children) or single claimants with a child of qualifying age	20000.00	20000.00
Single adult households without children	13400.00	13400.00
Monthly equivalent (Greater London)		
Couples (with or without children) or single claimants with a child of qualifying age	1916.67	1916.67
Single adult households without children	1284.17	1284.17
Monthly equivalent (Rest of Great Britain)		
Couples (with or without children) or single claimants with a child of qualifying age	1666.67	1666.67
Single adult households without children	1116.67	1116.67
Weekly equivalent (Greater London)		
Couples (with or without children) or single claimants with a child of qualifying age	442.31	442.31
Single adult households without children	296.35	296.35
Weekly equivalent (Rest of Great Britain)		
Couples (with or without children) or single claimants with a child of qualifying age	384.62	384.62
Single adult households without children	257.69	257.69
CAPITAL LIMITS - rules common to Income Support, income based Jobseeker's Allowance,		

income-related Employment and Support Allowance, Pension Credit, andHousing Benefit, and Universal Credit		
unless stated otherwise		
upper limit	16000.00	16000.00
upper limit - Pension Credit and those getting Housing Benefit and Pension CreditGuarantee Credit	No limit	No limit
Amount disregarded - all benefits except Pension Credit and Housing Benefit forthose above the qualifying age for Guarantee Credit	6000.00	6000.00
Amount disregarded - Pension Credit and Housing Benefit for those above thequalifying age for Pension Credit	10000.00	10000.00
Child disregard (not Pension Credit, Employment and Support Allowance norHousing Benefit)	3000.00	3000.00
Amount disregarded (living in RC/NH)	10000.00	10000.00
Tariff income		
£1 for every £250, or part thereof, between the amount of		
capital disregarded and the capital upper limit		
Tariff income - Pension Credit and Housing Benefit where claimant / partner is over Guarantee Credit qualifying age		
£1 for every £500, or part thereof, above or between the amount of		
capital disregarded and any capital upper limit applicable		
CARER'S ALLOWANCE	62.70	64.60
DEDUCTIONS - rules common to Income Support, Jobseeker's Allowance,		
Employment and Support Allowance, Pension Credit and Housing Benefit		
unless stated otherwise		
Non-dependant deductions from housing benefit and from IS, JSA(IB), ESA(IR) and Pension Credit		
aged 25 and over in receipt of IS and JSA(IB),		
or any age in receipt of main phase ESA(IR),		
aged 18 or over, not in remunerative work	14.80	15.25
aged 18 or over and in remunerative work		

- gross income: less than £139	14.80	15.25
- gross income: £139 to £203.99	34.00	35.00
- gross income: £204 to £264.99	46.65	48.05
- gross income: £265 to £353.99	76.35	78.65
- gross income: £354 to £438.99	86.95	89.55
- gross income: £439 and above	95.45	98.30
Deductions from housing benefit		
Service charges for fuel		
Heating	28.80	30.30
hot water	3.35	3.50
Lighting	2.30	2.40
Cooking	3.35	3.50
Amount ineligible for meals		
three or more meals a day		
single claimant	27.10	27.90
each person in family aged 16 or over	27.10	27.90
each child under 16	13.75	14.15
less than three meals a day		
single claimant	18.05	18.60
each person in family aged 16 or over	18.05	18.60
each child under 16	9.10	9.35
breakfast only - claimant and each member of the family	3.35	3.45
Amount for personal expenses (not HB)	24.25	25.00
Third party deductions from IS, JSA(IB), ESA(IR) and Pension Credit for;		
arrears of housing, fuel and water costs	3.70	3.70
Council Tax etc. and deductions for ELDS and ILS.		
child support, contribution towards maintenance (CTM)		
standard deduction	7.40	7.40
lower deduction	3.70	3.70
arrears of Community Charge		
court order against claimant	3.70	3.70
court order against couple	5.75	5.75
fine or compensation order		

standard rate	5.00	5.00
lower rate	3.70	3.70
Maximum deduction rates for recovery of overpayments (not JSA(C)/ESA(C))		
ordinary overpayments	11.10	11.10
Fraud Overpayments		
Housing Benefit/ CTB only	18.50	18.50
Benefits (not HB or Council Tax)	29.60	29.60
Deductions from JSA(C) and ESA (C)		
Arrears of Comm. Charge & overpayment recovery		
Age 16 - 24	19.30	19.30
Age 25 +	24.36	24.36
Arrears of Council Tax & Fines		
Age 16 - 24	23.16	23.16
Age 25 +	29.24	29.24
Maximum deduction for arrears of Child Maintenance		
Age 16 - 24	19.30	19.30
Age 25 +	24.36	24.36
DEPENDENCY INCREASES		
Adult dependency increases for spouse or person looking after		
children - payable with;		
State Pension on own insurance (Cat A)	66.35	68.35
State Pension (non-contributory, Cat C)	39.70	40.90
long term Incapacity Benefit	61.80	63.65
Unemployability Supplement.	62.70	64.60
Severe Disablement Allowance	37.10	38.20
Carer's Allowance	36.90	38.00
short-term Incapacity Benefit (over state pension age)	59.50	61.30
short-term Incapacity Benefit (under State Pension age)	48.15	49.60
Child Dependency Increases - payable with;		
State Pension; Widowed Mothers/Parents Allowance;	11.35	11.35

Appendix 1: UK Benefits & Pensions Rates 2018-19

short-term Incapacity benefit - higher rate or over state pension age;		
long-term Incapacity Benefit; Carer's Allowance; Severe Disablement		
Unemployability Supplement.		
NB - The rate of child dependency increase is adjusted where it is payable for the eldest child for whom Child Benefit is also paid. The weekly rate in such cases is reduced by the difference (less £3.65) between the ChB rates for the eldest and subsequent children.	8.00	8.00
DISABILITY LIVING ALLOWANCE		
Care Component		
Highest	83.10	85.60
Middle	55.65	57.30
Lowest	22.00	22.65
Mobility Component		
Higher	58.00	59.75
Lower	22.00	22.65
DISREGARDS		
Housing Benefit		
Earnings disregards		
standard (single claimant)	5.00	5.00
Couple	10.00	10.00
higher (special occupations/circumstances)	20.00	20.00
lone parent	25.00	25.00
childcare charges	175.00	175.00
childcare charges (2 or more children)	300.00	300.00
permitted work higher	120.00	125.50
permitted work lower	20.00	20.00
Other Income disregards		
adult maintenance disregard	15.00	15.00
war disablement pension and war widows pension	10.00	10.00
widowed mothers/parents allowance	15.00	15.00
Armed Forces Compensation Scheme	10.00	10.00
student loan	10.00	10.00
student's covenanted income	5.00	5.00
income from boarders (plus 50% of the balance)	20.00	20.00

aged 18 or over and in remunerative work		
- gross income: less than £139	14.80	15.25
- gross income: £139 to £203.99	34.00	35.00
- gross income: £204 to £264.99	46.65	48.05
- gross income: £265 to £353.99	76.35	78.65
- gross income: £354 to £438.99	86.95	89.55
- gross income: £439 and above	95.45	98.30
Deductions from housing benefit		
Service charges for fuel		
Heating	28.80	30.30
hot water	3.35	3.50
Lighting	2.30	2.40
Cooking	3.35	3.50
Amount ineligible for meals		
three or more meals a day		
single claimant	27.10	27.90
each person in family aged 16 or over	27.10	27.90
each child under 16	13.75	14.15
less than three meals a day		
single claimant	18.05	18.60
each person in family aged 16 or over	18.05	18.60
each child under 16	9.10	9.35
breakfast only - claimant and each member of the family	3.35	3.45
Amount for personal expenses (not HB)	24.25	25.00
Third party deductions from IS, JSA(IB), ESA(IR) and Pension Credit for;		
arrears of housing, fuel and water costs	3.70	3.70
Council Tax etc. and deductions for ELDS and ILS.		
child support, contribution towards maintenance (CTM)		
standard deduction	7.40	7.40
lower deduction	3.70	3.70
arrears of Community Charge		
court order against claimant	3.70	3.70
court order against couple	5.75	5.75

fine or compensation order		
standard rate	5.00	5.00
lower rate	3.70	3.70
Maximum deduction rates for recovery of overpayments (not JSA(C)/ESA(C))		
ordinary overpayments	11.10	11.10
Fraud Overpayments		
Housing Benefit/ CTB only	18.50	18.50
Benefits (not HB or Council Tax)	29.60	29.60
Deductions from JSA(C) and ESA (C)		
Arrears of Comm. Charge & overpayment recovery		
Age 16 - 24	19.30	19.30
Age 25 +	24.36	24.36
Arrears of Council Tax & Fines		
Age 16 - 24	23.16	23.16
Age 25 +	29.24	29.24
Maximum deduction for arrears of Child Maintenance		
Age 16 - 24	19.30	19.30
Age 25 +	24.36	24.36
DEPENDENCY INCREASES		
Adult dependency increases for spouse or person looking after		
children - payable with;		
State Pension on own insurance (Cat A)	66.35	68.35
State Pension (non-contributory, Cat C)	39.70	40.90
long term Incapacity Benefit	61.80	63.65
Unemployability Supplement.	62.70	64.60
Severe Disablement Allowance	37.10	38.20
Carer's Allowance	36.90	38.00
short-term Incapacity Benefit (over state pension age)	59.50	61.30
short-term Incapacity Benefit (under State Pension age)	48.15	49.60
Child Dependency Increases - payable with;		
State Pension; Widowed Mothers/Parents Allowance;	11.35	11.35

short-term Incapacity benefit - higher rate or over state pension age;		
long-term Incapacity Benefit; Carer's Allowance; Severe Disablement		
Unemployability Supplement.		
NB - The rate of child dependency increase is adjusted where it is payable for the eldest child for whom Child Benefit is also paid. The weekly rate in such cases is reduced by the difference (less £3.65) between the ChB rates for the eldest and subsequent children.	8.00	8.00
DISABILITY LIVING ALLOWANCE		
Care Component		
Highest	83.10	85.60
Middle	55.65	57.30
Lowest	22.00	22.65
Mobility Component		
Higher	58.00	59.75
Lower	22.00	22.65
DISREGARDS		
Housing Benefit		
Earnings disregards		
standard (single claimant)	5.00	5.00
Couple	10.00	10.00
higher (special occupations/circumstances)	20.00	20.00
lone parent	25.00	25.00
childcare charges	175.00	175.00
childcare charges (2 or more children)	300.00	300.00
permitted work higher	120.00	125.50
permitted work lower	20.00	20.00
Other Income disregards		
adult maintenance disregard	15.00	15.00
war disablement pension and war widows pension	10.00	10.00
widowed mothers/parents allowance	15.00	15.00
Armed Forces Compensation Scheme	10.00	10.00
student loan	10.00	10.00
student's covenanted income	5.00	5.00
income from boarders (plus 50% of the balance)	20.00	20.00

Appendix 1: UK Benefits & Pensions Rates 2018-19

additional earnings disregard	17.10	17.10
income from subtenants (£20 fixed from April 08)	20.00	20.00
Income Support, income-based Jobseeker's Allowance,		
Income-related Employment and Support Allowance (ESA(IR)) and PensionCredit		
Earnings disregards		
standard (single claimant) (not ESA(IR))	5.00	5.00
couple (not ESA(IR))	10.00	10.00
higher (special occupations/circumstances)	20.00	20.00
partner of claimant (ESA(IR))	20.00 (maximum)	20.00 (maximum)
Other Income disregards		
war disablement pension and war widows pension	10.00	10.00
widowed mothers/parents allowance	10.00	10.00
Armed Forces Compensation Scheme	10.00	10.00
student loan (not Pension Credit)	10.00	10.00
student's covenanted income (not Pension Credit)	5.00	5.00
income from boarders (plus 50% of the balance)	20.00	20.00
income from subtenants (£20 fixed from April 08)	20.00	20.00
EARNINGS RULES		
Carer's Allowance	116.00	120.00
Limit of earnings from councillor's allowance	120.00	125.50
Permitted work earnings limit - higher	120.00	125.50
- lower	20.00	20.00
Industrial injuries unemployability supplement	6240.00	6526.00
permitted earnings level (annual amount)		
Earnings level at which adult dependency (ADI) increases are		
affected with:		
short-term incapacity benefit where claimant is		
(a) under state pension age	48.15	49.60
(b) over state pension age	59.50	61.30
state pension, long term incapacity benefit,		
severe disablement allowance, unemployability		
supplement - payable when dependant		
(a) is living with claimant	73.10	73.10

(b) still qualifies for the tapered earnings rule	45.09	45.09
Earnings level at which ADI is affected when dependant		
is not living with claimant;		
state pension,	66.35	68.35
long-term incapacity benefit,	61.80	63.65
unemployability supplement,	62.70	64.60
severe disablement allowance	37.10	38.20
Carer's allowance	36.90	38.00
Earnings level at which child dependency increases		
are affected		
for first child	230.00	235.00
additional amount for each subsequent child	30.00	31.00
Pension income threshold for incapacity benefit	85.00	85.00
Pension income threshold for contributory Employment Support Allowance	85.00	85.00
EMPLOYMENT AND SUPPORT ALLOWANCE		
Personal Allowances		
Single		
under 25	57.90	57.90
25 or over	73.10	73.10
lone parent		
under 18	57.90	57.90
18 or over	73.10	73.10
Couple		
both under 18	57.90	57.90
both under 18 with child	87.50	87.50
both under 18 (main phase)	73.10	73.10
both under 18 with child (main phase)	114.85	114.85
one 18 or over, one under 18 (certain conditions apply)	114.85	114.85
both over 18	114.85	114.85
claimant under 25, partner under 18	57.90	57.90
claimant 25 or over, partner under 18	73.10	73.10
claimant (main phase), partner under 18	73.10	73.10
Premiums		

enhanced disability		
Single	15.90	16.40
Couple	22.85	23.55
severe disability		
Single	62.45	64.30
couple (lower rate)	62.45	64.30
couple (higher rate)	124.90	128.60
Carer	34.95	36.00
Pensioner		
single with WRAC	57.20	60.85
single with support component	49.70	52.25
single with no component	86.25	89.90
couple with WRAC	99.35	104.90
couple with support component	91.85	96.30
couple with no component	128.40	133.95
Components		
Work-related Activity	29.05	29.05
Support	36.55	37.65
HOUSING BENEFIT		
Personal allowances		
Single		
under 25	57.90	57.90
25 or over	73.10	73.10
entitled to main phase ESA	73.10	73.10
lone parent		
under 18	57.90	57.90
18 or over	73.10	73.10
entitled to main phase ESA	73.10	73.10
Couple		
both under 18	87.50	87.50
one or both 18 or over	114.85	114.85
claimant entitled to main phase ESA	114.85	114.85
dependent children	66.90	66.90
Pensioner		
single/lone parent has attained the qualifying age for Pension Credit but under 65.	159.35	163.00

couple – one or both has attained the qualifying age for Pension Credit but bothunder 65	243.25	248.80
single / lone parent – 65 and over	172.55	176.40
couple – one or both 65 and over	258.15	263.80
polygamous marriage		
for the claimant and the other party to the marriage where no members of the marriage have attained the age of 65	243.25	248.80
for each additional spouse who is a member of the same household as the claimant and no members of the marriage have attained the age of 65	83.90	85.80
for the claimant and the other party to the marriage where one or more of the members of the marriage are aged 65 or over	258.15	263.80
for each additional spouse who is a member of the same household as the claimant and one or more of the members of the marriage are aged 65 or over	85.60	87.40
Premiums		
Family	17.45	17.45
family (lone parent rate)	22.20	22.20
Disability		
Single	32.55	33.55
Couple	46.40	47.80
enhanced disability		
Single	15.90	16.40
disabled child	24.78	25.48
Couple	22.85	23.55
severe disability		
Single	62.45	64.30
couple (lower rate)	62.45	64.30
couple (higher rate)	124.90	128.60
disabled child	60.90	62.86
Carer	34.95	36.00
ESA components		
work-related activity	29.05	29.05
Support	36.55	37.65
INCAPACITY BENEFIT		

Appendix 1: UK Benefits & Pensions Rates 2018-19

Long-term Incapacity Benefit	106.40	109.60
Short-term Incapacity Benefit (under state pension age)		
lower rate	80.25	82.65
higher rate	95.00	97.85
Short-term Incapacity Benefit (over state pension age)		
lower rate	102.10	105.15
higher rate	106.40	109.60
Increase of Long-term Incapacity Benefit for age	11.25	11.60
higher rate	11.25	11.60
lower rate	6.25	6.45
Invalidity Allowance (Transitional)		
higher rate	11.25	11.60
middle rate	6.25	6.45
lower rate	6.25	6.45
INCOME SUPPORT		
Personal Allowances		
Single		
under 25	57.90	57.90
25 or over	73.10	73.10
lone parent		
under 18	57.90	57.90
18 or over	73.10	73.10
Couple		
both under 18	57.90	57.90
both under 18 – higher rate	87.50	87.50
one under 18, one under 25	57.90	57.90
one under 18, one 25 and over	73.10	73.10
both 18 or over	114.85	114.85
dependent children	66.90	66.90
Premiums		
family / lone parent	17.45	17.45
pensioner (applies to couples only)	128.40	133.95
Disability		
Single	32.55	33.55

Couple	46.40	47.80
enhanced disability		
Single	15.90	16.40
disabled child	24.78	25.48
Couple	22.85	23.55
severe disability		
Single	62.45	64.30
couple (lower rate)	62.45	64.30
couple (higher rate)	124.90	128.60
disabled child	60.90	62.86
Carer	34.95	36.00
Relevant sum for strikers	40.50	40.50
INDUSTRIAL DEATH BENEFIT		
Widow's pension		
higher rate	122.30	125.95
lower rate	36.69	37.79
Widower's pension	122.30	125.95
INDUSTRIAL INJURIES DISABLEMENT BENEFIT		
Standard rate		
100%	169.70	174.80
90%	152.73	157.32
80%	135.76	139.84
70%	118.79	122.36
60%	101.82	104.88
50%	84.85	87.40
40%	67.88	69.92
30%	50.91	52.44
20%	33.94	34.96
Maximum life gratuity (lump sum)	11260.00	11600.00
Unemployability Supplement	104.90	108.05
increase for early incapacity		
higher rate	21.70	22.35
middle rate	14.00	14.40
lower rate	7.00	7.20
Maximum reduced earnings allowance	67.88	69.92

Appendix 1: UK Benefits & Pensions Rates 2018-19

Maximum retirement allowance	16.97	17.48
Constant attendance allowance		
exceptional rate	135.80	139.80
intermediate rate	101.85	104.85
normal maximum rate	67.90	69.90
part-time rate	33.95	34.95
Exceptionally severe disablement allowance	67.90	69.90
JOBSEEKER'S ALLOWANCE		
Contribution-based JSA - Personal rates		
under 25	57.90	57.90
25 or over	73.10	73.10
Income-based JSA - personal allowances		
under 25	57.90	57.90
25 or over	73.10	73.10
lone parent		
under 18	57.90	57.90
18 or over	73.10	73.10
Couple		
both under 18	57.90	57.90
both under 18 - higher rate	87.50	87.50
one under 18, one under 25	57.90	57.90
one under 18, one 25 and over	73.10	73.10
both 18 or over	114.85	114.85
dependent children	66.90	66.90
Premiums		
family / lone parent	17.45	17.45
Pensioner		
Single	86.25	89.90
Couple	128.40	133.95
Disability		
Single	32.55	33.55
Couple	46.40	47.80
enhanced disability		
Single	15.90	16.40
disabled child	24.78	25.48
Couple	22.85	23.55

severe disability		
Single	62.45	64.30
couple (lower rate)	62.45	64.30
couple (higher rate)	124.90	128.60
disabled child	60.90	62.86
Carer	34.95	36.00
Prescribed sum for strikers	40.50	40.50
MATERNITY ALLOWANCE		
Standard rate	140.98	145.18
MA threshold	30.00	30.00
PENSION CREDIT		
Standard minimum guarantee		
Single	159.35	163.00
Couple	243.25	248.80
Additional amount for severe disability		
Single	62.45	64.30
couple (one qualifies)	62.45	64.30
couple (both qualify)	124.90	128.60
Additional amount for carers	34.95	36.00
Savings credit		
threshold - single	137.35	140.67
threshold - couple	218.42	223.82
maximum - single	13.20	13.40
maximum - couple	14.90	14.99
Amount for claimant and first spouse in polygamous marriage	243.25	248.80
Additional amount for additional spouse	83.90	85.80
Non-State Pensions (for Pension Credit purposes)		
Statutory minimum increase to non-state pensions	1.00%	3.00%
PERSONAL INDEPENDENCE PAYMENT		
Daily living component		
Enhanced	83.10	85.60
Standard	55.65	57.30
Mobility component		
Enhanced	58.00	59.75
Standard	22.00	22.65

Appendix 1: UK Benefits & Pensions Rates 2018-19

SEVERE DISABLEMENT ALLOWANCE		
Basic rate	75.40	77.65
Age-related addition (from Dec 90)		
Higher rate	11.25	11.60
Middle rate	6.25	6.45
Lower rate	6.25	6.45
STATE PENSION		
New State Pension		
Full rate	159.55	164.35
Transitional rate below full rate	2.5056%	3.0085%
Protected Payment	1.00%	3.00%
Increments - own (based on deferred new State Pension)	1.00%	3.00%
Increments - inherited (based on deferred old State Pension)	1.00%	3.00%
Old State Pension		
Category A or B basic pension	122.30	125.95
Category B (lower) basic pension - spouse or civil partner's insurance	73.30	75.50
Category C or D - non-contributory	73.30	75.50
Additional pension	1.00%	3.00%
Maximum additional pension (own + inherited)	167.26	172.28
Increments to:-		
Basic pension	1.00%	3.00%
Additional pension	1.00%	3.00%
Graduated Retirement Benefit (GRB)	1.00%	3.00%
Inheritable lump sum	1.00%	3.00%
Contracted-out Deduction from AP in respect of	Nil	Nil
pre-April 1988 contracted-out earnings		
Contracted-out Deduction from AP in respect of		
contracted-out earnings from April 1988 to 1997	1.00%	3.00%
Graduated Retirement Benefit (unit)	0.1343	0.1383
Increase of long term incapacity for age	1.00%	3.00%
Addition at age 80	0.25	0.25
Increase of Long-term incapacity for age		
higher rate	21.70	22.35
lower rate	10.90	11.25

Invalidity Allowance (Transitional) for State Pension recipients		
higher rate	21.70	22.35
middle rate	14.00	14.40
lower rate	7.00	7.20
STATUTORY ADOPTION PAY		
Earnings threshold	113.00	116.00
Standard Rate	140.98	145.18
STATUTORY MATERNITY PAY		
Earnings threshold	113.00	116.00
Standard rate	140.98	145.18
STATUTORY PATERNITY PAY		
Earnings threshold	113.00	116.00
Standard Rate	140.98	145.18
STATUTORY SHARED PARENTAL PAY		
Earnings threshold	113.00	116.00
Standard rate	140.98	145.18
STATUTORY SICK PAY		
Earnings threshold	113.00	116.00
Standard rate	89.35	92.05
UNIVERSAL CREDIT (monthly rates)		
Universal Credit Minimum Amount	0.01	0.01
Universal Credit Amounts		
Standard allowance		
Single		
Single under 25	251.77	251.77
Single 25 or over	317.82	317.82
Couple		
Joint claimants both under 25	395.20	395.20
Joint claimants, one or both 25 or over	498.89	498.89
Child amounts		
First child (born prior to 6 April 2017)	277.08	277.08
Second/ subsequent child (born on or after 6 April 2017)	231.67	231.67
Disabled child additions		
Lower rate addition	126.11	126.11

Appendix 1: UK Benefits & Pensions Rates 2018-19

Higher rate addition	372.30	383.86
Limited Capability for Work amount	126.11	126.11
Limited Capability for Work and Work-Related Activity amount	318.76	328.32
Carer amount	151.89	156.45
Childcare costs amount		
Maximum for one child	646.35	646.35
Maximum for two or more children	1108.04	1108.04
Non-dependants' housing cost contributions	70.06	72.16
Work allowances		
Higher work allowance (no housing amount)		
One or more dependent children or limited capability for work		
Lower work allowance	397.00	409.00
One or more dependent children or limited capability for work	192.00	198.00
Assumed income from capital for every £250 or part thereof, between capital disregard and upper capital limit	4.35	4.35
UC Daily Reduction		
100% reduction - High, medium or low-level sanctions apply - claimants aged 18 or over		
Single		
Single under 25	8.20	8.20
Single 25 or over	10.40	10.40
Couple		
Joint claimants both under 25 (per sanctioned claimant)	6.40	6.40
Joint claimants, one or both 25 or over and one is sanctioned (per sanctionedclaimant)	8.20	8.20
40% reduction - Lowest level sanction applies		
Single		
Single under 25	3.30	3.30
Single 25 or over	4.10	4.10
Couple		
Joint claimants both under 25 (per sanctioned claimant)	2.50	2.50

Joint claimants, one or both 25 or over (per sanctioned claimant)	3.20	3.20
Third Party Deductions at 5% of UC Standard Allowance (excludes deductions for rent and service charges included in rent)		
Single		
Single under 25	12.59	12.59
Single 25 or over	15.89	15.89
Couple		
Joint claimants both under 25	19.76	19.76
Joint claimants, one or both 25 or over	24.94	24.94
Maximum deductions for Fines	108.35	108.35
Minimum deductions for rent and service charges included in rent at 10% of UC Standard Allowance (10% minimum introduced from Nov 2014)		
Single		
Single under 25	25.18	25.18
Single 25 or over	31.78	31.78
Couple		
Joint claimants both under 25	39.52	39.52
Joint claimants, one or both 25 or over	49.89	49.89
Maximum deductions for rent and service charges included in rent at 20% of UC Standard Allowance (20% maximum introduced from Nov 2014)		
Single		
Single under 25	50.35	50.35
Single 25 or over	63.56	63.56
Couple		
Joint claimants both under 25	79.04	79.04
Joint claimants, one or both 25 or over	99.78	99.78
Overall Maximum deduction Rate at 40% of UC Standard Allowance:		
Single		
Single under 25	100.71	100.71
Single 25 or over	127.13	127.13
Couple		
Joint claimants both under 25	158.08	158.08
Joint claimants, one or both 25 or over	199.56	199.56

Appendix 1: UK Benefits & Pensions Rates 2018-19

Fraud Overpayments, Recoverable Hardship Payments and Administrative Penalties at 40% of UC Standard Allowance		
Single		
Single under 25	100.71	100.71
Single 25 or over	127.13	127.13
Couple		
Joint claimants both under 25	158.08	158.08
Joint claimants, one or both 25 or over	199.56	199.56
Ordinary Overpayments and Civil Penalties at 15% of UC Standard AllowanceSingle		
Single under 25	37.77	37.77
Single 25 or over	47.67	47.67
Couple		
Joint claimants both under 25	59.28	59.28
Joint claimants, one or both 25 or over	74.83	74.83
Ordinary Overpayments and Civil Penalties at 25% of UC Standard Allowance if		
claimant's and/or partner's earnings are over the Work Allowance		
Single		
Single under 25	62.94	62.94
Single 25 or over	79.46	79.46
Couple		
Joint claimants both under 25	98.80	98.80
Joint claimants, one or both 25 or over	124.72	124.72
WIDOW'S BENEFIT		
Widowed mother's allowance	113.70	117.10
Widow's pension		
standard rateage-related	113.70	117.10
age 54 (49)	105.74	108.90
53 (48)	97.78	100.71
52 (47)	89.82	92.51
51 (46)	81.86	84.31
50 (45)	73.91	76.12
49 (44)	65.95	67.92
48 (43)	57.99	59.72

47 (42)	50.03	51.52
46 (41)	42.07	43.33
45 (40)	34.11	35.13

Appendix 1: UK Benefits & Pensions Rates 2018-19

Appendix 2. UK Tax & Tax Credit Rates 2018-19

UK Tax & Tax Credit Rates 2018-19[524]

The current UK tax year is from 6 April 2018 to 5 April 2019.

Tax-free Personal Allowance

The standard Personal Allowance is £11,850, which is the amount of income you don't have to pay tax on.

Your Personal Allowance may be bigger if you claim Marriage Allowance or Blind Person's Allowance. It's smaller if your income is over £100,000.

Income Tax rates and bands

The table shows the tax rates you pay in each band if you have a standard Personal Allowance of £11,850.

Band	**Taxable income**	**Tax rate**
Personal Allowance	Up to £11,850	0%
Basic rate	£11,851 to £46,350	20%
Higher rate	£46,351 to £150,000	40%
Additional rate	over £150,000	45%

You do not get a Personal Allowance on taxable income over £123,700.

Scottish rates and bands for 2018/19

On the 20 February 2018 the Scottish Parliament set the following income tax rates and bands for 2018/19.

Bands	**Band name**	**Rates (%)**
Over £11,850*-£13,850	Starter Rate	19

524. Source: https://www.gov.uk/government/publications/tax-and-tax-credit-rates-and-thresholds-for-2016-17/tax-and-tax-credit-rates-and-thresholds-for-2016-17.

Appendix 2: UK Tax & Tax Credit Rates 2018-19

Bands	Band name	Rates (%)
Over £13,850-£24,000	Basic Rate	20
Over £24,000-£43,430	Intermediate Rate	21
Over £43,430-£150,000**	Higher Rate	41
Above £150,000**	Top Rate	46

* Assumes person is in receipt of the Standard UK Personal Allowance
** Personal Allowance is reduced by £1 for every £2 earned over £100,000

Working Tax Credit rates

Rates (£ per year)	2018 to 2019	2017 to 2018	2016 to 2017
Basic element	£1,960	£1,960	£1,960
Couple and lone parent element	£2,010	£2,010	£2,010
30 hour element	£810	£810	£810
Disabled worker element	£3,090	£3,000	£2,970
Severe disability element	£1,330	£1,290	£1,275

Childcare element of Working Tax Credit

The maximum weekly childcare costs you can claim for and percentage of costs covered are shown below.

Rates (£ per week)	2018 to 2019	2017 to 2018	2016 to 2017
Maximum eligible cost for 1 child	£175	£175	£175
Maximum eligible cost for 2 or more children	£300	£300	£300
Percentage of eligible costs covered	70%	70%	70%

Child Tax Credit rates

The maximum annual Child Tax Credit rates are shown below.

Rates (£ per year)	2018 to 2019	2017 to 2018	2016 to 2017
Child Tax Credit family element	£545	£545	£545
Child element	£2,780	£2,780	£2,780

Rates (£ per year)	2018 to 2019	2017 to 2018	2016 to 2017
Disabled child element	£3,275	£3,175	£3,140
Severely disabled child element	£1,325	£1,290	£1,275

Tax credits income thresholds and withdrawal rates

The annual tax credits income thresholds and withdrawal rates are shown below.

Rates and thresholds (£ per year)	2018 to 2019	2017 to 2018	2016 to 2017
Income threshold	£6,420	£6,420	£6,420
Withdrawal threshold rate (%)	41%	41%	41%
Threshold for those entitled to Child Tax Credit only	£16,105	£16,105	£16,105
Income rise disregard	£2,500	£2,500	£2,500
Income fall disregard	£2,500	£2,500	£2,500

Child Benefit rates

The weekly Child Benefit rates are shown below.

Rates (£ per week)	2018 to 2019	2017 to 2018	2016 to 2017
Eldest/only child	£20.70	£20.70	£20.70
Other children	£13.70	£13.70	£13.70

Guardian's Allowance rates

The weekly Guardian's Allowance rates are shown below.

Rates (£ per week)	2018 to 2019	2017 to 2018	2016 to 2017
Guardian's Allowance	£17.20	£16.70	£16.55

UK Benefit cap amounts

If you live outside Greater London, the cap is:

- £384.62 per week (£20,000 a year) if you're in a couple, whether your children live with you or not.
- £384.62 per week (£20,000 a year) if you're single and your children live with you.
- £257.69 per week (£13,400 a year) if you're single and you do not have children, or your children do not live with you.

If you live in Greater London, the cap is:

Appendix 2: UK Tax & Tax Credit Rates 2018-19

- £442.31 per week (£23,000 a year) if you're in a couple, whether your children live with you or not.
- £442.31 per week (£23,000 a year) if you're single and your children live with you.
- £296.35 per week (£15,410 a year) if you're single and you do not have children, or your children do not live with you.

Selected Bibliography

Source Materials for British Social Security Law

There is a vast amount of literature on the British social security system. The Government itself produces considerable amounts of official information about the benefits and how they are administered. Related to these official sources are reports about aspects of the social security system or particular benefits published by a variety of Government-appointed Advisory Committees as well as Parliamentary Select Committees. Second, many bodies working with specific groups of claimants produce *rights guides* – technical analysis of the rules as they apply to particular categories of claimant. Third, there is the analytical work of scholars working in the area of social security law.

This bibliography does not purport to be comprehensive but does provide an introduction to the different sources of literature, which have been mentioned in the previous paragraph. Much of this material is available online. Government published material is available free. For a list of material published on different aspects of the social security system, go to www.dwp.gov.uk.

I. Official Sources

A. Law and Guidance

See: *The Law Relating to Social Security* (www.dwp.gov.uk/publications/specialist-guides/law-volumes/the-law-relating-to-social-security/); and *The Law Relating to Child Support* (www.dwp.gov.uk/publications/specialist-guides/law-volumes/the-law-relating-to-child-support/). There used to be a separate volume relating to War Pensions – special benefits for service personnel injured in action, but these are now administered by the SPVA within the MOD: *see* (www.veterans-uk.info/index.htm) (*See* www.hmrc.gov.uk/ni/index.htm for information about National Insurance Contributions).

These sources contain all the law on social security. Although authoritative and comprehensive, they are very hard to use in practice since the statutes and regulations are simply reprinted without any annotations or guidance about what the material means. Staff working in the three principal service delivery agencies – JobCentre Plus, the Pensions Service and the Disability and Carers Service use more informal guidance, including some of the commercially published material such as the works listed in the 'Rights Guides' – *see* below.

Neligan, D., *Social Security Case Law – Digest of Commissioners' Decisions.*

This contains summaries of the Social Security Commissioners' decisions on points of social security law, grouped together under subject matter. These are increasingly supplemented by decisions of the Upper Tribunal (Administrative Appeals Chamber) which, from November 2008, has taken over the functions of the Social Security Commissioners.

For *Social Security Commissioners' Decisions* and decisions of the *Upper Tribunal (Administrative Appeals Chamber)* which deal with social entitlements *see* https://www.judiciary.gov.uk/about-the-judiciary/who-are-the-judiciary/judicial-roles/tribunals/tribunal-decisions/.

These are the official 'law reports' of the Social Security system, comprising the reported decisions of the Social Security (formerly National Insurance) Commissioners, and the decisions of the Upper Tribunal (Administrative Appeals Chamber).

The Decision Makers' Guide (Looseleaf, 12 volumes, TSO) available online at www.dwp.gov.uk/publications/specialist-guides/decision-makers-guide/ /.

Technically not a statement of the law, but rather guidance prepared within the DWP for the benefit of staff. It does set out in more or less clear English the rules applicable in social security law. It also lays down procedures that must be followed by staff in a wide variety of situations.

Housing Benefit Guidance Manual www.dwp.gov.uk/local-authority-staff/housing-benefit/performance-and-good-practice/hbctb-good-practice-guide/ and A guide to Housing Benefit and Council Tax Benefit https://www.gov.uk/government/publications/housing-benefit-and-council-tax-benefit-guidance-part-b.

Similar official accounts of the Housing Benefit and Council Tax Benefit schemes prepared by the DWP for local authority Housing Benefit/CTB staff.

Social Fund Commissioner, *Annual Report for [year] on the Standards of Review by Social Fund Inspectors* (TSO, annual from 1989). *See* now also www.irs-review.org.uk/infocent/reports/areports.htm (Independent Review Service).

Self-explanatory, similar reports for Northern Ireland are also published each year.

Department of Work and Pensions, Statistics and Research http://statistics.dwp.gov.uk/asd/index.php?page=statistics.

Website providing detailed information about social security benefits together with tables showing longer-term trends in claiming patterns and expenditure.

Social Security and Child Support Appeals.

This website provides information to appellants and others. *See* www.justice.gov.uk/guidance/courts-and-tribunals/tribunals/sscs/index.htm.

B. Reports of Government Advisory Committees

Social Security Advisory Committee. *See* https://www.gov.uk/government/organisations/social-security-advisory-committee.

Established in 1980 by an amalgamation of the former National Insurance Advisory Committee and Supplementary Benefits Commission, the Advisory Committee produces reports on:

Draft Regulations

As will be seen in the main body of the text, a great deal of social security legislation is brought into force by the creation of regulations (Statutory Instruments or Orders in Council) rather than by primary legislation. Thus the opportunity for Parliamentary scrutiny of the bulk of social security law is very limited. Many regulations, however, have to be referred to the Social Security Advisory Committee for comment, before they can be brought into effect. In practice, the SSAC often invites comment on draft regulations from a wider panel of consultees. When it has finished its consultations and come to its view on the specific proposed regulations, it publishes a report commenting on the draft regulations and may make recommendations, which on occasion differ from what the Government had originally proposed. The Government is obliged to publish a reply indicating those points on which it has agreed with the SSAC and those which it has not accepted. This provides some measure of extra-parliamentary accountability that would not otherwise be available through the Parliamentary system.

Regular Reports

The SSAC publishes annual reports on its work which include commentary on what it regards as significant issues facing the social security system. This is tendered as advice to the Secretary of State, though it may of course also contain criticism of Government policy.

Other Reports

A series of research reports was published in the 1990s. This has now been replaced by a series of Occasional Papers, discussing policy issues of concern to the Committee.

Industrial Injuries Advisory Council. *See* https://www.gov.uk/government/organisations/industrial-injuries-advisory-council.

This committee performs a somewhat similar task to the SSAC in the specific context of the industrial injuries scheme. In particular, it has to consider whether new industrial diseases should be added to the list of prescribed diseases for the purposes of the industrial injuries scheme.

C. Official Research Reports

The Department of Work and Pensions commissions research and publish reports of the outcomes of such research. Details of the full list of research reports may be obtained from http://research.dwp.gov.uk/asd/asd5/.

D. Parliamentary Reports

Regular reports on the Department of Work and Pensions are issued by the Work and Pensions Select Committee of the House of Commons. *See* www.parliament.uk/business/committees/committees-archive/work-and-pensions-committee/.

II. Rights Guides

All of the works in this category are published by social reform groups active in the area of social security. Most of the books listed are revised annually to take account of changes in social security legislation. *See also* www.cpag.org.uk/; www.lag.org.uk/; and www.citizensadvice.org.uk/.

Child Poverty Action Group. *Welfare Benefits and Tax Credits Handbook.* Annual, London: CPAG. This publication, which is updated every year, is published by the leading anti-poverty pressure group. This book is however not a campaigning volume but a clear and straightforward analysis of the benefits available in the British social security system. Although ostensibly written for claimant use, it is likely that it is of more practical utility for welfare rights advisers and others who deal with claimants. This is a highly recommended core text.

Child Poverty Action Group. *Housing Benefit and Council Tax Reduction Legislation*, 30th edn, edited by Findlay, L. et al. Annual, London: CPAG, 2017–2018. This is a Handbook that comprehensively deals with housing benefits and an array of related issues.

Child Poverty Action Group. *Universal Credit.* London: CPAG, 2017. This is a Handbook provides the rules on claiming benefits and explains the welfare reform changes.

Child Poverty Action Group. *Child Support Handbook.* Annual, London: CPAG. This is a Handbook dealing with the new arrangements for child maintenance brought about by the introduction of the Child Support scheme in 1991.

Child Poverty Action Group. *Benefits for Migrants Handbook.* 6th edn, 2013.

Guidance on the specific issues relating to benefit entitlements which affect those advising European Union (EU) and non-EU immigrants and members of the ethnic minorities and also asylum seekers.

Child Poverty Action Group specialist handbooks on: *Council Tax, Debt Advice, Paying for Care, Fuel Rights and Social Inclusion.*

Disability Rights Handbook. Annual, London: Disability Alliance, April 2015. Well-established guide, published by the Disability Alliance, on benefits and services available to disabled people.

III. Academic and Other Independent Commentaries and Books

This third category lists a sample of the principal textbooks and research monographs which have been written, primarily by scholars working in universities, but some also written by lawyers practising in the relevant area of law.

Bonner, D. & I. Hooker, et al. (eds). *Social Security Legislation 2017-18, Volume I: Non Means-Tested Benefits and Employment Support Allowance*. London: Sweet and Maxwell.

This contains the full text of all the relevant legislation relating to non-means-tested benefits, together with commentary on the provisions which helps the reader follow through the complexities of the legislation and also summarizes the decisions of the Social Security Commissioners on the many points of law raised by social security law. These volumes are now used widely in DWP offices as well as by tribunals. The authors are academics but with practical experience sitting as judges in the First-Tier Tribunal. The annotations are their independent view of the meaning of the regulations.

Wood, P. & J. Mesher, et al. (eds). *Social Security Legislation 2017-18, Volume II: Income Support, Jobseeker's Allowance, State Pension Credit and the Social Fund*. London: Sweet and Maxwell, 2017. Similar in concept to volume 1.

Rowland, M. & R.C.A. White. *Social Security Legislation 2017-18, Volume III: Administration, Adjudication and the European Dimension*. London: Sweet and Maxwell.

Similar in format to the above two books, this is also an annotated collection of the relevant statutory material, commissioned by the Tribunal Service for Tribunal Judges and members.

Wikeley, N., D. Williams & Hooker, I., *Social Security Legislation 2017-18, Volume IV: Tax Credits and HMRC-Administered Social Security Benefits*. London: Sweet and Maxwell.

This is the fourth in the series of annotated statutory materials published by Sweet and Maxwell. They are revised and republished annually; Sweet and Maxwell also publish an updating supplement to keep the main texts up-to-date.

Mesher, J., R. Poynter et al. (eds), *Social Security Legislation 2015-16, Volume V: Universal Credit*. London: Sweet and Maxwell.

This is the fifth and final volume in the series of annotated statutory materials published by Sweet and Maxwell on the latest, emerging key benefit – UC.

Wikeleye, N. *Social Security Legislation 2017-18, Volume I: Universal Credit*. London: Sweet and Maxwell.

Findlay, L., et al. *CPAG's Housing Benefit and Council Tax Benefit Legislation*. Annual: CPAG.

Authoritative annotations and analysis of the Housing Benefit and Council Tax Benefit schemes by legal practitioners, updated by specialist team.

Buck, T. *The Social Fund: Law and Practice*. 3rd edn, London: Sweet and Maxwell, 2009.

Analysis by academic lawyer who was formerly legal adviser to the Social Fund Review team of the Social Fund scheme.

Jacobs, E. *Tribunal Practice and Procedure*. 3rd edn, London: Legal Action Group, 2014.

Analysis by a Judge of the Upper Tribunal on practice and procedure in the reformed tribunal system – in which social security tribunals are by some distance the largest single component.

Selected Bibliography

A. Principal Text Books

Harris, N. et al. *Social Security Law in Context.* Oxford: Oxford University Press, 2000.

This academic account of British social security law and its sociopolitical context. It treats early developments resulting from the coming to power of the Blair Labour Government particularly well. It is not up-to-date.

Ogus, A.I., E. Barendt & N. Wikeley. *The Law of Social Security.* 6th Revised edn, London: Butterworths, 2002.

The book both analyses the law, and sets it in its social, political and economic context. Very strong on the history of British social security law. It is not up-to-date.

B. Specialist Texts and Monographs

Note that the following selection is particularly selective. Other texts are referred to in the footnotes to chapters of the book.

Lewis, R.I. *Compensation for Industrial Injury.* Abingdon: Professional Books, 1987. It is a detailed study of the industrial injuries scheme and the interaction with the law on personal injuries.

Wikeley, N.J. *Compensation for Industrial Disease.* Farnham: Dartmouth Publishing, 1993. It is a detailed study of the history and rules relating to compensation for industrial disease.

Stapleton, J. *Disease and the Compensation Debate.* Oxford: Oxford University Press, 1986.

Scholarly analysis of the interface between common law damages and the social security system.

Partington, M. 'Secretary of State's Powers of Adjudication in Social Security Law.' School for Advanced Urban Studies, University of Bristol, Working Paper No. 96, 1991.

Report of a research study into the adjudicative functions of the Secretary of State for Social Security, falling outside the mainstream adjudicative structure, and includes an account of the historical development of social security adjudication.

Sainsbury, R. *Survey and Report into the Working of the Medical Appeal Tribunals.* London: HMSO, 1992.

Report commissioned by the President of the Independent Tribunal Service into the working of MATs, with particular emphasis on the perceptions of appellants.

Sainsbury, R. *Deciding Social Security Claims: A Study in the Theory and Practice of Administrative Justice*. Edinburgh, Scotland, UK: University of Edinburgh, 1988.

It is an unpublished but brilliant PhD thesis, examining in detail the workings of decision-making processes within the social security system.

Genn, H. & Y. Genn. *The Effectiveness of Representation at Tribunals.* London: Lord Chancellors Department, 1989.

Report of a detailed and influential survey of the impact of representation on decision outcome in four areas of administrative justice, including social security.

Classic critique of (then) SBATs which contributed to the thinking which led to the restructuring of social security adjudication from 1984 (under the HASSASSA Act, 1983).

Baldwin, J., N. Wikeley & R. Young. *Judging Social Security: The Adjudication of Claims for Benefit in Britain.* Oxford: Oxford University Press, 1992.

First major survey of the system of social security adjudication since the creation of the reformed structure for adjudication under the HASSASSA Act 1983 and contains helpful bibliography.

Buck, T., D. Bonner & R. Sainsbury. *Making Social Security Law: The Role and Work of the Social Security and Child Support Commissioners.* Farnham: Ashgate, 2005.

C. Law and Practice Journals

Welfare Rights Bulletin published every other month by Child Poverty Action Group.

Written for Welfare Right workers, this provides in effect an updating service for the CPAG rights guides. Largely contains descriptions and analyses of developments in the law.

Journal of Social Welfare and Family Law published six times a year by Routledge.

This is a more academic journal. It contains a notes and development section and fuller articles on policy and research. It also has summaries of unreported Commissioners' decisions and also decisions of the Social Fund Inspectorate.

Journal of Social Security Law published quarterly by Sweet and Maxwell since 1994.

Legal Action published monthly by Legal Action Group.

Contains regular updates of developments in social security law, as well as other areas of law in the general social welfare area.

Industrial Law Journal published four times a year for the Industrial Law Society.

Contains occasional articles and notes on social security law especially in the interface with Labour Law and industrial relations matters.

Poverty is a Quarterly Journal of the Child Poverty Action Group primarily devoted to discussion of policy issues relating to social security.

D. Other Bibliographies

O'Higgins, P., M. Partington & S. Hughes, *Social Security Law in Britain and Ireland: A Bibliography.* London: Mansell, 1986.

Detailed collection of reference to literature on British and Irish social security law until 1985 and primarily of value to scholars interested in historical aspects of social security law.

IV. Useful Websites

www.dwp.gov.uk.
www.ons.gov.uk.
www.dsdni.gov.uk.
http://lawvolumes.dwp.gov.uk/the-law-relating-to-social-security/.
http://www.cpag.org.uk/.

Index

The numbers here refer to paragraph numbers.

Index

Index

www.ingramcontent.com/pod-product-compliance
Lightning Source LLC
LaVergne TN
LVHW011119300926
849160LV00008B/447